99 YEARS OF NAVY

Previous books by Sam Morley

Start off Smashed!
In Search of Eastern Promise
Victory in Site!
If it wasn't for Golf ...!
By Yon Bonnie Links!
Durban's Lady in White (update of her 1964 autobiography)
Back to Durban – 50 Years On!

99 YEARS OF NAVY

SAM MORLEY

Quiller Press

Copyright © 1995 Sam Morley
ISBN 1 899163 07 7

First published 1995 by
Quiller Press Limited
46 Lillie Road
London SW6 1TN

Designed by Jim Reader
Jacket illustration by Ted Hughes

Produced by Book Production Consultants PLC
25–27 High Street, Chesterton, Cambridge.
Printed and bound by Biddles Limited, Guildford

Contents

Introduction

I first met Lt. Comdr. Woods R.N. when interviewed for membership of the Eccentric Club of St. James's in 1958. He was Club Secretary. A slightly built, quietly-spoken gentleman of 66. Ten years later I was invited to start a Club magazine, by which time we had become firm friends with the Royal Navy as our common link.

My six years during World War II bore no comparison to his 50 years from 1897 which started as Boy 2nd Class at HMS *Ganges*, Shotley, to the wardroom and staff of Admiral Air, Lea-on-Solent, and on to 'Civvy Street' with an honourable retirement and pension at the age of 57. We would sit for hours over a decanter of port after lunch at the Club, while he regaled me with vivid recollections of a much earlier life afloat than I knew.

So much so, that when he retired from Club duties and settled down in Brighton at the age of 78, I persuaded him to start from the beginning and set down his naval life in chronological order, to be run as a series in the half-yearly editions of the Magazine. Like everything else he ever did, he tackled the project methodically, searching through his possessions, cupboards and loft at home for long-forgotten links, and would sit for hours at his typewriter producing his spellbinding story of a bygone era.

But with each batch of typescript would come a note to say it was becoming increasingly difficult to dig up more. He died on Easter Monday 1972, at the age of 80. When attending his funeral, I met his widow, a slightly-built, gracious lady. She said how much he'd enjoyed re-living his forgotten early days when trying to write them up and thanked me for encouraging him to persevere as long as he did. I asked if there was anything among his possessions that might help continue his story in the Club magazine. To go on printing it after his death would be a tribute to his memory. She believed there was nothing left that he hadn't already covered, but if anything turned up, she would let me know.

Sure enough, a few weeks later she wrote enclosing a sixty-year-old exercise book. Its edges a bit tattered, it was his handwritten diary of his involvement in the opening year of World War I aboard the battle cruiser HMS *Princess Royal*. The inside front cover showed a photograph of the ship, the relevant technical data, and some of his explanatory notes, all handwritten clearly and methodically by this young man of 22, who was obviously so proud of being one of the 1,160 men that formed its crew. It started in clear detail on the 27th July 1914, but by the date of the last entry on the 16th March 1915 the laconic comments were almost indecipherable. One could sense the strain and despondence of those awful wintry conditions at sea with a daily toll of lost ships and boyhood friends.

I paraphrased what I could from that diary and had a lot of help from the Imperial War Museum, National Maritime Museum and Naval History Library in pursuit of photographs and information to supplement the continuation of his story, but there was never enough to finish the book.

The story then sat on the 'back burner' for twenty years waiting for a rush of creative blood to the head and some way of coupling his lifetime in the Navy with my own meagre six years whereby a title such as the one chosen would be justified.

Then I published *Durban's Lady in White* in 1991 and wrote *Back to Durban ... 50 Years On!* in 1992. They brought in hundreds of letters and phone enquiries from ex-Royal Navy veterans, many of whom had written their own book of naval experiences and wondered about publication.

One in particular – Bill Dunlevey's "Under an Umbrella", told of his life spent under the R.N. 'umbrella' from 1936 to 1974 (part of it was under a Japanese one as a prisoner of war after his ship, HMS *Exeter*, was sunk in the Java Sea). But what made his story so different to any other war book, and compulsive reading for any wanting to know more about the deadly 'knock-out punch' that won us the fight, is that he was part of a slave labour squad in the shipyards of Nagasaki and as such became unique. HE IS THE ONLY ENGLISH EYEWITNESS I'VE EVER HEARD OF, LET ALONE MET, THAT WAS RIGHT THERE ON THE SCENE WHEN THE SECOND ATOM BOMB OF WORLD WAR II FELL ON THAT ILL-FATED CITY! Having survived it he tells of all he witnessed in dramatic detail.

Despite a less than fair share of equitable treatment from a grateful nation on getting out from under his 'umbrella' his final paragraph reads:

> *"The ships I knew are now long gone. I feel a certain regret about it but the memories of all those ships, shipmates, POW friends, establishments and faraway places will always be with me. They will never fade because once they pulsated with life, laughter, sadness and fun.*
> *YES, Life was Great under that Large Umbrella!"*

The first two stories feature the history of two professional sailors with over ninety years in the 'Andrew' between them. The third is the tale of an enthusiastic amateur who opens his story with the following three paragraphs:

"With an appetite whetted by seven years of naval stories from the local library came the decision, one Friday afternoon, that running away to sea was the only means of escape from a fate far worse than death. I was thirteen at the time.

Fate, at that time and if I remember correctly, was embodied by a sinister physics master radiating icy malevolence at my failure to produce a backlog of written-up exercises based on his lectures, and the puerile excuses offered each week for their absence. Unless the paperwork presenting my version of his teachings over the past ten weeks was on his desk by Monday, the consequences, I was informed, would be dire. Very dire.

There was a Royal Navy recruiting office in our High Street, into the windows of which I would often gaze on my way home from school, fascinated by the quality of seafaring life portrayed. On that fateful Friday it seemed to offer sanctuary from the impending wrath of Mr Andrews. I walked in and asked if they could find me a ship – quick!"

The story goes on to tell how they did – ten years later – and describes countless experiences on many waters and in many lands over the next six years.

An ex-Marine friend with whom I share a love of golf and epic English poetry took part in the abortive Combined Ops. raid on Dieppe in August 1942. As it occurred when I was between ships – doing an LTO course across the Channel at Roedean School for Girls! – I got his permission to feature his story. And what an awesome feature it is.

The book takes us on to Royal Navy experiences in recent years, right up to my current involvement through writing and/or publishing three books: "Durban's Lady in White"; "Back to Durban …50 Years On!"; "Just Nuisance A.B." and promoting a monument in Durban to the Lady in White. All of which put me well behind in earlier attempts to get on with this one. But having now completed the Introduction, the rest should be downhill!

Sam Morley
Christmas 1994

PART ONE

THE ROYAL NAVY OF LIEUTENANT COMMANDER W.E.V. WOODS, R.N. from 1897 to 1915

CHAPTER ONE

Victoriana to Boy 1st Class

My generation was born when Great Britain and the Empire dominated the world. Queen Victoria was on the throne, her subjects and enormous amount of overseas possessions protected by the Army and the greatest Navy in existence.

We youngsters were proud to be British and deeply stirred by the Naval and Military displays which took place from time to time. Each year we took part in the national commemoration of the Battle of Trafalgar and the death of Nelson, sang "Rule Britannia" (and meant it) and came away brimming over with patriotic love for our great country.

The first Naval Review that I remember was Queen Victoria's Diamond Jubilee Review held at Spithead in the early summer of 1897. News of this event – just a part of the celebrations taking place throughout the Empire – had been discussed with great anticipation by my school friends. We were, together with children from other schools, to take part in a procession through the colourfully decorated streets, each child bearing a flag on a pole and to be given a very special tea in the grounds of the Canoe Lake, Southsea.

Just how I managed to carry a bamboo stick – with what seemed the largest Union Jack in the world attached to it – for over two miles, I do not know – for I had just turned five (we commenced school at three years of age in those days).

However, the task accomplished and tea-fight over, each child was given a Diamond Jubilee goblet, embossed with a portrait of Queen Victoria to mark the occasion, and then marched to the seafront to see the Fleet.

What a tremendous spectacle it was – there at anchor, three miles offshore, with the Isle of Wight forming a picturesque background, lay line upon line of warships stretching for miles well out into the Solent. All were gaily dressed with flags.

Great squat battleships, armoured cruisers, light cruisers, torpedo boats with their black hulls, white upper works and yellow funnels freshly painted and glistening in the sun, sailing brigs and auxiliary vessels – all berthed equi-distant in perfect formation and their white ensigns streaming in the breeze.

After dark, at a signal flashed in Morse from the masthead of the flagship – and as if controlled by a single switch – the whole Fleet sprang to life. Each ship's hull, super-structure, masts and guns were highlighted by thousands of coloured lamps. Cries of appreciation could be heard from the thousands of people lining the seafront.

It was a great show, terminating with a searchlight display at midnight. All the more impressive and unique because in those days there were no newsreel or TV camera crews recording the scene for re-presentation in cinema or home.

One of the advantages of living in Portsmouth was to watch from close quarters the daily movement of warships entering and leaving harbour; gliding through those same channels traversed for hundreds of years by their predecessors, often bearing the same names and making for the same destinations.

Standing at Sallyport, near the mouth of the harbour and where the press gangs used to operate, sometimes – when the air was still – strains of the Admiral's salute, sounded on a bugle, came floating over the waters. It would be a passing warship saluting the flag of the Commander-in-Chief at Portsmouth which was then flying on HMS *Victory*.

Growing up in this heady atmosphere, and with the unpleasant alternative of an apprenticeship in the dockyard followed by a lifetime of monotony working there, it is no wonder that the more adventurous life in the Navy, with prospects of seeing the world, appealed to so many youngsters of my era.

R.N. SCHOOL, GREENWICH 1903 – 1907

Thus it was, that having made up my mind to join the Navy when I was old enough to do so, I was fortunate to be accepted for pre-Naval training into the Royal Hospital School, Greenwich. I entered at the age of 11½ years and remained there for four years.

A book could be written about the Royal Hospital School, the former Palace of William and Mary, and of its complement of 1,000 boys – all sons of sailors. But other than saying that it was affectionately known as the 'Navy Cradle', whose lessons I remembered in varying degrees forever, I will pass on to the next stage in my Naval career.

In October 1907, the day arrived for my class to join the Royal Navy. With a last backward glance at HMS *Fame*, we marched through the gates of the school and were on our way to HMS *Ganges*, the newly-built Boys Training Establishment at Shotley, Suffolk. 'Life on the Ocean Wave' was about to commence but, in point of fact, it had really begun on HMS *Fame* which merits more than a passing mention.

In 1873, HMS *Fame* was built on concrete in the grounds of the Royal Hospital School, Greenwich and was recognised as the largest model sailing ship in the world. It accommodated 55 boys during their last six months at the school.

Under the supervision of instructors who had spent most of their naval careers in sailing ships, the boys had to work her as a ship at sea – running aloft over the masthead barefooted, manning and laying out on the yards, setting and furling sails, and sleeping in hammocks. Negotiating the ice-encrusted masthead and slippery rigging early on a winter's morning could be a frightening experience. It brought home the fact that one's safety was one's own responsibility – nobody else could help.

She was built into the ground with nets around her to break the fall of anybody unlucky enough to fall. As for size, she was longer and wider in the beam than the *Cutty Sark*, now permanently berthed in dry dock nearby.

When the school was transferred to Holbrook in 1926, and the buildings taken over for the National Maritime Museum, *Fame* was broken up. Pieces of her oak structure were made into paperweights and given to those who had 'sailed' in her. I have one on my desk as I write, inscribed *"Fame – 1873-1926"*.

HMS *GANGES* – 1907

When we arrived at Shotley, it having been clearly established that each boy had engaged himself to serve His Majesty King Edward VII in the Royal Navy for 12 years from the age of 18, we were formally entered as Boys 2nd Class, and issued with our kit.

We were fortunate in joining *Ganges* after 1st October 1907, and thereby qualifying for a free kit. Formerly it had to be bought through deductions from pay made over a period. As pay was 6d a day it must have been like paying off a mortgage on a house. There certainly couldn't be a lot left over for maintaining a wife in every port – if the widely-held image of 'Jolly Jack' is to be believed!

HMS *IMPREGNABLE*, DEVONPORT 1907 – 1908

Automatic promotion to Boy 1st Class would be at the end of 9 months training, but accelerated promotion was given to boys with good educational marks and reports. They would qualify for the Advanced Class, established on HMS *Impregnable* at Devonport. I was one of those selected to be drafted there a week after joining *Ganges*.

The purpose of the Advanced Class was to train and earmark selected youths for promotion to Petty Officer and eventually to Warrant Officer early in their career, a requirement made necessary by the installation of a great deal of scientific equipment in the many warships currently under construction due to the International Arms Race – mainly against Germany. Many of the older Petty Officers, although first class seamen, had never received much schooling and were unable to master the calculations required to operate some of the new instruments.

Impregnable was one of the last of the old 'wooden walls' in commission and looked most impressive. Her upper works remained rigged the same as when she had sailed the seven seas, excepting there were no sails. The four decks – upper, main, lower and orlop – were wide and unencumbered, and the gunports gave ample ventilation and sufficient light – but there were no power winches or mechanical aids of any kind.

Provisions, stores, coal, accommodation, ladders, etc., all had to be hoisted aboard by manual labour. Water for drinking, cooking and sanitation had to be pumped by hand – sometimes from sheer necessity, and sometimes as a punishment.

Each evening the boats were hoisted by the port and starboard watches each vying against the other. A healthy competitive approach to most duties and exercises was adopted to prevent what might otherwise have proved to be just arduous drudgery.

Courses of instruction on *Impregnable* were spread over the year we were to spend aboard her before being drafted onto a seagoing ship and included seamanship, gunnery and mechanical training.

Our day commenced at 5.30am. We'd be rudely awakened by the bosun's pipes and the quartermasters' "All hands heave out, heave out, heave out, lash up and stow hammocks". A frantic scramble ensued, all being aware that the last six to stow hammocks would get a touch of the rope's end – always carried by the instructors – and would qualify automatically for the pumping party or other unpopular tasks.

After "Hands to cocoa" had been complied with (despite an eighth of an inch of cocoa butter floating on it) came scrubbing the upper deck – barefooted of course – then general cleaning of the ship, and then the cleaning of ourselves in a screened-off section of the upper deck.

Breakfast was at 7.00am and consisted of 8oz. bread, ½ oz. butter and a basin of coffee. In addition, on two mornings a week boiled salt pork was issued. It wasn't very nice and didn't look it, but it was something to eat and we looked forward to the pork days with relish. How much one got depended on seniority. The senior boy sat at the ship's side under the mess shelf (the seat of honour) and by custom took the first cut before passing the pork down the table. By the time it reached the juniors at the other end very little remained. The best that can be said of this system is that it taught us not to criticise our seniors, to be thankful for small mercies, and to hope for better times. We always rose from the table with a good appetite!

Inspection and morning prayers finished at 9.00am and instruction commenced. Lectures in seamanship, combined with 'do-it-yourself', taught us about knots and splices, anchors and cables, boxing the compass in quarter-points – to be recited backwards – and later how to handle a 14' fir oar without catching a crab, and heaving the lead.

Later, theory was put into practice when, as cutter's crew, we pulled five miles on the routine trips to the dockyard for stores.

Boat sailing was more popular and, once we had learned to keep clear of running tackle, it was great fun. Competition to be picked for the racing crews was keen. Masthead drill formed part of the course, with instructors stationed at intervals on the rigging to urge us ever upward. A lash of the rope's end for the slow ones always accelerated progress.

In the gunnery classes, every order was carried out at the double on the principle that "a smart No. 1 makes a smart No. 2 and a smart No. 2 makes a smart gun's crew!" The positions of gunlayer, trainer, range finder, loader, etc., were taken by each boy in turn and practiced until everyone worked together as a team. Mechanism of the gun was explained at great length and each crew, as part of it's training, would have to strip down and re-assemble the weapon on which they had exercised that day.

Fieldgun exercises, based on the activities of the Naval Brigade in South Africa not so long before, called for a great deal of physical exertion and took place in the playing fields ashore. Forenoon instruction ceased at 11.50am when the bugler sounded "Cooks to the galley", followed at noon by "Hands to dinner".

It was always a good substantial meal and included 12oz. of meat followed by figgy or plum duff or some other pudding. The meal over, we would go on deck and watch for the ships due to come up harbour – maybe *Adventure* from the West Indies, *King Alfred* from China, or *Espiegle* from the Persian Gulf, flying paying-off pendants after long commissions abroad. With starry eyes we looked forward to the days when we too would form part of the crew of similar vessels.

School commenced at 1.30pm. The Naval schoolmasters were dedicated officers who, from the start, impressed upon us the importance of obtaining educational certificates as a prerequisite to promotion. As a result of their high pressure methods, we were advanced to Boy 1st Class after three months service, six months ahead of our pals left behind at Shotley! It involved a test of our knowledge of algebra, applied mechanics, trigonometry, logarithms and simple problems in navigation. I have always felt that the consequent increase in pay from 6d to 7d a day was fully justified!

Mechanical training consisted of practical instruction in the use of tools, working with metals, and lectures on boilers and pumping systems in seagoing ships. The syllabus was arranged to include a daily period of physical training, and for football, cricket and water polo in season.

Tea at 4.00pm was the last meal of the day – 8oz. bread, 1oz. jam and tea. Alas, the 8oz. bread was what we had left of that issued for our breakfast that morning. It depended on whatever we had managed to save from the breakfast ration and had locked away in a secure place – usually a ditty box. Failure to do this resulted in its disappearance and in it's place a note with KYBEO written on it. This meant "Keep Your Blue Eyes Open" – poor comfort, but excellent advice.

The evenings were spent washing clothes (and almost invariably a re-scrub, if you were not up to the high standard of cleanliness required by the instructors), peeling potatoes, writing letters home, boxing, fencing and playing chess or draughts.

At 8.00pm the boats were hoisted, each watch in competition with the other. A succession of varying trills – long since forgotten – would signify the following commands to those manning each set of boat falls (the two ropes passing through pulleys at the boat davit heads and linked to the forward and after ends of the boat): "Haul taut singly"; "Marry"; "Hoist away"; "Avast heaving"; "Unreel and coil down boat falls".

Thereafter hammocks were slung, the mess made tidy for the night and, after rounds and inspection of the decks, "Pipe Down" at 9.00pm. We were glad to turn in.

So the routine went on. We settled to it and tried hard to keep out of trouble. Discipline was strict but not harsh. Minor offences involved stoppage of local leave on Saturday and Sunday afternoons or No. 10a punishment. More serious offences meant up to twelve cuts with the cane – a degrading punishment and a relic from the days of flogging with the birch. 10a was generally awarded for a period of 7 days but could be more. The offenders were called at irregular intervals to face the paintwork in silence for thirty minutes with a lashed up hammock resting on the shoulder, and to have meals on deck standing up. They were detailed off for all the pumping and coaling parties. It has been known for a boy or seaman under such punishment to observe in bitter tones that he "wished he had never joined!"

Pay-day was once a week. It was a cruel blow to find that, instead of the 3s 6d earned, only 6d pocket money was paid. The idea was to encourage thrift and build up a credit. This would help to pay for replacement of kit and for railway fares when proceeding on long leave before joining a seagoing man of war, but any credit balance would be paid in full before leaving *Impregnable.*

Prices from the ship's stores were in relation to the low pay, for example first quality Turkish towels were 8d each, blankets 6s 0d, boots 7s 6d, socks 10d per pair, and a railway fare cost 1d per mile return. We squandered the pocket money on lemonade, buns and stamps from the canteen.

The courses completed, we were granted 10 days leave before joining the Seagoing Training Squadron.

HMS *EURYALUS*, 1908 – 1909

I was in a party drafted to HMS *Euryalus*, the flagship lying alongside at Portsmouth. She was an armoured cruiser of 14,000 tons, built in 1902, with four very tall funnels rising high above the superstructure and bridge. Large cowls for trimming into the wind to provide ventilation to the stokeholds and engine-rooms ran the length of the boat deck. Single 9.2" guns in turrets were on the fo'c'sle and quarter deck, and along each side were two pairs of 4.7" guns, one superimposed above the other. Each pair was in a single casemate, with the lower only a few feet above the water-line. Viewed from the jetty she looked grim.

On reporting aboard, we each received a card showing our individual allocation of mess, boat, part of the watch, and special duty station at sea, and also a handbook giving particulars of the ship, which we were to study and learn. It was good to find that on account of our youth and numbers a bakery had just been installed as well as a small refrigerator compartment for meat. Thus we would have fresh bread and meat throughout the cruise, instead of ships biscuit and salt pork. These were very special features which did not become standard in later ships for some years.

Compared with *Impregnable* the ship seemed strange and cheerless with a labyrinth of water-tight compartments, cramped accommodation and the noise of pumping machinery working day and night.

OUTWARD BOUND

Being fully stored and under sailing orders *Euryalus* set out for the Mediterranean on 7th October 1908, just a year after we had left Royal Hospital School at Greenwich. For the first time we heard the time-honoured pipes of "Secure ship for sea"; "Close B and C water-tight doors"; "Special sea dutymen to your stations"; "Hands to stations for leaving harbour".

From the bridge came a succession of orders: "Let go for'ard", "Starboard 10"; "Slow ahead port"; "Let go aft"; etc. All links with the shore now severed she was a warship underway with the Trinity House pilot conning her through the channels towards the open sea.

The ship's company was formed up on deck standing to attention, and the Royal Marine Guard and Band did likewise on the quarter deck. With the Admiral's flag flying at the fore, it was saluted as we went by other ships. Passing *Victory* flying the flag of the Commander-in-Chief, the band played the Admiral's salute and course was set for the harbour mouth where, years before, I had watched other ships departing.

I had hoped to see the Sallyport on this special occasion but it was not to be. I was stationed well below the water-line as one of the emergency hand steering party – but I did hear the propellers!

Having dropped the pilot, the trip down Channel commenced with the order "Off boots". These were not worn on board again for four months.

The sky was overcast, the sea choppy and soon there was a slight motion on the ship. We wondered whether we would be seasick. It was not until the next day, having run into bad weather in the Bay of Biscay that we got the answer.

With the bow plunging deep into the water and the propellers racing in the air, the ship, pitching violently, embarked on an endless succession of nose dives with mountainous seas looming up on each side. In the course of recovery, aided by cross winds and tall funnels, she shuddered and lurched heavily sideways, shipping water in the process. At times it came as high as the knees before escaping into the scuppers, forcing us to hold onto anything handy to avoid being swept there ourselves. This rhythm, with ballet-like variations, continued unabated. The screaming of the wind in the rigging, the noise of clanging anchor cables, crashing fitments dislodged by the movement of the ship and the occasional whiff of hot lubricating oil from the reciprocating engines, combined against us. Our will to resist cracked – first as a trickle and then with a mad rush, 430 budding Nelsons suffered the ultimate in the miseries of *mal-de-mer*!

There was no let-up – it got worse instead of better – but no one, however ill, was excused answering the call to muster. The Petty Officers made sure we were there –

it was all part of the cure. Our prayers that the ship would go down and take us with her were not answered. We felt most unhappy.

Our arrival at Vigo on the north-west corner of Spain – and the sensation of being on an even keel again – cheered us immensely. We made up for those meals we were unable to eat on the passage down, supplemented by the plentiful supply of cheap fruits brought from shore. I well remember that peaches were twelve for a penny.

The weather *en route* to Gibraltar was much better, we were not so seasick and commenced to acquire both good appetites and our sea-legs.

Off Sardinia we rendezvoused with the newly built HMS *Dreadnought* whose revolutionary design, mighty guns and heavy armour had rendered all other warships obsolescent, and had led to the International Naval Arms race. We were privileged to witness her battle practice trials, to hear the thunder of her ten 12" guns fired simultaneously at a target being towed some miles distant, and to watch the fall and ricochet of the one-ton projectiles.

Proceeding eastward the weather became finer each day and on the ship "Hove-to" exercises took place in dropping and manning the boats. After having pulled some distance, the boats were recalled in pairs and hoisted aboard by their respective watches – the watch taking the longest time having to lower their boat and re-hoist it!

There was no Echo Sounding Equipment or other depth finding apparatus in those days. The depth of water had to be ascertained by heaving the lead and reading the markings in fathoms on the lead line. The lead weighed 10 lbs., and the knack of heaving it without letting it fall on one's head – which it did if looked up at during the heave – was acquired only after much practice!

Standing on a small platform not far above the water with the ship under way, a choppy sea, and hampered by oilskins, it was an unenviable job. For this reason the leadsman was usually relieved each hour, often soaked through and frozen despite the oilskins.

During the cruise each boy did at least one trick (1 hour) as a leadsman. Other special duties included a full watch (4 hours) as a lookout and a trick as a helmsman. The bridge was open with no protection from the weather at the wings where the look-outs were stationed. Periodically, in the reply to the Officer of the Watch on the upper bridge, they would report "Bow and steaming lights burning brightly. Nothing in sight. Optional light on" (unless it had been switched off to test alertness).

To see the day break at sea, with the sun rising slowly on the horizon was well worth turning out at 3.45am to keep the morning watch (4.00am to 8.00am). It was more comfortable at the wheel, as the helmsman was protected by glass screens, but there was a great sense of responsibility in keeping the ship's head on course – and nervousness when altering the helm. We were, of course, under constant observation with the experienced seamen always at hand to take over in emergency. This was as well, for it fell to my lot to be at the wheel when approaching Malta. Although miles from the narrow entrance to the breakwater I'd already convinced myself that a terrible naval disaster was imminent when, to my great relief, I heard behind me the gruff voice of the quartermaster saying, "Hop it, Sonny." As his horny hands closed over the spokes he called up the voicepipe, "Repeat course, sir, Chief QM at the wheel."

WITH THE MED. FLEET, MALTA

On arrival at Malta we were allotted a good berth in the grand harbour, enabling us to see the many ships of the Mediterranean Fleet moored there. Watching their activities was of great fascination to all us budding First Sea Lords.

Small vessels bringing fresh provisions, mail, etc., made their way alongside, but perhaps the most welcome was the lighter with fresh water. For most of the trip drinking water tanks had been kept locked and water for washing severely rationed, as the distillation plant could not produce enough to meet normal requirements.

Coaling ship was particularly arduous and dirty work, the dust finding it's way everywhere – especially into the throat. It was a matter of "All hands in" – breaking bulk in the collier and filling hundred-weight bags until 400 tons had been hauled aboard. Hosing down the decks followed and then the task of trying to wash the grime off ourselves. Trying to do this from small tubs of cold water on the upper deck left much to be desired and the rims of our eyes remained black for days. There were no bathrooms for the boys – we always washed from the tubs on the upper deck.

After a short spell in harbour, training at sea commenced. In rough weather we were exercised in drills for dealing with collisions, surprise action stations, man overboard, or fire in ship. This required that steel crankshafts stowed in positions in various parts of the ship had to be carried on the shoulders through a number of compartments and fitted to Downton pumps permanently secured to the deck. It took six boys on each crankshaft to heave round and start the pumps. Simultaneously a party would be struggling with a 20' x 20' paunch mat trying to place it over an imaginary hole in the ship's side caused by the 'collision'. With the ship rolling, much time was spent doing all this and there were many injured hands. Chances of survival in a real collision would have been slim.

Gunnery practice took place frequently and points were awarded for hits on the targets when firing 12 pounder and 4.7" guns. Many of those scoring the highest points found themselves gunlayers of 15" guns in the battleships of the 1914 war.

Watchkeeping in the stokeholds enabled us to appreciate the hard life of the stokers. Shovelling coal continuously and removing clinkers from the furnaces by means of a 12' steel slice for 4 hours at a stretch required experienced men of great strength. It was beyond the capabilities of the average boy. Our job was to transport ashes to the hoists for tipping overboard and to obtain the coal required for the furnaces from the bunkers at each side of the stokeholds. In bad weather the stokehold decks were usually awash and after pushing a skid with its one hundredweight of coal uphill at one stage, it frequently happened that on the rebound one finished up, complete with skid, in the opposite bunker. How different it must have been when oil fuel was introduced!

Euryalus anchors were of old fashioned design with stocks (the cross piece at the top), and each weighed 4 tons. Unlike stockless anchors in use today, which are drawn up into and secured within the hawsepipes, they had to be 'catted' into and stowed in a perpendicular position on a bed projection from the hull. This was done by a series of manoeuvres with derricks and wire hawsers, an ever present danger to the crew of the boat working below to help guide the anchor into position. It was always a long job.

At the conclusion of the exercises our sister ships *Cressy* and *Hogue* joined us (both were sunk when together again in the 1914 war) and we returned to Malta.

EARTHQUAKE IN SICILY, 1909

Almost immediately came news of the earthquakes in the Straits of Messina. The squadron was ordered to embark supplies for the relief of the victims and to proceed at full speed to render assistance. Approaching the scene of the disaster, the sea was found strewn with bodies and debris of all kinds. Navigation became tricky due to the eruption of the seabed. Ashore massive devastation had taken place, the dead lay all about, few buildings survived and there was great sorrow among the survivors. For most, relatives, friends, homes and personal possessions had all gone. It was heart-breaking to behold.

Depots were set up for the distribution of the food, clothing and bedding landed from the ships, and field hospitals established. The local authorities proclaimed the penalty of death by shooting for looting.

Rescue parties searched buildings, the heaps of rubble and chasms where once roads had been, thus saving the lives of many victims who otherwise would have per-ished. Burial parties dealt with the dead – the stench and fumes of sulphur were nau-seating.

When nothing more could be done locally, refugees were transported by the Navy to southern Italy. *Euryalus* took aboard 180 badly injured persons who were operat-ed upon, many for the amputation of limbs which were dropped overboard on pas-sage to Syracuse. During the voyage the injured had to be placed in rows on the upper deck – it was the best that could be done in the circumstances and their cries remained with us for a long time. It was a sad experience for all concerned.

Altogether, 77,000 persons were killed as a result of the earthquakes which wrecked Messina, Calabria, Reggio and Terromoto. The battery decks, where in nor-mal conditions we slept in our hammocks, had been piled high with relief stores, and latterly had accommodated the injured. During this period we had slept with our clothes on in the ammunition passages running alongside the boiler rooms well below the water line. It was hot and there was always the sickly smell of cordite from the magazines. It left us with a head like a thimble on a pin in the mornings, so we were glad to sleep on deck again in the fresh air.

After a spell of sightseeing in Malta, we were pleased to hear that the ship had been recalled to England and, to add to the excitement, was to carry out a full-power steam trial from Gibraltar.

This time, no longer suffering from seasickness, we were able to watch the wash and wake of the ship travelling at 20 knots. Thus it was we reached Spithead one very cold January morning, and had our last shivering wash from the tubs on the upper deck.

Our training was over. We felt very fit, had learned and seen a lot, and were discharged as fully-trained ratings to await instructions to join one of the ships of the Fleet. Before leaving we were informed that His Majesty, King Victor Emanuel III of Italy, had conferred upon us a medal for the rescue work at Messina. That was over 60 years ago and the medal, like its owner, is a bit battered now!

HMS *Vengeance*, an old battleship that had taken part in the Diamond Jubilee Review twelve years earlier, was in dry dock undergoing an extensive refit. The draft of boys to which I belonged was sent to live on board while waiting to be accommodated elsewhere.

A worse choice for this purpose would have been hard to find. With boilers out of action there were no sanitary or cooking facilities, and no electricity. The interior lighting – by candlelight in those compartments in use – was dismal and quite insufficient to show up obstacles in the gangways as we groped and tripped in the semi-darkness, dragging our kitbags and hammocks. The decks were littered with wire hawsers, gas cylinders and auxiliary machinery opened up for examination, and here and there areas under repair or alteration were roped off. The smell of hot resin, tallow, red lead and anti-fouling compositions was overpowering.

It was obvious that the ship was in no state to accommodate anybody and that someone, somewhere, had blundered. Realising this, the officer-in-charge obtained permission to send us on leave until required. This indeed was welcome news. An idyllic fortnight was to pass, recounting experiences to admiring family and friends, before instructions arrived to join the newly built HMS *Bellerophon*.

The bright morning of 20th February 1909 saw us, light of heart and light of step, pulling heavy handcarts containing our worldly possessions over the renowned cobble stones in Portsmouth Dockyard. We were on our way to commission the largest and most powerful battleship in the world.

CHAPTER TWO

HMS **Bellerophon:** *1st Battle Cruiser Squadron*

*B*ellerophon, the second ship of the *Dreadnought* class to be completed, lay berthed at the South Railway Jetty – towering over adjacent buildings and the slipway upon which she had been built.

A score or so of horsedrawn wagons, having discharged their loads of baggage, passed by as we approached the ship. It therefore came as no surprise to find several hundreds of the crew already assembled alongside. Having been checked in and allocated duties on board, we joined them to await the arrival of the remainder of the crew from Naval Depots.

This gave us an opportunity to pick out the main features of the ship: the great hull; her two huge funnels through which a railway train could be driven; the recently designed tripod type masts with gunnery control and range-finding towers built at their apex. The main armament of ten 12" guns, mounted in pairs in armoured turrets was easily discernible, but not the sixteen 4" guns which were screened. Heavy armour ran the length of the ship, and to provide protection against torpedo attack, steel-meshed nets were attached to booms along the hull. She was of 20,000 tons displacement and the turbines drove her at a top speed of 20 knots.

The traditional ceremony of commissioning took place at 9.00am with the ship's company of 900 officers and ratings being called to attention on the quarter deck whilst the Admiralty authority to commission was read out by the Captain. Simultaneously, Drake's Whip was broken at the fore masthead, to fly there day and night as long as the commission lasted, and the colours saluted as they were hoisted for the first time.

Thus HMS *Bellerophon* was formally in commission, and had joined the Fleet.

An address by the Captain followed, emphasising the importance of getting the ship to the highest pitch of efficiency as rapidly as possible in order to exercise with the battle squadrons. There was much to be done in testing out the new equipment throughout the ship, and with enthusiastic specialist officers and petty officers straight from courses at the gunnery and torpedo schools, those of the ship's company directly concerned were kept very busy in this respect.

Meanwhile, steamboats, sailing launches, pinnaces and other boats complete with their outfits, were obtained from the dockyard, tested and hoisted aboard. Storing ship – a seemingly unending operation – involved drawing thousands of items of varying descriptions from the dockyard. Working parties transported these to the ship in handcarts or horsedrawn wagons – there were no motor vehicles.

The range for the bosun included such items as spare lengths of anchor chain, to holystones, sailmaker's needles, cordage, the birch and cat o'nine tails, cleaning gear, etc. For the carpenter came timber, paints, boats, oars, etc. Cylinders of industrial gases, lubricating oils, firebars and firebricks, as well as spare machine parts and all manner of tools were requisitioned for the engineer. Outfits of flags for signalling and ceremonial use were provided for the signals branch, and electrical spares, explosive charges and wireless telegraphy equipment for the torpedo division.

As the stores were brought alongside they were unloaded onto the jetty, checked by those responsible for their custody, and then taken aboard for stowage. During these activities the internal economy was being attended to: outfits of cooking implements and utensils were issued to the Galleys, and skewers, cleavers, knives, chopping blocks and the like for the butcher's shop!

Messtraps (table appointments, etc) were provided to the officers messes, of fine quality china, glass, electro-plated cutlery and table linens, on an adequate scale to cater for the lavish and high standard of hospitality a Fleet battleship could be obliged to provide in diplomatic exchanges of mutual 'goodwill' during its commission.

Modest outfits for petty officers (greatly improved in later years) included one earthenware cup and saucer each – a recently introduced improvement in lieu of the one pint earthenware basins formerly supplied, and at that time still issued to other ratings, whose previous entitlement was an enamel one.

The tenant for the canteen had been appointed from the official list of Approved Tenants. To be on the Approved List they were obliged to donate 5% of their turnover to the ship's canteen fund which in turn made grants for sports gear, concert parties, benevolence, etc. This list included firms such as Wm Miller, Dickinson's and Army and Navy Stores. These were the nucleus of the Canteen Board which, in turn, was the forerunner of the NAAFI.

The canteen stores supplemented the items obtainable from the ship's stores and were of great variety. Stocks to meet requirements for several weeks were delivered aboard daily. Similarly, wine merchants were embarking wines, spirits, cigars and cigarettes for the officer's mess.

The navigating officer obtained chronometers, charts, notices to marines, etc. The Paymaster was responsible for the receipt of confidential books and Admiralty Orders, books of instruction, libraries, stationery, etc. Complete with a buoy, buoy-rope and canvas bag, he went ashore – accompanied by an armed escort – to draw the golden sovereigns and half-sovereigns he would need to pay the ship's company. The buoy and buoy-rope would be securely fastened to the canvas bag. This procedure went back to the time when, it is alleged, an officer returned from such duty and reported that the money had been lost over the side of the gangway while staggering up the incline!

The medical officer was just as busy, obtaining his surgical instruments and completing his pharmacy, first aid boxes, bedding and furniture for the sick bay, and checking the medical history sheets of the crew.

Everyone was kept on the move, but there still remained the major tasks of embarking torpedoes, shells and ammunition, three months provisions and clothing, not forgetting sacramental wine for the Chaplain, and 1,500 tons of coal.

Eventually everything was inboard and stowed away. Coaling was the worst operation, employing "All hands". Always an unpleasant and backbreaking job, it was marginally eased by having wide open decks and built-in coal shutes. Looking back, it was a hefty programme, but with an eager ship's company things went well from the start.

Our Captain was one of the most senior in the Navy and had around him first class officers, mostly specialist, keen on the drive for efficiency taking place. It should be noted that with the introduction of *Dreadnought* a new epoch had begun. Since Trafalgar the supremacy of the Royal Navy had gone unchallenged. The pride of old Admirals and Captains and indeed the men, centred around the ability to sail, to ride out storms, and not only to maintain but to vie with each other in enhancing the pristine appearance of their ship. I remember once admiring a cruiser coming up-harbour with a polished copper stern right down to her water-line. Pure seamanship counted above all else and was the sure road to promotion. Firing a gun at a flag attached to a buoy didn't seem important in those pre-*Dreadnought* days, and long range gunnery controlled by instruments had not even been thought of.

But with the rivalry brought about by building *Dreadnought*-type battleships by other nations, particularly Germany, and the growing size of their fleets, new schools of thought and awareness had emerged. Specialisation in the new scientific techniques of gunnery and torpedo control was the order of the day, and became the road to promotion seized upon by younger officers and men.

With an arms race unprecedented both in extent and character, millions of pounds were being spent on defence. Not only were the Royal dockyards in this country building battleships, battle cruisers, destroyers and submarines to capacity, but the great shipbuilding firms of Vickers, Armstrong-Whitworth, Fairfields, Swan & Hunter and others were doing the same. Not for this country alone, but also for Australia, New Zealand, Canada, Malaya, Japan and Turkey. No less than 7 warships were under construction in Portsmouth Dockyard and six improved *Dreadnought* battleships were nearing completion in other Royal yards. The object was to have a Navy twice the strength of any other two Navies.

Such was the atmosphere in which the 'shake-down' cruise of HMS *Bellerophon* commenced, and having swung for adjustment of compasses at Spithead, course was

15

set for Berehaven, Bantry Bay, for calibration of the guns. A permanent base had been established there for this purpose and was used by all new ships, or any others when fitted with new armament.

Advantage was taken of the calm waters in this anchorage to carry out Evolutions – a traditional series of arduous exercises laid down by the Admiralty and devised to teach sailors to cope with disasters and emergencies at sea.

Unshackling the sheet anchor (5 tons) and taking it by pulling boat to an imaginary flagship was high on the list, as it was known the Commander-in-Chief was keen on making a signal to individual ships saying, "For exercise, bring sheet anchor to flagship." A ship aground in a real emergency might try to pull itself off at high tide by sending its sheet anchor away in a small boat, dropping it in deeper water and then winching-in the attached cable.

"Out torpedo nets", involving a maze of wires and electric winches, had given trouble in the early exercises. The huge rolls of steel mesh, running almost the length of the ship, had sometimes taken charge when, wriggling like snakes, they dropped into position in the water, snapping the controlling brail wires. The sudden release of tension would cause the wires to whiplash across the deck inflicting serious injury to anyone in their path.

"In nets" was equally hazardous, but with repetitive practice efficiency increased until the cumbersome nets and wire ropes could be handled without incident.

With the calibrations completed, "Spit and polish" commenced on a grand scale. The decks were sanded and scored with holystones, but the grime left by the dockyard seemed impossible to shift. So it was a case of 'keep on keeping on', and we did – on our knees – for a half hour or more at a stretch. Luckier ones scored with sharkskin the beading around the upper deck. It took a long time before the decks came up to the snow white standard for which the Navy has always been renowned. The modern powers that shift dirt biologically overnight had, unfortunately, not yet been discovered. But even if they had it is doubtful if 'My Lords' of those days would have approved their use. "Bad for good order and naval discipline", they would have growled at the thought of traditional hardships being eased.

Brasswork was another matter. It had all been lacquered and this had to be sandpapered off before applying the old fashioned metal polish paste. Results were poor, possibly because of lack of enthusiasm and insufficient time to rub it in long enough, so we found ourselves in trouble.

In the worst situations it sometimes happens that deliverance comes from an unexpected quarter, and so it was with us. There was a well-known, widely advertised sauce retailing at 1/- for a monster bottle – the cheapest on the market – with but one instruction, vis: "Take plenty with everything". It proved to be the finest and most rapid polish in existence, giving a brilliant finish on brasswork, and was used regularly until liquid polish was issued at a later date.

16

With the ship painted and smartened in appearance generally, leave was given one Saturday afternoon. Experienced and far-seeing sailors took the waiting jaunty cars for the two mile journey to Castletown Bere. On arrival, they would set to with a will, rapidly reducing the stocks of Irish porter laid in by Mother Sullivan in her little bar. It could not have been very long after the 'foot-sloggers' arrived that she'd be putting up her 'Sold Out' notices!

The Navy always looks after its young. We boys were granted leave to go ashore, but for recreation purposes only and under the supervision of an officer. So, with our Divisional Officer, twenty or so of us were landed for a paperchase. We chased away merrily until, losing the trail we stumbled into a bog. Getting out was extremely difficult and by the time the last one was extricated we were a pretty soiled, cold and miserable lot. Our officer showed great initiative in finding a small local hotel where resources were taxed to the limit in providing us with hot baths, bed sheets to dry on, and a fine high tea. All very kindly paid for by our Divisional Officer from his own resources.

A number of Mother Sullivan's erstwhile customers missed the liberty boat back to the ship and were punished for breaking their leave – forfeiting a day's pay and a day's leave for each three hours or part thereof of absence. Excuses that the driver of the jaunty car was drunk, a wheel had come off *en route*, or that the horse had dropped dead, were of no avail! Leave-breaking was always regarded as a serious offence and, in addition to the punishment quoted, often carried a further sting when ships visited interesting ports of call. Leave in such cases would then be restricted to those men who had not broken their leave during the previous six months.

It was an opportunity to emphasise the Naval Discipline Act which, in accordance with King's Regulations and Admiralty Instructions, had to be read to the ship's company quarterly. The lower deck having been cleared and the officers and ship's company drawn up on the quarter deck with their caps off, the Captain would read the Act which ranged from the instruction for the public worship of Almighty God, the punishment applicable for cowardice in the face of the enemy, and finally the penalty for committing the most heinous crime of all – that of striking a superior officer! Hearing for the first time the awesome words: "Every person subject to this Act who shall strike or attempt to strike his superior officer, he being in the execution of his office, shall suffer DEATH, or such punishment as may be hereinafter mentioned" left an indelible impression.

There seemed but little chance of escape anyway, and Captains of warships still had the power when outside territorial waters to impose the death penalty, although I doubt whether any Captain in those days would have gone so far. On the other hand, some had the reputation of considering the punishment did not go far enough, since it could only be carried out once!

Any serious offence would not have gone undetected for long as the ship's police were also specialists in their duties of observing any breach of the ship's orders or Kings Regulations. They had been associated with the severe disciplinary measures brought into force in the Royal Naval Barracks, Portsmouth, following the incident of a stoke and an officer. Seamen, being trained in field exercises, knew that when addressing a body of men an officer sometimes gave the order "Front row on the knee". In that way he could ensure being seen by all when trying to make a point during instruction. Although this was a legitimate order, stokers did not know of it as they received no training in gunnery drill. The order having been given to a mixed assembly of seamen and stokers, one stoker remained standing, saying he only bent his knee to God. He was eventually tried by Court Martial and sentenced to five years penal servitude.

None of this delayed the constant exercising of "Action Stations" during the latter period in Bantry Bay. The crew learned to react instantly to the now familiar panic call that would reverberate through the ship without warning at any hour of the day or night. The time taken between the Officer of the Watch sounding the alarm and his report to the Captain 'Ship close up at Action Stations', was carefully monitored. And woe to he whose tardiness resulted in the last guns-crew to close-up getting one hour's extra gun drill in the dog-watches.

Finally, the ship and its crew was judged to be sufficiently efficient to join the 1st Battle Squadron for night exercises off Portland.

CHAPTER THREE

Showing the Flag

*B*ellerophon attracted much attention when passing through the lines of war-ships to pick up her berth, astern of *Dreadnought*. The harbour was crowded. We identified eight powerful battleships of the King Edward VII class, many earlier types and countless cruisers and destroyers. Many had been recalled from for-eign stations to build up the Home Fleet, currently being assembled in local waters. In the distance could be seen the port depot and several colliers.

Ships recently at sea were coaling and taking aboard fresh provisions. Others were leaving harbour for exercises in the Channel. Hoists of flags fluttered from the yard-arms, indicating course, speed, formation position, etc. Wireless telegraphy was in it's infancy and had not yet supplanted signalling by semaphore and flashing lamp, which took place continuously, at speeds far too fast for the average sailor to read.

Boats seemed to be everywhere – steamboats delivering and obtaining des-patches from the flagship, other boats sailing or under oars on various missions or exercises.

One cutter's crew coming alongside with oars tossed (in an upright position) received an unpleasant reminder that *Bellerophon* was fitted with automatic ash ejec-tors. Owing to lack of coordination between deck and stokehold, the ejectors had opened up full force just as the cutter came abreast of them, knocking the oars flat and smothering the crew with a mixture of cinders and ashes.

Flag officers of squadrons, looking regal in impressive uniforms, were afloat in their highly polished barges, flying their personal flags, to attend conferences aboard *Dreadnought*, the Fleet flagship.

The routine at Portland was based on battle practice and manoeuvres. As a fleet, and individually, the ships were kept exercising at sea as much as possible. It was gun-nery, gunnery – day and night.

During manoeuvres at night the Fleet would be blacked out under simulated war conditions and, if located, mock attacks would be made by the destroyer flotillas. With some 30 years to go before the invention of radar, one can picture the tension as scores of eyes searched for and tried to monitor movement of friend or foe in the Stygian blackness.

The story went that on one particularly dark night, Captain (D) in the flotilla leader was fortunate enough to spot the flagship and, regardless of discipline, broke the darkness by flashing the message "How do you like your eggs done?" The reaction of the Admiral is not known but Captain (D) was required to report to the flagship on arrival in harbour, in frock-coat and sword.

Few sights in the world could equal that of the Home Fleet at sea. Squadrons of battleships, like castles of steel, led by *Dreadnought*, steaming in stately formation, or manoeuvring as ordered by signal, with cruisers and destroyers spread out ahead as far as the eye could see. It was truly a magnificent spectacle. Here was Britain's might upon which the fate of the country and the Empire would ultimately depend.

There were regular periods in harbour for coaling, putting right minor defects and recreation. Shore leave to Portland or Weymouth was granted from early evening until 7.00am the following day. Other than an opportunity to stretch the legs and have a good meal there were few attractions at either place. To provide entertainment, a theatrical touring company occasionally leased a hall and put on a series of shows – not up to West End standard perhaps, but all good workers. One of the favourites was "The Bad Girl of the Family", the elderly star of which always received great applause, especially in the second house. Long wooden forms provided the seating on the sawdust covered floor and the price of admission was 1/- for the first three rows, 9d for the remainder.

Sometimes ships with good concert parties would stage a shore performance almost to professional standard – these were very popular both with the Fleet and the local people. There was the added pleasure of watching talented shipmates who, judging by the quality of their performances, had chosen the wrong vocation in joining the Royal Navy! Or one could witness the exhibition of one rather starchy ship's bandmaster, dressed in his best uniform, who, having raised his baton to place his orchestra 'under starter's orders' deliberately delayed the 'off' for the sake of effect – only to have his dignity shattered and the pregnant silence broken by a ribald shout of "Swankpot!" from the back of the hall.

One ship even produced dramatic plays, and to see the Master-at-Arms, or one of his unpopular minions (a Regulating Petty Officer) portraying Shylock, or able-seaman MacHammock-Lashing as Uriah Heep, was something never to be missed and well worth the inconvenience of catching the 11.30pm boat back aboard.

There were no music halls or theatres in Weymouth, neither were there any cinemas – then known as Electric Theatres – as they were only just making their début in the big cities. Therefore these enthusiastic attempts at providing entertainment filled a great need.

Other amenities were the Mission to Seamen, which did good work in providing beds, meals or a game of billiards for those who did not wish to visit the wide range of pubs, each with its own following of regulars from the Fleet. Generally speaking, that was the main purpose for the run ashore. Sailors liked beer, but there was none for them aboard their ships – one reason being the lack of space to stow it. About 75% of those entitled (at the age of 20) drew the daily rum ration consisting of $1/2$ gill of spirit – only 4.5% under proof – to which water was added to make up half a pint. It was a dreary and drowsy mixture, unpleasant to the taste, but in the absence of anything else very welcome! Given the choice, most of those drawing their rum ration would have preferred a beer.

Prominent temperance workers with the welfare of the sailor at heart induced the authorities to grant a payment of 3d a day in lieu of the rum ration to those who foreswore their grog and registered as temp. But once entered as 'G' or 'T', there was no changing over for twelve months. The 3d a day credited to temp personnel was a more generous concession than was generally known as, quoting from memory, the cost of rum was 3s $6^1/2$d a gallon.

If staying ashore for the night it was important to book a bed on landing, as the demand often exceeded the supply. Most houses near the harbour had notices in the window "Good Beds – Early Call" and the prices ranged from 6d to 1/-. One very good hotel on the seafront charged 1s 6d and provided clean linen each night!

Occasionally weekend leave was given. This enabled those with families in Portsmouth to visit them. Although much appreciated, it meant returning from Portsmouth at midnight on Sunday to arrive in Weymouth at 3.30am on Monday. No beds being available at that hour, and the ship being moored at a buoy about a mile or more offshore, it was a case of sleeping on the beach or walking around until the first boat came to collect returning libertymen from the jetty at 7.00am. In due course the Railway Company put on an excursion whenever 500 passengers could be guaranteed and arranged for the train to reach Weymouth at 6.45am, whereby one could meet the boat and arrive aboard all the fresher for the Fleet Evolutions – a masochistic rehearsal for emergencies and usually sprung without warning on ships in harbour on Monday mornings.

There was a keen rivalry between individual ships and squadrons performing these exercises, for which points were awarded, so if one could beat a 'chummy ship' or maintain a record, so much the better.

All eyes were directed to the flagship, hoping to read the signal ordering the exercise for the morning. It could be anything from "Out collision mat over port bow below water-line"; "Out torpedo nets"; "Hoist out and raise steam in second picket boat"; "Land field guns"; "Send sheet anchor to Flagship in pulling cutter"; or even "Land sailmaker in Neil-Robertson stretcher" (a patent device for transferring a severely wounded or sick person from a vessel at sea).

Designed to test the efficiency and the serviceability of equipment, all was generally fair and above board, but dodges to save time were not unknown. One old battleship was always first in the sheet anchor exercise until it was discovered this was due

21

to using a wooden replica, made by her carpenters, which weighed less than half that of the original!

Whatever the job, there was always the urge to excel, whether it be gunnery, torpedo work, boat sailing, Evolutions or even coaling, which in spite of its unpopularity was tackled with zest. Each hour flags denoting the number of tons taken aboard were hoisted and the result compared with those of other ships. Hopes of night leave rose or fell according to these results as the day wore on. There were trophies for efficiency and sporting events, which often went to the same ship. It was a very proud ship indeed that won the 'Silver Cock' as the best all-rounder.

The Fleet was based at Portland for the winter months, the ships dispersing to their Home Ports – Portsmouth, Devonport, Chatham – in time to give 10 days leave to each watch for Christmas. In the spring, cruises were made to Vigo, Aranci Bay, Gibraltar and into the Mediterranean as far as the Balearics, tactical and gunnery exercises taking place *en route*.

During the early summer, courtesy visits were made to seaside resorts around the British Isles. These were followed by war exercises at sea for ten to fourteen days in which most ships in home waters and sections of the Royal Naval Reserve participated. Then came a few days leave before moving to Scottish waters for the remainder of the summer and early autumn.

In 1909 the naval estimates had reached, for those days, the astronomical figure of around sixty million pounds (the pound was stable against the American dollar at $4.80 to the pound!) and probably influenced the decision to show the Fleet to those who had seldom had the chance to see it. So, in June 1909, led by the Commander-in-Chief, Admiral Sir William May in *Dreadnought*, the greatest ever amount of warships assembled and anchored off Southend. Nearest the pier, and heading several lines of ships of all types, were *Dreadnought*, *Bellerophon* and the two latest Dreadnought-class, *Superb* and *Temeraire*.

The Fleet was due at 1.00pm and it was a matter of comment in the newspapers that it anchored precisely to the minute, a very fine performance on the part of those responsible. There was a tremendous welcome and the visit was a great success, with several thousands of visitors coming aboard the ships each afternoon and being shown around. Southend, agog with gaiety, took the sailors to heart and organised all manner of entertainment for them. It was a jolly occasion and stories of enthralling (and no doubt exaggerated) personal adventures were told among messmates long after the visit was over – well worth the cleaning and painting that had gone into getting the ships ready for inspection by their 'owners'.

Northern bases were at Rosyth, Cromarty, Invergordon and Scapa Flow, each being visited in turn by sections of the Fleet. Periods at Rosyth were chiefly for recreation. The optical illusion that the mast would strike the Forth Bridge as the ship passed underneath was always something to watch with bated breath as we steamed

ABOVE: *HMS* Impregnable.

RIGHT: *Lt. Commander WEV Woods, RN in his full dress uniform in 1942 at the age of fifty.*

ABOVE: *HMS* Fame *built on concrete in the grounds of the Royal Hospital School, Greenwich which was established in the 17th century for the sons of sailors and demolished in 1926 when the school was moved to Holbrook.*

LEFT: *An aerial view of Maritime Greenwich. The* Cutty Sark *appears in the right foreground.*

ABOVE: *HMS* Euryalus. *Woody's first ship 1908–1909.*

BELOW: *HMS* Iron Duke – *Admiral Jellicoe's flagship at the Battle of Jutland, 1916*

Earthquake at Messina, Sicily 1909. The horror of Messina's end: panic-stricken inhabitants in mad flight between earthquake and flood. (From an artist's impression of the scene.)

ABOVE: *HMS* Bellerophon *in 1909.*

BELOW: *HMS* Princess Royal *of the First Battle Cruiser Squadron, 1914.*

— H.M.S. "Princess Royal" —

First Commissioned   13th November 1912

Built at Barrow by Vickers, Son & Maxim.

Length	700 ft.	
Beam	90 ft.	
Displacement	26,350 tons	
Speed (on Trials)	34·4 Knots.	This photograph, taken
Coal Capacity	4000 tons	after the action off
Oil	1150 / 2500 tons	Heligoland, shows the
Burns Coal at Full Speed	100 tons per hr.	peculiar method adopted to deceive
Armament	8 — 13·5"	the Enemy in their endeavours to get a Range.
	16 — 4"	All ships were painted
Armour	12" Harvey Steel	after the same style.
Horse Power	70,000 (Has developed 100,000)	Note: The dark colour paint is the usual slate. Ships are painted.
Crew (Normal)	1000 men	
(Max)	1160 men	

Woody's statistics on the ship he commissioned in 1912.

LEFT: *The King of Italy thanking British officers for the work accomplished by rescue parties off HMS* Euryalus.

BELOW: *This map indicates some of the places mentioned in his story of his first sea-going venture on the* Euryalus *by Boy 1st Class WEV Woods.*

slowly toward our anchorage. At that time the new immense naval dockyard was under construction at Rosyth and the noise from where we were berthed half a mile away was indescribable.

Leave to visit Edinburgh with its amenities and many places of interest, only twenty miles away by train, was always welcome. The boys, not being allowed night leave, were taken there by the Ship's Chaplain, visiting the castle, Holyrood Palace, John Knox's house, etc., during the afternoons. Alternatively, a brisk walk to Dunfermline, five miles distant, to see the cottage in which Andrew Carnegie was born, and to listen to the fine band playing in the attractively laid out park, both maintained by the Carnegie Trust.

Gunnery exercises took place in the Moray Firth. High battle-practice targets of latticework built on hulls, costing £3,000 each (£25,000 today?) were fired at from great distances. When acting as spotting-ship astern of the target, the sharp flashes of explosion from the firing ship's guns were seen minutes before the approaching one-ton projectiles, hurtling towards the target with terrifying express-train shrieks, causing us to duck instinctively. From the spotting position several cable-lengths astern, they still seemed to be making a bee-line for the tip of one's nose. As they hit the sea great white water spouts erupted to a height of 200 feet or more, often ricocheting before going to the bottom.

After the exercises the ships would anchor off Cromarty – then a small fishing village at the mouth of Cromarty Firth – where the population was less than the complement of any of the ships. It was a close-knit community, whose peaceful way of life had been intruded upon by the establishment of a naval base – almost like visitors from outer space. They were very devout and were rather shocked by football being played in their midst on Sundays while all the villagers were at church.

I have never forgotten the kindness of the Captain of the fishing fleet who preached in the chapel on Sundays, afterwards taking a party of sailors to his cottage for tea. His wife, a matronly Scots lady with a round rosy face, silver grey hair brushed flat and parted in the middle, wearing a large white apron, presided at her table, heavily laden with freshly baked scones, pancakes, oatcakes, white bread, brown bread and home-made jams and jellies. What a feast for hungry boys! So different to their tea aboard – and how they did appreciate it!

Invergordon, at the other end of the Firth and on the main line to London, was more thickly populated. Midway between Invergordon and Cromarty was where HMS *Natal*, a four funnelled cruiser with 9.2" guns caught fire and blew up in 1915. Her upturned, half-submerged wreck remained in the Firth for many years after – a memorial to the hundreds of her crew and the tragic children's party taking place on board at the time.

Scapa Flow, a magnificent natural harbour, was bare, bleak and uninviting (when drafting these memoirs 60 years or so after my first glimpse of the place, I still remember those first impressions and can picture lunar astronauts training there for their moon walk!) Mails were delayed and fresh foods, other than fish, were obtainable only in small quantities. Many of us were destined to spend four years of our lives there, but first impressions remained – we never liked it.

The weekend routine at Scapa, without leave, seemed more unpleasant than ever. Although the upper deck and mess decks were scrubbed daily, on Saturdays the whole morning was devoted to extra cleaning in preparation for the Captain's Rounds on Sunday. Special attention was given to the burnishing of knives and forks with emery paper and the polishing of spoons and tin-plated utensils. After a final polish on Sunday – following the custom handed down from sailing days – the cutlery was set out in geometrical patterns, spaced to allow the other messtraps to be laid out, type-by-type, and lined up with those on the tables of other messes, like guardsmen on parade. 'Cooks of Messes', a duty rota involving two from each mess doing the daily housekeeping chores of the mess until the next pair took over 24 hours later, were responsible for all of this. It usually involved them in a race against time to get the job finished and then changed into their 'Number Ones' before the Captain commenced his rounds.

This was a ceremony in itself – preceded by the Master-at-Arms carrying a candle-lit lantern and a bugler sounding the "Still". The Captain, attended by the Commander, 1st Lieutenant, Senior Medical Officer and other Heads of Departments, all wearing frock-coats and swords, would enter and make a minute inspection of each mess. Taking his time, he would carefully examine item after item, lifting the lids of wooden bread barges, opening drawers in the mess shelves, looking under tables, passing a white doeskin gloved hand along overhead racks searching for dust, and asking questions involving 'Cooks of Messes' to heads of departments. Never any hurry – a thorough inspection always took place, and woe to he whose personal gear was not stowed clean and neat in any locker into which the Captain chose to peep.

Meanwhile, on the upper deck in their Sunday best, having been inspected by divisional officers, the ship's company remained fallen in awaiting inspection by the Captain and hoping that he would soon appear. There were always hazards – hair too long, bad shave, rows of tape on the collar too close together, silk handkerchief tied the wrong way, bow over the left eye or pimples on the face! Names having been taken and delinquents given orders, the ship's company was called to attention while the Commander saluted the Captain and the order given for the ranks to be dismissed.

Immediately after the Sunday inspection came the pipe, "Hands rig Church on the quarter deck". This meant that heavy mess stools of solid oak, with collapsible metal legs at each end – which had a knack of getting in the way – had to be unshipped from their anchorages and transported up ladders and through narrow hatchways to the quarter deck. It was usually more hazardous than it sounds, involving as it did hordes of heavily-laden sailors making for the same hatchways at the same time. The shoving and jostling resulted in crushed fingers and blows on the head from stools, which brought forth torrents of blasphemy and nautical oaths such as never would be heard in the precincts of a church ashore. Old salts fervently prayed that the text would not be 'Cleanliness is next to Godliness', avowing that in other ships this had sometimes led to "Clean Guns" after the service!

Finally, the stools were taken back below and hands piped to dinner. Unless anything unforeseen occurred, and with the exception of watchkeepers, the ship's company had the rest of the day to themselves.

This was as far as Lt. Comdr Woods got with his story when trying to put it together for the first time at the age of 80. He died three weeks later in April, 1972.

From naval records, it was learned that he was promoted from Boy 1st Class to Boy, Supply Stores, and drafted back to Portsmouth from HMS Bellerophon, *where he joined HMS* Grafton *on 5th January 1910. From June 1910 he served on HMS* Cochrane *until August 1911, and then on HMS* Arrogant *until August 1912. From there he went to HMS* Dolphin *until November 1913 when he was one of 1,000 officers and men selected to commission the brand new battle cruiser HMS* Princess Royal *at Barrow-in-Furness.*

'Woody' then takes up his story again, thanks to a 60 year old diary discovered by his wife a few weeks after his death. The inside front cover showed a picture of HMS Princess Royal *with some of its technical data he'd compiled. The faded script started boldly with the heading as shown, but became increasingly difficult to decipher. He seemed to lose interest in keeping his diary as depression crept in with the war taking its daily toll of friends and ships he knew. But he gives graphic word-pictures depicting the tension of days immediately prior to the declaration of war and the early false alarms.*

The mind boggles at the verbal picture he paints of coaling and provisioning ship at Scapa Flow on the first day of war. From 6.00pm on the 5th until 7.00am on the 6th they loaded and stowed 850 tons of coal, 10,540 lbs of meat and 10,080 lbs of potatoes. Everybody on board – regardless of rank – took part in this prodigious backbreaking task.

Now for the diary ...

CHAPTER FOUR

War!

The diary opens:-

SUNDAY, 26TH JULY 1914

Wire from Admiralty cancelling mid-summer leave. Ships already on passage recalled to Portland. Fleet now awaiting instructions. There is great disappointment at having holidays so abruptly stopped.

MONDAY, 27TH JULY

3am – "Reveille"; "Hands secure collier"; 3.30am -"Coal Ships" 1,250 tons. During the forenoon oil lighter supplied oil. Urgent demands for provisions forwarded to Deptford, thus cancelling previous ones on Portsmouth for Friday next. All available stores for engineer, carpenter and bo'sun being hurriedly passed into the ship. Rumours of war everywhere.

TUESDAY, 28TH JULY

Have completed with coal and oil to war-stowage. Now awaiting further orders. Every ship here in Portland is taking aboard all manner of stores with the utmost despatch, both day and night. Parties of men are removing coal from the wharf to lighters. These are being emptied by ships faster than they can be filled. Every tug or steam vessel procurable is being utilised. Portland has never been so busy before.

Leave given to all ships coaled. I went intending to remain until 7.00am tomorrow. 8.30pm the patrol was hurrying all over Weymouth with orders for all men to return to their ships as soon as possible. From Weymouth Parade great activity was noticed amongst the squadrons in Weymouth Bay, many small ships were getting under way. Caught a steam pinnace leaving at 10.00pm. There was great excitement everywhere, crowds waiting to see us off, some laughing and making jokes and saying we should be ashore again tomorrow, others crying. What a send off they gave us as we left, singing and cheering in turns. Never in my experience has there been such a show of feeling at

Weymouth towards the Fleet. Evidently they think we are going to war, and we wonder if it really is true and whether we are gazing at the lights of Weymouth for the last time as we leave the pier.

Passing through the lines we noticed that ships not yet finished coaling were getting the coal inboard as fast as possible and that there were few ships still waiting for a collier. Signal had been made saying all ships were to be coaled without fail by the morning. Getting on board once more it was apparent steam was being raised. Special parties had gone ashore to bring off the ten days fresh provisions, 7,500 lb. meat and 15,000 lb. potatoes. This was brought alongside at 2.00am and at 3.00am another lighter came filled with lubricating oils, fire bricks and many articles for the engineers' stores. All these were being stowed away during the small hours, and those people trying to snatch a bit of shut-eye did not get much sleep owing to the din and bumping as the above mentioned stores were dragged under their hammocks.

Then we heard a boatload of choristers sailing around the Fleet singing hymns.

WEDNESDAY, 29TH JULY

I'll start today's account from 4.00am when the bugle called all hands to get the ship under way. Some had not had any sleep since Sunday night. I managed to get a letter posted home explaining that I should not be on leave as anticipated. We followed the Battle Squadron. The last ship to leave harbour was the "Iron Duke" and as she took station astern of us, the 1st Battle Cruiser Squadron, it was evident that the Commander-in-Chief, Admiral Sir George Gallagher, was not aboard, his position being at the head of the Fleet. After passing the Shambles lightship the whole Fleet steamed west for two hours. This, it is certain, was to prevent any interested busybody knowing our course, for at 8.00am all ships turned 16 points and proceeded east at slow speed. An air of mystery overhung the Fleet, which looked grand and impressive.

The first signal of importance was "Clear ship for action". This made us fully aware we were not going on a Cook's tour! Every moveable piece of structure above deck was taken down: boats, davits, ladders, rigging, parts of bridges and hundreds of fittings – all necessary, yet not worth the danger they would become in action. This accomplished, 'service' ammunition was got up from the shell rooms and magazines and put in position by the 4" guns. In the afternoon 'War Routine' was brought into force, thereby giving the chance of a nap to all off watch. We availed ourselves of this opportunity, especially those who had not seen their hammocks for three nights.

During the dog-watches (which are the watches from 4.00 to 6.00pm and from 6.00 to 8.00pm), all wooden furniture, desks and library cupboards were smashed up. These would be used as firewood. At 8.00pm the guns were manned by part of the watch and a keen look-out kept for any signs of any ships. Fleet is steaming with all lights out and any German vessels on the prowl will certainly receive a warm welcome. Misty weather makes navigation dangerous. Great excitement everywhere.

THURSDAY, 30TH JULY

Midnight – The watch called to relieve the guns crew and navigational parties. I was relieved from my station, which during the war is on the decoding staff – my duties are to decode all signals made by wireless. These signals are made in secret codes and cyphers with a special officer is in charge of the code books.

At 2.00am the Fleet passed through the Straits of Dover. The nerve strain throughout the dark hours is very severe, not knowing at any moment if we shall be fired upon. At 4.00am all 4" ammunition re-stowed in the shell rooms and magazines. This has to be wheeled along under the hammocks, thus waking the occupants. Searchlights re-stowed below armour. These have now to be fitted into position each night, a most cumbersome operation.

At 7.00am men who had kept the first and middle watches were called (these are the watches from 8.00 to 12.00pm and from 12.00pm to 4.00am). About this time the Fleet increased speed and got into battle formation. The 1st Battle Cruiser Squadron took up its position about 10 miles ahead of the Battle Squadron, immediately behind the Light and Armoured Cruisers. The only ships sighted during the day were the *Jeane Barte* and the *Glorie* – both French ships. Rifles, chests, history sheets and all documents stowed down the holds right at the bottom of the ship. The rigging was rattled down, i.e. lashed with wire to prevent the ends flying about if struck by a shell. Cabin furniture and all internal fittings such as library cases, desks, etc., smashed up. It seemed a pity that so much good gear should be sacrificed. This done, operating tables were rigged, stretchers and surgical instruments were made ready and placed in convenient positions. Anything likely to catch fire easily was stowed away or burned in the ship's boilers. Curtains, covers and table cloths were collected and placed in a store below the water-line.

6.00pm – The ammunition operation was again repeated and the light guns manned at 8.00pm. Of course, the big guns are always manned both day and night. Everybody is cheerful, but excited and anxious. The officers have been issued with revolvers.

FRIDAY, 31ST JULY

5.00pm – Fleet anchored Scapa Flow. Coaled ship on arrival 800 tons.

SATURDAY, 1ST AUGUST

I little thought this time last week that I would be in dreary Scapa Flow. There are great hills all around which are at present obscured by fog. On one of these is a tree and it is the pride boast of the inhabitants of Kirkwall, a small fishing town four miles from the landing stage, as it is the only one around. Well, I think that while daylight holds that tree will be our only non-naval living companion, as it were.

A signal announced that until further orders, all private correspondence from the Fleet would have to pass the censor. In our case the Chaplain was detailed off for that duty. All ships' boats, with the exception of two steam boats and a sailing launch, were put ashore and stowed in a field. Also gangway ladders, wooden targets, wardroom pianos and the like. "Out torpedo nets" is the order at night and this has a straining effect on the nerves. We are not frightened – on the contrary – but the atmosphere of suspense generates tension throughout the ship.

SUNDAY, 2ND AUGUST

The war news is alarming and today seems any day but a normal peacetime Sunday. Distinguishing bands around funnels have been painted out.

MONDAY, 3RD AUGUST

Early this morning, the 1st Battle Cruiser Squadron received orders to raise steam for full speed. At 1 o'clock our Rear Admiral, who was promoted to Vice-Admiral last night at the early age of 43, came aboard and, throwing aside all the pomp and ceremony that usually marks the approach of a flag officer, stepped onto a raised hatch and said, "I've just come aboard to have a look at you", in a most friendly and disarming fashion. After outlining the situation he remarked that "we are not yet at war, but it's a £1,000 to a gooseberry that we will be by tomorrow." In which case, he said "you ought to be pleased to be in the *Princess Royal*", which had carried off all the squadron prizes in gunnery and he was sure that "the reputation held in time of peace would be upheld to the last in the event of war". He looked upon her as the eldest child of the squadron and one to which he could confidently entrust any duty. We were about to reap what our fathers had sewn, and the world's eyes would be upon us in these finest fighting machines man had ever produced. His very inspiring speech, of which I have given only a few extracts, made us very proud and the lusty cheers he got as he stepped over the gangway resounded around the harbour.

6.30pm – Armoured cruisers proceeded.

7.30pm – 1st Battle Cruiser Squadron proceeded at 28 knots. Sea rough.

Three German transports had been reported making for the Shetland Isles under escort of cruisers and destroyers. "At last!" we exclaimed. "Now we're going to see what our guns will really do!" Although no ships were visible, heavy firing was heard and we thought that the armoured cruisers were having a go. On we sped, throwing masses of foam over the decks, with every man at his station ready. Shots were falling just in front of the *Lion*, our flagship, and we eagerly awaited the signal to "open fire". All eyes were strained to see the enemy.

No signal to "open fire", and no ships came, however. The firing was the RGA doing a practice shoot, thinking we had passed. Thus ended our first exciting experience.

During this time I was in the engine-room and hearing the explosions thought we were actually under fire, so was much surprised on reaching the upper deck and finding no smashed-up enemy. We started patrolling an area through which the transports would have to pass near Fair Island. No encounter. Signal received announcing that Admiral Sir J. Jellicoe would assume command of the Home Fleet: Vice-Sir G. Gallagher.

TUESDAY, 4TH AUGUST

No sign of the transports although we have been scouring the sea all day. Evidently they have not ventured this way after all. The armoured cruisers have been patrolling one side of Fair Island and the 1st Battle Cruiser Squadron the other, so it would have been impossible to have slipped both of us. My afternoon watch.

3.30pm – "Wireless" from Admiralty stating that the British ultimatum to Germany would expire at midnight tomorrow, at which hour war would be declared by telegram. This caused great excitement but appeared to be just a taster, for at 6.00pm a telegram stated that the ultimatum would expire at midnight tonight. How often have I pictured to myself what an awful experience the night before would be, and yet here we are actually about to start and it is so totally different to my fancy. Everyone is jolly and not a bit disturbed.

WEDNESDAY, 5TH AUGUST

I went on watch at midnight. At 1.10am the fatal telegram arrived. I decoded it. It was short and grim and read as follows: "Admiralty to all ships. Commence hostilities at once against Germany."

Although war has only just been declared one wonders if the Germans have stolen a march on us, and if there are any of their ships lurking around. If there are, they would get a warm reception as all guns are now loaded and vigilant watch is being kept.

During the forenoon the Fleet surgeon addressed a few words of advice to the ship's company regarding the most suitable underclothing to be worn to assist in cleaning shell splinter wounds. The tension is great as we expect to see the enemy at any minute and are waiting for the "action" bugle to sound off. The first incident of war was our interception of the British steamship *Ailsa*, which was boarded and her documents and cargo examined. This was the first news those on board her had heard of 'war'.

Our next was a little more exciting – a vessel under sail flying the German ensign was sighted. We signalled to her to "heave to", an order she did not obey owing to not having a qualified signaller on board. We soon caught her up and, speaking to her in German, made her lower sail. An armed boat's crew was despatched and they searched the vessel.

The German crew disclaimed all knowledge of war and stated that they had been on the Dogger Bank for five weeks, salting their own fish. There were no traces of this being carried out however, and they could offer no explanation as to why they were so far north (this occurred off the Shetlands). There were two carrier pigeons on board, both with English markings, which were said to have been picked up at sea. The crew of 13 were taken prisoners and we recalled the steamer Ailsa to tow our first prize, the *Berlin von Ernden* to Kirkwall. It was said that four pigeons were sent off as the *Ailsa* made for the fishing vessel.

3.00pm – We proceeded into Scapa Flow at 25 knots, arriving at 6.00pm. Collier immediately secured and 850 tons taken aboard. Also provision ship alongside and those not on coal started getting the food in. This included officers, as everything was being done as fast as possible. We were only allowed to provision ship for three hours so the more we got aboard in that time the better we were going to eat in the days to come. Another boat came alongside from the frozen meat ship Jaffa, with 10,540 lb. meat and 10,080 lb. potatoes. Owing to the necessity of getting as much inboard as possible, every available man, irrespective of rank, was busily employed stowing until 7.00am. Coal was inboard at 3.30am.

During this operation a light cruiser patrolling the entrance signalled that some torpedo boat destroyers, presumably German, were becoming visible. There was a rush from the collier to man guns, lights were extinguished and those too long in being switched off were quickly smashed. It was a false alarm, but not before a rumour passed round the ship that six of the eight *King Edward III* class – which had left harbour only a few hours earlier – had been torpedoed by this supposed flotilla and had been sunk with all hands. We were much relieved to hear later that such was not the case. No sleep for anyone.

THURSDAY, 6TH AUGUST

It will be of interest to note the following signals which passed last night between the Commander-in-Chief and His Majesty King George V.

From George R.1 to Admiral Sir John Jellicoe:-

"At this grave moment of our nation's history I send to you and all officers and men of the Fleet, of which you have assumed command, the assurance of my confidence that, under your direction, they will revive and renew the old glories of the Royal Navy, and prove once again the sure shield of Britain, and of her Empire in the hour of trial."

Admiral Sir John Jellicoe – Admiralty. "Please submit following to HM King George V":-

"On behalf of the officers and men of the Home Fleet I beg to tender our loyal and dutiful thanks to Your Majesty for the gracious message, which shall inspire all with determination to uphold the glorious traditions of the past."

These messages gave general satisfaction and were much appreciated.

7.00am – "In nets". 1st Battle Cruiser Squadron proceeded 18 knots. Passed three ships *Crescent* class (old light cruisers). *Crescent* reports having captured two steam ships. Exercised "General Quarters". Everybody is dead beat – some, including myself, have been up since midnight Tuesday 4th.

10.00am – Two light cruisers joined up the Squadron. Ships spread out to search. Several fishing vessels flying Dutch ensign were passed about noon. They were allowed to proceed unmolested.

3.00pm – We joined up with a section of the Battle Squadron, including ships of the *Iron Duke*, *King George V*, *Colossus* and *St Vincent* classes. Reported that hostile submarines are active. Sharp look-out being kept. We don't relish being bowled out in that fashion – a stand-up fight is fairer. Message received that German minelayer *Koenigen Louise* has been sunk by destroyer *Lance*. The Lance is a new boat. Survivors state that they have laid a line of mines several miles in length from Hull. Vigilant "night defence" stations. The weather is fine, sea smooth, just the thing for the submarines. It is very trying dropping off to sleep at night under these new conditions. We are always expecting a sudden call (or lift!).

FRIDAY, 7TH AUGUST

1st Battle Cruiser Squadron was despatched with flotilla of destroyers to search a section of the Norwegian coast. It had been reported that the Germans had established a torpedo and light cruiser base, also a sort of depot. The destroyers went right in close to the land but reported that they had seen nothing. A large whale was sighted and thought to be a submarine. It really looked like one and if it had not shot up a steam of water when it did, it would probably have got a 4" shell for it's supper! Stopped and examined a Norwegian trawler. She proved satisfactory and was permitted to proceed.

SATURDAY, 8TH AUGUST

Midnight – Received report of the loss of the *Amphion* light cruiser with the paymaster and 130 men. Paymaster Gedge passed me in my last examination. She was blown up by a mine laid by the *Koenigen Louise*. Passed the Battle Squadron this morning which had just coaled.

1.30pm – Anchored Scapa. The entrance channels are being swept continually. Fresh provisions drawn from *Jaffa*, coal in by 11.30pm (800 tons).

The diary continues with a daily picture of life at sea sixty years ago. Long arduous sleepless patrols with numerous false alarms of enemy shipping and submarines, back-breaking coaling and provisioning against the clock at all hours and in all weathers, and back on patrol as soon as this was achieved. Huge fleets of ships, the likes of which will never be seen again, scouring the Home Waters for an enemy that preferred to lie low and wait.

Then, on Thursday 27th August, the Princess Royal *with the remainder of the 1st Battle Cruiser Squadron, leave Scapa Flow at 2.00am and proceed east all day at 22 knots. We pick up the diary again:-*

FRIDAY, 28TH AUGUST

Most exciting 24 hours.

8.00am – Reports from our destroyers that they were just going into 'action' against a strong force of German destroyers. It was part of a pre-arranged scheme that this flotilla should creep well into the enemy water and lure to sea as big a squadron as possible so that the 1st Battle Cruiser Squadron and 1st Light Cruiser Squadron could polish them off.

We heard firing ahead and shortly came up to the German cruiser Mainz on fire, with masts and one funnel shot away, and flag struck. Everybody still alive on her was hurriedly boarding a raft they had launched. A thick mist suddenly shut three more German cruisers out of sight and we were uncertain of their position until they opened fire on us. Not being able to see them (they were well into the mist, whilst we were only just on the edge of it with the light behind, which made us faintly visible to them) our only course was to fire at the flashes of their guns. Despite the fact that shells were falling all around us we were only hit twice – one smashed through upper deck battery, causing many steel splinters and finally tearing it's way through a steamboat before bursting; the other hit the side of the ship.

Our superior and heavier gun fire soon sunk one ship, which made a brave fight until the last. When she saw all was lost she steamed full speed towards us and was within a 2 mile range. A turret was blown completely out of her, the gun firing up in the air about 50 ft. She quickly sunk and the last seen of her was the smoke from her guns which were still firing as the water closed over her. Another German ship, the *Ariadne*, hauled down her flag and immediately firing ceased. She then turned and, firing a salute, tried to escape into the mist. A few salvos soon finished her and the last seen of her was flames shooting in all directions and her stern out of the water. The whole action lasted about one hour.

Thanks to the skill of our Admiral, we received no damage from the Heligoland Forts which were at times only 11 miles off. The fog also proved a friend to us in this respect.

The signal to retire was made at 1.30pm. The *Southampton* and *Viking* picked up nine German officers and 81 men, survivors of the *Mainz*.

Casualties on our side numbered 69. The *Arethusa* was badly damaged and the destroyer *Laertes* was put out of action at the beginning when hit in her engine-room. She was towed into port. None of our ships were lost.

The following wireless report was made to the Commander-in-Chief:

"Destroyers today heavily engaged enemy destroyers. Results satisfactory, details unknown.

1st Light Cruiser Squadron sank *Mainz* and received slight damage.

1st Battle Cruiser Squadron sank one cruiser *Koln* class and another cruiser disappeared in the mist on fire in a sinking condition.

1st Battle Cruiser Squadron attacked by submarines and floating mines during afternoon, but is undamaged."

Commander-in-Chief to ships engaged:- "Splendid – well done."

SATURDAY, 29TH AUGUST

Had a pleasant sleep after the excitement. Steaming at 21 knots through thick misty weather. 1st Light Cruiser Squadron fired at submarine this afternoon. Arrived Scapa 7.30pm and the whole Fleet in harbour "manned ship's side" and cheered us all madly. Colliers alongside.

SUNDAY, 30TH AUGUST

7.00am – Finished coaling. Everybody tired out. 9.00am provisioned and filled up with ammunition. 81 rounds fired during the action. Paint ship. Hands had had no sleep for 48 hours.

(That was the Battle of Heligoland Bight, in which my history book states that the Admiral Beatty's Battle Cruiser Squadron, Commodore Tyrwhitt's Light Cruiser Squadron and a flotilla of destroyers sunk the German cruisers Mainz, Ariadne *and* Koln, *together with one destroyer, and that no British ships were sunk or badly damaged. The wearisome patrols continue:-)*

CHAPTER FIVE

With Admiral Beatty at the Battle of Dogger Bank

MONDAY, 31ST AUGUST 1914
1st Battle Cruiser Squadron ordered to raise steam for 20 knots and proceed 4.30pm.

TUESDAY, 1ST SEPTEMBER
The merchant ships *Skuler* of Bergen and *Rolf Jare* carrying provisions were boarded during the day and passed as harmless. Both were flying Norwegian flags.

WEDNESDAY, 2ND SEPTEMBER
Boarded British trawler early this morning. They were good enough to give us enough fish for the ship's company. Fired two rounds of blanks in order to make the *Canfoa Chine* heave to at 9.00am. She was British.

FRIDAY, 4TH SEPTEMBER
Have been making a careful search for bases, mines and any suspicious craft all day off the Danish coast. The only suspicious things encountered were a number of small vessels all flying neutral flags. We are getting tired of seeing so many of the same colour, as it is certain that these craft are laying the mines. The *Rolf Jare*, which we searched last Tuesday was afterwards found to have, under her innocent cargo of bacon, another and more sinister cargo of 'eggs', in the form of large quantities of explosives. In addition she had five ensigns of different countries. It is of course most difficult to bowl these offenders out as in every case they have sets of 'dud' papers. Sea rough and ship rolling heavily. *Speedy* struck a mine and foundered.

SATURDAY, 5TH SEPTEMBER
Our arrival at Rosyth at 7.00am was marked by the rousing welcome we received from the Territorials stationed in the shore batteries, and civilians. There were also large numbers on the Forth Bridge. 1,500 tons of coal taken in and about two hundred miners came on board to give some of our fellows a spell.

35

Provisioned with fresh meat and veg. Read the reports of the 'action' of Heliogoland in the newspapers.

SUNDAY, 6TH SEPTEMBER

Ship's company busily employed all day cleaning ship after coaling, etc. The seven days overdue mail reached us today. There was plenty of excitement when it was issued.

10.30pm – "Action" sounded. Submarines reported entering harbour. The 'nets' were out as a precaution and guns were quickly manned. False alarm so one watch turned in at midnight. Reported that German cruiser had captured and sunk fifteen English fishing trawlers.

MONDAY, 7TH SEPTEMBER

This is the longest stay we have had in harbour since I started the diary. Officers allowed ashore for exercise. Still taking more stores aboard.

5.00pm – Left harbour at 10 knots and received hearty cheers as we passed under Forth Bridge. A screen of TBDs escorted us as far as May Island where we increased speed to 25 knots.

WEDNESDAY, 9TH SEPTEMBER

Squadron in battle formation: *Invincible* and *Inflexible* ahead; *Lion* and *Queen Mary* centre; and *Princess Royal* and *New Zealand* astern. A destroyer ahead of each ship, who are line abreast screening from submarine attacks. TBD examined steam trawler at 5.00pm – she was permitted to proceed. Our orders are to be off the Borkum and Norderney lightships at 4.00am tomorrow. Our submarines report that a large squadron is at anchor in Emden Harbour. The light cruisers and TBs are to pass the lightships and endeavour, as before, to draw the enemy out. Great difficulty was experienced last time in distinguishing our own submarines so they have been ordered to leave the immediate vicinity. The Battle Fleet will be 90 miles astern of us at 4.00am. We are all on the tiptoe of expectation and hope to be able to give a good account of ourselves tomorrow.

THURSDAY, 10TH SEPTEMBER

It was a glorious sight this morning to see our ships. Every available halyard had the white ensign on it, the Union Jack being forward on the stay. We have two ensigns nailed to the mast.

The TBDs and light cruisers crept round the islands in sight of Emden and thence along the coast to the Norderney Light. We anxiously waited to hear gunfire but it did not come. At 8.00am we observed our light cruisers steaming through the haze at high speed towards us. In vain we looked for the enemy who ought to be chasing them.

Shortly after this a string of flags on the *Lion* ordered the squadron to turn 16 points and we knew there was nothing doing. The TBDs found the harbour cleared, which meant the Germans had news of our movements and must have cleared off between the time our submarines left and the time the advance squadron arrived.

11.00am – Joined up with Battle Fleet, after carrying out high speed manoeuvres, and proceeded at 10 knots in company.

FRIDAY, 11TH SEPTEMBER

Parted company with Battle Fleet just after 1.00am. Sea rough and choppy and a thick mist about. 1st Battle Cruiser Squadron steaming line abreast. Rejoined squadron 9.00am.

New Zealand examined steam trawler which, according to papers, was English. Reported that one of our gunboats has captured a trawler, formerly belonging to Grimsby, with 200 mines aboard. The Admiralty gave a list of these vessels with the names and numbers. They were purchased by the German government about six months ago and they still have their old names and register number on them.

A very black night – not a star out. Squadron in single line ahead.

SATURDAY, 12TH SEPTEMBER

Midnight – Parted company with Battle Fleet. A proper hurricane raging with the ship doing the 'Cake Walk'. Everything toppling about and crockery rolling in all directions.

5.00am – Arrived at Scapa Flow. Even in harbour a very rough sea was running. Procded to coal ship – 1,750 tons – which was made doubly irksome by the heavy rain and cold wind. Coal in by 5.00am, "Out nets" as soon as collier had cast off. We expect to sail tomorrow night.

The months go by and Princess Royal *crosses to the West Indies to assist* Invincible *and* Inflexible *to search the southwest Atlantic for a German squadron which had sunk our ships* Good Hope *and* Monmouth *in action off Coronel. But 'the two Is', under the command of Admiral Sturdee, had already succeeded in destroying the* Scharnhorst, Gneisnau *and* Leipzig *at the Battle of Falkland Islands before the* Princess Royal *could join them.*

They carried on with patrols on the western side of the Atlantic Ocean operating from Halifax, Nova Scotia where, from 4.00 to 10.00pm on November 22nd 'Woody' had his first run ashore since he left Weymouth on July 28th.

On Christmas Day, Princess Royal *left Nova Scotia to return to Scapa Flow after many more patrols, searching in vain for German surface raiders and their supply ships. They carry on with patrols in those cold northern waters, alert for subs., ships and Zeppelins, hungry for action, until Saturday, 23rd January when they left Scapa at 6.16pm at 24 knots. The diary goes on:-*

SUNDAY, 24TH JANUARY 1915

7.00am – Dark with a dirty grey sky. No signs of surface raiders which, it has been rumoured, were coming across the Wash. Presently large clouds of smoke were visible as our destroyers came toward us and the light cruiser *Aurora* signalled "Enemy in sight consisting of four battle cruisers, three light cruisers and sixteen destroyers". Occasionally there were gun flashes and then 34 miles off the Norfolk coast we sighted the smoke of the enemy and then their masts. Chase was given and immediately the whole enemy squadron turned and fled. Speed was worked up to 28 knots and by gradually overhauling at 8.30am the Lion was able to try a few range shots.

9.00am – *Princess Royal* opened fire at 22,000 yards and a running fight commenced. The enemy wired for assistance and we received news that the High Seas Fleet were on their way out. The position now was the enemy's light and battle cruisers were being chased by our light cruisers and four battle cruisers – the *Lion*, *Princess Royal*, *Tiger* and *New Zealand*. As near an equal match as could be desired. The *Indomitable*, owing to her inferior speed, had dropped astern.

Salvos and broadsides were exchanged. Our speed, reaching 29 knots. At about 7.30am, through the concentrated fire of the enemy, the *Lion* was badly damaged and was forced to drop out of line. She had developed a heavy list and we heard she had been torpedoed. *Princess Royal* was detailed to lead the line and heavy fighting continued until 12.50. The result was one German battle cruiser sunk, two set on fire and in a sinking condition, plus six or seven destroyers sunk.

We were repeatedly attacked by subs. and enemy-dropped floating mines. The *Princess Royal* hardly had a scratch on her and *Tiger* had a few splinter wounds about the funnels. The fire which occurred on her upper deck was quickly extinguished. The action over, we passed the last battle cruiser – a total wreck, a mass of flames and smoke shooting from her. She quickly sank and our torpedo boats took off survivors. About this time a Zeppelin made it's appearance, taking care not to come within decent range. Being only about 60 miles from Germany at this time we now turned back to base. On passage back, the squadron was again attacked by subs., to no avail. Admiral Beatty came alongside in a TB, having hauled down his flag in *Lion*, and was heartily cheered as he was helped over the side by grimy stokers just up from below. He was very pleased with our work and congratulated the ship. We now fly the flag.

Picked up with the *Lion* at 2.30pm. She can just manage 8 knots and is being escorted by destroyers and light cruisers and screened by ourselves and remainder of 1st Battle Cruiser Squadron. The Germans made a mistake this time.

Our casualties:-

Tiger	10 killed	11 wounded
Lion	Nil	12 wounded
Indomitable	Nil	?

New Zealand	Nil	Nil
Princess Royal	Nil	Nil

MONDAY, 25TH JANUARY

Steaming on various courses all day to screen *Lion* which is being towed by *Indomitable* at 8 knots. There have been several unsuccessful submarine attacks. They are after the *Lion.*

TUESDAY, 26TH JANUARY

Rosyth 5.00am – Thick fog. *Lion* anchored on Queensferry side of the Bridge. The Admiral hoisted his flag aboard her before she entered the harbour where she was cheered by ships present.

Coal ship, 1,400 tons and oil. Ammunition all night. Papers arrived with photos of ships.

That was what the history books called the "Battle of Dogger Bank". Another highly successful action which kept the High Seas Fleet in hiding until Jutland confirmed our sovereignty of Home Waters.

WEDNESDAY, 27TH JANUARY

Paint ship and complete stores. Harbour.

THURSDAY, 28TH JANUARY

The Admiral, Sir David Beatty, KCB, DSL, MVO, hoisted his flag on *Princess Royal.* All his staff came on board during afternoon. I went aboard *Lion* and was shown round and saw damage, which was very severe in places. Huge masses of steel torn like pieces of paper. Really incredible.

11.30pm – proceeded to sea with *Queen Mary* and 1st Battle Cruiser Squadron. Some special operation on. Calm water.

FRIDAY, 29TH JANUARY

Sea rough, snow storms during afternoon. Operations postponed. Carried out firing during afternoon. Heading for Rosyth. Reports received say the German cruiser *Koberjn* was sunk on Sunday, also the *Moltke* sunk on reaching harbour.

SATURDAY, 30TH JANUARY

Reached Rosyth 7.00am. Coaled 600 tons and oiled ships, finished by 11.00am. Another spasm at 4.00pm. Submarines sighted coming up the Forth. "Out nets" and armed boats. Nothing afterwards sighted although several signals during my watch, 8.00 to 12.00 midnight, re sinking of three merchantmen.

SUNDAY, 31ST JANUARY

"In nets" 11.00am. Provisioned store ship came alongside 5.00pm, took on board six weeks' stores. Finished 11.00pm. *Tiger* left 8.00pm for dockyard.

MONDAY, 1ST FEBRUARY

Harbour, the First Lord of the Admiralty came on board and remained all day. The Admirals came on board to hold conference.

The diary went on with more alarms and excursions, a visit and inspection by His Majesty King George V to Princess Royal in Rosyth Harbour, promotion for 'Woody's captain to commodore for his part in the Dogger Bank action, a coaling ship record of 287 tons per hour for 5^1/2 hours, and a depressing daily toll of more U-boat sinkings. The diary gets spasmodic and its last laconic entry is:-

TUESDAY, 16TH MARCH 1915

German submarine sighted between the Forth Bridge and Inchkeith and fired at. It is not known whether she was disabled. Must have passed boom when raised to admit steamer.

With nothing further to draw on for first-hand information of Lt. Comdr. Woods's naval history, all I can do is finish with the schedule of his service as provided for me by the naval authorities:-

28th April 1915 to 31st march 1916	HMS *Foxglove*
1st April 1916 to 6th October 1918	HMS *Neptune*
16th February 1917	Promoted Victualling Chief Petty Officer
17th January 1919 to 6th June 1920	HMS *Enchantress*
1st October 1920 to 10th November 1922	HMS *Philomel*
11th November 1922 to 29th October 1923	Portsmouth Depot (HMS *Victory*)
30th October 1923 to 26th November 1925	Torpedo School (HMS *Vernon*)
27th November 1925 to 16th May 1927	HMS *Princess Margaret*
17th May 1927 to 6th June 1929	Portsmouth Depot (HMS *Victory*)
7th June 1929 to 18th May 1931	HMS *Bee* (China Station)
19th May 1931 to 4th June 1931	HMS *Vindictive*
4th June 1931	Discharged to a Commission
1939 to 1940	Staff Admiral Air, Lea-on-Solent
1940 to 1943	R.N. Air Station Astroth
1943 to 1947	R.N. Air Station Eglinton

PART TWO

UNDER AN UMBRELLA

By ex-Chief Petty Officer Bill Dunlevey, D.S.M., B.E.M

To our wives and families who, over the past fifty years, have done so much to help we returning Far Eastern Prisoners of War along that rocky road to recovery.

Foreword

*L*ooking back on my life, I realised the greater part of it has been spent under an umbrella , so to speak, sheltered from the nitty-gritty of everyday life by the administrative hierarchy of schools, institutions, naval establishments, ships, and last but by no means least, Japanese prisoner of war camps.

Under an Umbrella, therefore, is a fitting title for the book in which I do my best to describe it all.

Bill Dunlevey
September 1994

CHAPTER SIX

En route to a Life Afloat

I was born a Shropshire lad on 10th July 1919, in a small hamlet called Milson near Cleobury Mortimer in the county of Salop. My mother and father were of Irish stock originating from Foxford in County Mayo, Ireland. I was the youngest of five brothers and four sisters and we lived in a small cottage overlooking the lovely Shropshire countryside, my father working on one of the local farms. The few recollections I have of my early days are of being bathed in a small metal tub; the smell of carbolic soap; riding with my father on several different agricultural machines, and sitting under the hedgerow with him while he drank cider from an earthernware jar, occasionally giving me a little sip.

Mother died when I was three and Father, unable to look after all of us after her death, sent me and my elder brother to an orphanage in Bebington, Cheshire.

He died while I was in the orphanage, when I was about seven. It was a Catholic Institution in Heath Road, Bebington, Cheshire, run by an order of nuns called The Sisters of Charity, who still wore big flowing white starched hats. There were about 120 boys altogether and the place was staffed by a Mother Superior, eight nuns, a bandmaster, a general handyman, a gardener, and some four or five maids, mostly Irish.

The orphanage was set in quiet, spacious grounds, with several fields cultivated to provide the home with vegetables, etc.

The main building consisted of a large refectory with long wooden tables, benches and a wooden floor, all of which we had to scrub at least twice a week. There was a large kitchen run by a nun and two maids – designated out of bounds to us unless working there. There were three dormitories housing some 40 boys each, a band room (as the orphanage had a Silver Band), a cobbler's shop where our boots were repaired by hand (we never, ever had shoes), a laundry, general farm building and outhouses, a Chapel (later a church was built in the grounds), an isolation building, and a large building which had a stage for the plays in which we had to partake. This was also used as a recreation hall whenever the weather was unsuitable for playing outside.

We wore boots and stockings, corduroy shorts, and a jersey. The band, when playing at engagements, wore blazers and caps.

Our daily routine was to be awakened at about 6.00am when beds were checked to see if any boy had wet his bed. This was considered by the nuns to be laziness and any boy found to have done so was made to duck six times in a cold water bath – even in the middle of winter. Then, depending on the nun on duty, the younger boys would receive 30 to 40 strokes on his hands with a cane. One nun used to give them on the backside; another when you came home at night, so that you brooded about it all day at school. I know these things because I was one of the unfortunates who wet the bed.

We then washed and went to Mass in the Chapel, cleaned our boots, had breakfast, which consisted of two rounds of dripping bread and a mug of tea – we had the same breakfast every day the whole year round. We then marched in a long column to school at St John's in New Ferry, Cheshire, a distance of some $2^1/2$ miles, with our bandmaster riding his motor cycle and keeping us in order. After school we marched back for dinner, which consisted of potatoes, meat and cabbage. On Wednesdays we had fish and twice a week we had rhubarb and custard. The pattern never changed for the whole eleven years we were in the orphanage. We were marched back to school again each day and then home in the late afternoon. For tea we had two rounds of jam and bread with a mug of tea – those who wet the bed did not get an evening mug of tea.

We worked on the farm if the weather was fine, or in the cobbler's shop repairing boots, or on knitting machines making the jerseys and stockings we wore, or went to band practice if one was in the band. Then we all washed and went to bed at about 8.00pm.

At the tender age of six I was put in the orphanage Silver Band and learned music the hard way. We had an ex-army bandmaster – Kennedy by name – an Irishman who would hit us on the fingers with his baton if the wrong valve was pressed. I started on second cornet, then on to baritone, then on to a euphonium. The one redeeming feature about being in the band was that we went out on engagements, playing in local parks, at garden fâtes, processions, and at Tranmere Rovers football ground when the great Dixie Dean played for them, and invariably were provided with a tea, with such luxuries as sandwiches, cakes, etc. The people who laid on these teas were always impressed by how quickly the plates were cleared. Probably thought we were starving and weren't far out at that!

One way we had of supplementing the diet was to take potatoes from the garden and put them under the central heating boiler ash pit to bake.

The local priest came to the Home each day to say Mass. He had his breakfast there and the boy who cleaned away the table used to get the crusts of the toast he had left.

We went to the local school where one of the boys, Teddy Penlington, whose father had a shop, would bring sweets to school – but we had to give him piggyback rides to get any from him. He became a great pal of mine along with another boy, Freddy Archibold. Years later, Teddy was lost on a bombing mission over Germany as a young pilot officer. This was a great blow when I called to see him and his family after the War. Freddy Archibold finished the war as a Squadron Leader.

Most of the boys from the orphanage never had pocket money and never saw a film show. Times were quite hard but it never seemed to bother us. The boys finished school at the age of fourteen and, leaving the orphanage, mostly went to farms in Southern Ireland, Canada, Australia and New Zealand. It was a great wrench leaving the home we had shared for so many years.

A Sea Training School in Liscard, Wallasey, offered to look after me for the next two years, as they were short of a euphonium player in their band. Once again the dice were thrown and my future decided for me. I was taken from the orphanage on the back of our bandmaster's motor cycle with just the clothes I wore.

Arriving at the Lancashire Sea Training School in 1933 I was kitted out with a sailor's uniform for the first time. During the day we attended classes taking such subjects as gymnastics, seamanship, signals and metalwork, training mainly for the Merchant Navy, although each year a few boys were accepted for the Royal Navy.

The food was a little better than at the orphanage. We even had a round of buttered jam and bread in the evening – a true luxury!

We were allowed out on Saturday afternoons and Sundays. My first Sunday off was spent walking all the way back to the orphanage, some ten or twelve miles, to see old friends and show off my uniform. I still had no pocket money. Sometimes I would call in at Port Sunlight to see the Donnellys – they would always give me a lovely tea and a sixpence for my fare back. A truly kind and caring family.

Most of our weekends off would be spent walking along the Promenade from Liscard to New Brighton on the Wirral Peninsula, meeting the local girls, and even having a cigarette – if the girls brought any! On the Promenade near Liscard was the Old Mariners' Home where we would talk to the old sailors about China, South America and various places around the world. It was fascinating, and little did I realise that one day I would be a seasoned mariner myself and talk of these places too.

It was a happy time with the band playing many engagements at fêtes, municipal parks, etc. On one occasion we played at the opening of the Mersey Tunnel in Liverpool by the late King George V and Queen Mary. We also used the free passes we were given to cross from Liscard, Wallasey on the ferryboats to Liverpool, pretending to be full-blown sailors!

When the time came to leave the Sea Training School, I wanted to join the Royal Marine Band, but the requirement in those days was to have a knowledge of string besides brass or silver instruments. This I did not have so, in February 1936, I was sent to Canning Place, Liverpool, to sit the exam and take a medical for the Royal Navy. I passed. Several weeks later I went over to Canning Place Recruitment Office and was given my railway ticket and two shillings and sixpence. The recruiter said, "Here's half a crown for joining the Royal Navy for twelve years." I told him that for five shillings I would sign on for twenty-two years. He remarked, "I think you had better do twelve years, son, and see what it's like." Had I known then that I was going to do thirty-eight I could have asked for a pound! My next elder brother, who joined the Sea Training School just before me went into the Merchant Navy.

I left Liverpool by train on 4th February 1936 to join HMS *Ganges*, the boys' training establishment at Shotley – the first 'port of call' for thousands of boys who entered the Royal Navy.

CHAPTER SEVEN

From Boyhood to 'Warhood'!

Several ships in the history of the Royal Navy have been named Ganges but the one with which the shore establishment is associated had been a sailing ship in Bombay in 1821.

In 1898, after nearly 80 years' active service – during which time she became the last sailing ship to wear an Admiral's flag; she was converted into a training ship and stationed at Harwich. In 1905, when the present buildings at Shotley were opened, the boys were transferred ashore and the old *Ganges* towed away. The establishment, which covered nearly 102 acres, was ideally situated for its purpose. It was bounded on two sides by the Rivers Orwell and Stour, with open country lying between it and the nearest town – Ipswich – eight miles to the north-west. The climate was healthy and rainfall among the lowest in England.

Boys between 15 and 16 years old were recruited from all over Great Britain and Ireland three times a term at intervals of five weeks. The year consists of three terms: Easter – 14 weeks; Summer – 15 weeks; and Christmas – 14 weeks, three weeks leave being granted to boys between each term.

There were roughly 2,000 boys under training at any given time. On arrival at HMS *Ganges*, boys were sent to a special new entry block – Nozzers – to carry out their joining routine and preliminary training. The training at this stage was elementary and consisted largely of instruction in the maintenance of kit, laundering, personal cleanliness, discipline and schooling. The main establishment was divided for administration and competitive purposes into a number of divisions, each named after a famous Admiral and headed by a Lieutenant Commander with the assistance of a branch officer and two petty officer instructors.

On arrival in the main establishment the boys were formed into classes and allocated to one of these divisions where, in the normal course of events, they remained for the rest of their time in HMS *Ganges*. The centre of a boy's domestic life was his dormitory (known as mess). Here he had his bed, clothes locker and in a special square in the dormitory known as the Mess Square, he ate his meals. The boys were called at 6.30am. After cleaning their mess and eating breakfast they cleaned the establishment from 7.40 to 8.40am, after which came ceremonial parade (Divisions) and prayers. Instruction started at 9.00am and continued until dinner at 12.50pm. Every afternoon was taken up by games with instruction starting again at 4.40 until 6.40pm. Supper was at 6.50pm, then lights out and in bed by 9.00pm.

And so it was that along with about another 20 boys I arrived at Harwich one cold February evening and embarked on a picket boat to Shotley and on to HMS *Ganges*. We must have looked a motley bunch to the instructor that met us, and all were filled with awe at the size of the establishment. In the foreground overshadowing the parade ground was the famous "*Ganges* Mast" – some 160 feet high, which we would later on be expected to climb. Taken to the Annexe, where all new boys stay for four weeks, we were issued uniforms and many other items of kit. We spent the first month sewing our names into each item, learning how to wash our clothes, how to iron them, and how to lay them out for inspection. Everything had to be rolled up to a certain size and stops (string) put on each end so that the name was uppermost. We learned how to clean our rooms, how to make our beds up, and how to drill. At the end of the month in the Annexe, our kit and our rooms were thoroughly examined. On passing inspection (as most of us did) we left the Annexe and the name Nozzer behind, and joined a new class in the main establishment.

I joined Anson Division to start another nine months training in seamanship, gunnery, rifle shooting, mast climbing, physical training, swimming, boat work (sailing and pulling) and had to take part in football, rugby, boxing, running, and every other conceivable sport. Great emphasis was placed on these sporting activities.

Pay was six shillings and three pence per week, of which we received only one shilling in actual payment, the rest being put to our credit. But that credit went mainly on purchasing new items of kit replacements.

Each class had two petty officer instructors. We were awakened in the morning by either of these instructors shouting at the top of his voice "Wakey, wakey! Rise and Shine! Morning's fine! Get the sleep out of your eyes!" Sometimes the early morning greeting was a little cruder than that and anybody not out of bed in a flash was tipped out of it. After a drink of cocoa and a hard tack biscuit, it was all hands on deck to clean the mess. When this was finished to the satisfaction of the instructor we'd have breakfast, which consisted of a couple of slices of bread and a small piece of fish (Yellow Peril), or a kipper, or a slice of fat bacon with tomatoes. Then off we went to instruction. A lot of the boys were not too impressed about their food, but to me – after the last two places I had been in – it was luxury! I think this poem by Cyril Towney called "Shotley Stew" is very appropriate (sung to the tune of "A Little bit of Heaven Fell From Out The Sky One Day"):

"Shotley Stew"

There's a half a pound of bully beef, left from the month before,
And half a yard of sausage, found on the canteen floor.
One or two old ham bones, which were minus of the meat,
And two old tins of meat and veg the dog refused to eat.

They took it to the galley, and they let it boil all day,
They topped it up with castor oil to pass the time away,
And when they finished boiling it, it tasted just like glue,
So they gave it to the *Ganges* boys, and called it "Shotley Stew".

We spent many hours on the River Orwell pulling and sailing boats – 32' Sloop rigged cutters and 27' Montague whalers. The swimming pool was down on the cold foreshore and if we weren't doing boatwork in the early mornings, we were down at the swimming pool. I remember my first morning there extremely well. It was very cold and we had to put on a wet duck suit. The swimming instructor said, "All the non-swimmers down the deep end." I enquired of him, "Excuse me, sir, don't you mean the shallow end?" "Hah!" he said. "We have a clever wee boy here." Then he shouted at the top of his voice: "When I said the deep end, I meant the deep end." I went to the deep end where he wasted no time in pushing me in. I could not swim or even float and when he saw me spluttering he stuck a long pole out to me, but as I reached for it he gave me a slight tap on the head. Before three weeks were out I could do six lengths of the bath, and what's more, could go on the trapeze over the bath!

Once the swimming test in the pool had been passed we were taken out onto the river in a boat, and had to jump or dive off and then swim around for about fifteen minutes before being picked up. This was with a sailor's suit on. Many years later I was to be very thankful for this part of my training.

The gymnasium was another tough place. The instructors barked their orders in such an aggressive fashion we would almost panic in our efforts to comply. "Across the floor without touching it – MOVE!" "I don't want you to run, I don't want you to walk, I want you to bloody-well fly!" What's more, they meant it.

The boxing instructor would get in the ring with you and didn't pull any punches. After three rounds you knew you had been in the ring with him!

After supper we went to evening instructions so our time was well occupied throughout the working day. We were not allowed to smoke and any boy caught was put over the box horse in the gym and given six cuts. Grace was said before meals and was compulsory. I well remember the unofficial grace we used to say before meals: "What has got to do with this side of the table has nothing to do with that side of the table – so keep your beady eyes off."

49

If you received punishment, it was called "Jankers". They used to have an instructor called the "Shotley Terror" and he certainly lived up to his name. I remember seeing him take the boys under punishment on the parade ground. While the other boys were at sport, they were made to squat on their haunches and jump forward continuously with a stick outstretched in their hands over their heads. This went on for quite some time. Then they were made to double backwards and forwards across the parade ground until they almost dropped. Quite tough treatment for 15 and 16 year olds.

The rifle range was another tough place. On a cold winter's morning if one did not take first pressure on the trigger of a 303 Lee-Enfield rifle, the instructor would rap one's fingers with a steel pull-through rod.

Another class punishment was to run up and down steep "Laundry Hill" until ready to drop. Looking back, it was all very good training as it taught endurance and self-discipline.

I remember one day all the boys were assembled and the Captain of HMS *Ganges*, Captain Enright (who we thought was God), spoke to us. He had joined the Navy as a Boy 2nd Class, and later (much later) became an Admiral. He said that if we reached down far enough into our kit bags we would find an Admiral's Sword. During my long service in the Royal Navy I never did find it. Either the kit bag was too big or my arm too short.

Having passed our exams at the end of nine months we were now considered ready to join the "Fleet" as young sailors, and I was one of a party of boys drafted to HMS *Rodney*. I was sad at the thought of leaving HMS *Ganges*, but life moves on.

I still look back with admiration to the Royal Naval Training Establishment at Shotley. It strengthened me physically, but above all provided a firm moral base and wide mental vision which no other school for a boy of my class could have given. It was the finest establishment ever conceived to build boys into real men.

This was the day of the battleship and HMS *Rodney* was a huge example. She displaced 35,000 tons, was 710 feet long and 106 feet wide. She had nine 16" guns, twelve 6" guns, 4.7"s and numerous others. She had a speed of 23 knots and her armour plating was 16" thick. I was put into the fo'c'sle division – the fo'c'sle officer was Lt. Comdr. Teddy Rowe, nicknamed the "Iron Man". The chief petty officer of the fo'c'sle division was "Dixie" Dean, a small man – but what he lacked in stature he made up for in other ways. He was responsible for the smooth running of the fo'c'sle division and the work programme.

We took over as flagship from HMS *Nelson*, a sister ship, and carried the flag of Admiral Sir Roger Backhouse. I remember seeing him for the first time, a tall distinguished figure, and to me as a young sailor he seemed like God. Everybody on the bridge of *Rodney* seemed to think likewise.

We left Portsmouth and rejoined the Home Fleet. I remember being anchored off Spithead and my job was to scrub and clean the huge lower boom which the ship's boats tied up to when in harbour. I had a long piece of spun yarn with a scrubber tied on one end and a cloth on the other. One dangled this over the boom and lowered the scrubber or cloth into the sea as required.

One day I finished quicker than usual and reported as much to CPO Dixie Dean who didn t happen to be too fond of the Irish. Having red hair and an Irish surname I came into that category, so when I said, "I've finished the boom, sir", thinking he would be pleased he said to me "Get your trousers rolled up (we were already in our bare feet) "and holystone the deck!" This consisted of getting down on one's hands and knees and pushing a rectangular piece of holystone (a kind of soft sandstone) backwards and forwards over the surface of the wooden deck. It was the most tedious and tiring job I had ever done, but the decks were always spotlessly clean.

Being still a boy on *Rodney* my education continued. We still attended school on board besides instruction in torpedoes, electrical work, and gunnery. There were constant kit inspections to see that our uniforms and accessories had been kept up to scratch.

I remember watching an Able Seaman by the name of "Tiddly" Stretch laying out his kit. It consisted of one set of underwear and a pair of socks, instead of the usual forty or so items. When his divisional officer asked him "What is the meaning of this, Stretch?", his reply was "Can I help it, sir, if the Royal Navy is composed of rogues and bloody vagabonds?" A reply, no doubt, that deserved an award for pithy wit but probably won poor Stretch a 14 days spell in the cooler!

Having very little money in those days, one had to find means of passing spare time without expense. One way was to learn some of the more decorative knots from older sailors, such as the Turk's Head, the Rose Knot, the Manrope Knot, Sinnets, and many more, and how to roll up leaf tobacco for the pipe smokers.

Another thing that fascinated me as a young sailor was listening to some of the older salts reciting poetry like "The Pigtail of Le Fang Fu" and "The Green Eye of the Yellow God", and "Dangerous Dan McGrew" and a few others. Most of these had two versions: the true one and the sailors' version.

Mah-jong was also popular in the Royal Navy, brought back by the old gunboat crews from the China Station. It was played widely in Hong Kong where you could hear the click of the pieces as you walked the streets of Wanchai. Uckers was another popular game – it was similar to Ludo, but not when played the sailors' way!

My action station was "A" Turret magazine where we pushed the red shalloon bags of cordite out into the handling room through flash tight scuttles. I always remember the gunnery instructor telling us that in case of fire we would not be able to get out of the magazine and all fireproof hatches would be locked from the outside. I was glad after a few months on this job to be moved to the handling room where we put the 16" projectiles on to hydraulic lifts to the gun house. Many months later I was moved into the gun house itself.

51

I must admit to being terrified when shut in the gun turret for the first time, the moving part of which weighed some 1,800 tons. The gun barrels were the length of a cricket pitch and there were three of these in each turret. The shells they fired each weighed a ton and could travel 21 miles. Aircraft were used for spotting fall of shot.

I enjoyed being on *Rodney*. We cruised to the fjords in Norway, visited Portugal, Algiers, Denmark and were out in the "Med" at the time of the Spanish Civil War. This ship was my home for roughly two and a half years. I ran in the ship's cross country team and used to enjoy the competition between ourselves and the Army, universities and many other teams.

I well remember running in Lisbon against a Portuguese team. In those days we did not have such things as track suits, just a vest and a pair of white shorts, held up by a naval belt with a money pouch on it. Our route took us through a street where the local ladies leaned from the windows enticing men in. I succumbed, nipped into one of the houses, spent 15 minutes there, and still managed to finish in the first 35 out of 50; my usual position in these races being in the first three as I was considered a good runner in those days. Needless to say, I was questioned by the officer in charge of the running team, Lt. Comdr. Teddy Rowe, on my poor showing. My excuse was that I had caught a "stitch" but it didn t go down too well.

At most of the places we visited, our ship was open to visitors in the afternoons and they would come in their thousands. One of the 16"projectiles would be stuck up for the visitors to see. It was just under one ton in weight, but a sign would be placed on it saying "Please do not remove!"

When HMS *Rodney* did a full 16" shoot, all crockery was taken out of the shelves in the messes and light bulbs were removed. Invariably quite a number of deck planks were ripped up after a shoot, after which the shipwrights were kept busy re-caulking and re-laying them.

It used to be a wonderful sight when the Home Fleet joined up with the Mediterranean Fleet for combined exercises. There were ships as far as the eye could see. Somewhere in the region of eight to ten battleships, four or five aircraft carriers, thirty or forty cruisers, about a hundred and forty destroyers and numerous auxiliary ships. Great Britain was the greatest sea power in the world prior to the War.

When exercises had finished, the two fleets would return to Gibraltar and when thousands of sailors had shore leave all hell broke loose in the famous bars like the Trocadero, the Café Royal, and others along Main Street. There were many shore patrols in evidence during these periods, including American. They carried sticks whereas the British did not. I did not visit these bars then as I had very little money being a boy seaman – nor had I become noticeably wealthier when promoted to Ordinary Seaman.

While in Gibraltar I payed a visit to the pocket battleship *Deutschland* when it put into Gibraltar to bury her dead. While patrolling off the Spanish coast, she had about ten sailors killed by Spanish Forces engaged in the Spanish Civil War. It was rumoured that after she had buried her dead, she went out and shelled Spanish coastal towns in retaliation.

I had been promoted to Ordinary Seaman by this time, earning the princely sum of 30 shillings a week.

At Algiers, local traders were allowed on board to sell their wares – it was the first time I had seen dirty postcards being sold – all unofficial of course. We visited the Atlas Mountains and the famous Chiffa Gorge, where hundreds of monkeys came down to feed out of our hands, paid a visit to a local vineyard and tasted the local wines, visited the "Casbah" and the famous Black Cat brothel. Tangier was our next stop (not much different from Algiers) and then home again.

At Portland I went aboard the Submarine H27 and spent a week at sea with her. It was an opportunity to get an idea of what submarine life was all about.

At Plymouth, our home base, I left HMS *Rodney*, my home for two years, and joined the light cruiser HMS *Diomede* on 6th May 1938. It was quite a wrench leaving old friends after two years.

Diomede, along with about eight other light cruisers, was laid up in the river at Devonport, tied up in pairs, head and stern to buoys. They were not in commission – just had maintenance crews consisting of eight to ten men on each ship in case they were required in an emergency.

There was not the same rigid discipline as on the ships of the Fleet and life was easier. I spent sailing weekends up the river in a 27' Montague whaler, along with one or two shipmates. No beer was allowed on board HM ships in those days, but we used to pull a small dinghy over to the shore on the quiet side of the river, take a big metal "fanny", fill it full of draught beer and take it back on board. We would get up early in the morning, pull the dinghy over to the shore, climb the banks into the fields around the area and collect fresh mushrooms to take back to the ship for a breakfast fry-up. Life was good and the going was easy.

One evening after doing my washing I took it down to dry in the boiler-room, where I found the duty engine-room artificer had hung himself. I quickly called the duty petty officer, who phoned Devonport Barracks and got an ambulance to come out to the ship. This was the second suicide I'd witnessed. While serving on the *Rodney*, I wanted to dodge church one Sunday morning so sneaked into the gyro room and an electrical artificer had done the same thing. It was the first and very last time I ever dodged church in the Royal Navy.

While on *Diomede* I volunteered for the Submarine Service along with a friend named Stanley Crumbleholme. I was a Seaman Gunner and Stanley a Seaman Torpedoman. They accepted him but turned me down. They only needed one or two gunners at the most on a submarine, whereas they always needed torpedomen with electrical experience. Stanley went to the ill-fated *Thetis*, which foundered with nearly all hands in Liverpool Bay on 1st June 1939. Evidently, the outer door of one of the torpedo tubes was open and unknowingly someone opened the inner tube door, thereby allowing the sea to flood in. There were, I believe, only four survivors, but my old shipmate was not one of them.

Since that awful disaster, the "Thetis Valve" was introduced on the inner door of a torpedo tube to prevent it ever happening again. *Thetis*, eventually salvaged and re-named *Thunderbolt*, was sunk off northern Sicily by the Italian Navy corvette *Cicogna* on 13th March 1943.

About July or August 1939, the Naval Reserves were called up and suddenly HMS *Diomede*, as all the ships in the reserve, came to life. Men of all walks of life – publicans, building workers, jewellers, shopkeepers, bank clerks, etc. became sailors again. The ship took on stores and ammunition, men were allocated to their different stations and duties before we went to sea for trials, and finally we went down to Portland for a review by King George VI. We never did get back to Plymouth after the review but proceeded to Scapa Flow. War was declared in September 1939.

Our ship was allocated to the Northern Patrol station, operating between the Shetlands, Faroes and Greenland. It was a bitterly cold area to patrol. One of our main tasks was to intercept merchant ships using the northern routes to Europe. We would stop a merchant ship and put a boarding party on board, search the ship, and if we thought they carried contraband likely to help the Germans, the boarding party would stay on board and the ship taken to Lerwick in the Shetlands.

I was now a Leading Seaman and one of my jobs was coxswain of the seaboat which had to be dropped anytime the boarding party had to board a ship. This was indeed a tough job in those northern waters, one of the toughest I had had to date, but it was good training.

The ships on our northern patrol were small light cruisers of some 3,000 to 4,000 tons like *Diomede, Cardiff, Calypso, Caradoc,* etc. They were not ideally suited to the weather in those parts and much later were relieved by converted armed merchant ships.

Had *Diomede* been torpedoed I doubt if we d have lasted five minutes up in those waters. I received a parcel one day when we put in to Solom Voe. It had been sent by the Hon. Diana and Jacqueline Law from London and contained a balaclava helmet and scarf for which I was most grateful. I wore it constantly during those cold Arctic patrols. They had also included a letter, in which one paragraph stated: "We hope you catch plenty of fish"! Obviously a little mistaken about what we did, there being precious little time for fishing on our job, but nevertheless many similar parcels came to the ship from kind people such as they.

During our time on the northern patrol, the armed merchant ship *Rawalpindi* was sunk with great loss of life while protecting a large transatlantic convoy from the German heavy cruisers *Gneisnau* and *Scharnhorst*. Captain Kennedy, father of Ludovic Kennedy, was awarded the Victoria Cross (posthumously).

HMS Ganges – *RN training establishment for boys and new entries at Shotley near Ipswich. Two shots of the famous mast that all were obliged to climb up and over.*

ABOVE: *HMS* Exeter *before leaving the UK never to return.*

LEFT: *HMS* Exeter *(marked x) being bombed by Japanese planes.*

BELOW LEFT: *The end of a great ship in Banka Straits, Java Sea, 1942.*

ABOVE: *Christened 'Fat Man', this 'Act of Retribution!' fell out of a B29 over Nagasaki on 9th August 1945.*

BELOW: *Some of the damage it did photographed four days later (note train in the centre chugging through the debris).*

ABOVE: *Bill Dunlevey on the fo'c'sle of HMS* Andromeda *under his beloved 'umbrella' when being interviewed by the* Evening Post, *Port Elizabeth, SA.*

LEFT: *Between decks on the same ship when presented with his British Empire Medal and Distinguished Service Medal by Admiral Sir John Bush.*

A MATELOT'S FAREWELL TO HIS TOT

You soothed my nerves and warmed my limbs
And cheered my dismal heart,
Procured my wants, obliged my whims –
And now its time to part.
'Mid endless perils of the deep
And miseries untold
You summoned sweet forgetful sleep,
Cocooned me from the cold.

Ten years ago, the "pound o' leaf",
That cast its fragrant spell
About the ship, expired in grief
And sadness of farewell.
Though guests might find the pantry bare,
Whene'er they chose to come
Your hospitality was there:
A tot of Pussers's rum.

Two hundred years and more you filled
The storm-tossed sailor's need.
Now you've been killed by spite distilled
From jealousy and greed,
And petty clerks with scrawny necks
Who never saw a wave,
Nor felt the spray nor heaving decks,
Consign you to your grave.

Alas! However I protest
To save myself from hurt,
They tell me that it's for the best –
To keep us all alert.
And so the time has come, old friend,
To take the final sup.
Our tears are shed. This is the end.
Goodbye, and bottoms up!

P.W.

One of the many doggerel laments at the passing of the daily rum issue in January 1971.

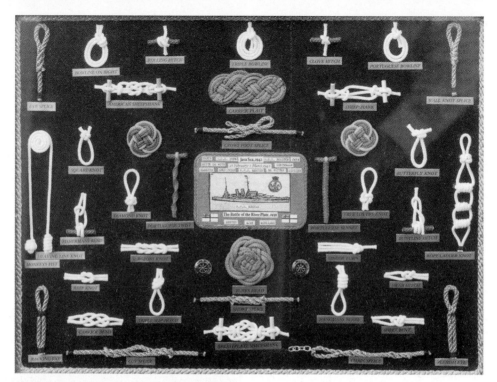

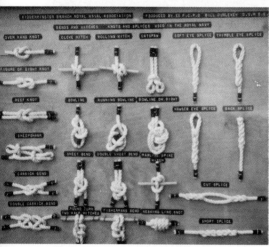

Naval knots and splices are Bill Dunlevey's speciality. A subject on which he still lectures and demonstrates to this day.

HMS Nubian *under full sail! Improvising with her upper-deck awnings when the prop shaft failed her in mid-Channel.*

ABOVE: *Bill aged 8 (circled second left, with his cornet) in the front row of St Edmund's Orphanage Band.*

LEFT: *At the age of 76.*

We were at sea when we learned that HMS *Royal Oak*, a battleship of some 29,000 tons, had been sunk at Scapa Flow at about 1.30am on 14th October 1939, an anchorage we had always thought safe. Evidently the German U-boat (U47) had navigated Kirk Sound, got into Scapa Flow, and torpedoed *Royal Oak* with a huge loss of life – some 800 out of a crew of 1,200 were lost. The Navy was shocked and grief-stricken. Most of us knew many of her crew. This was Germany's first real blow against Great Britain in the 1939 War. I believe U47 was later sunk by the destroyer *Wolverine* in March 1941.

I had now spent nearly two years on *Diomede*, and after six months on northern patrol was due to leave her. After a three month spell in Royal Naval Barracks, Devonport, I joined HMS *Periwinkle*, a new flower-class corvette, at Harland and Wolff, Belfast, on 1st April 1940. I was one of a pre-commissioning advance party and spent several weeks aboard her before the full commissioning crew joined us. Until they did I worked on the ship during the day and returned to digs in Newtownards Road at night, with a delightful landlady who used to make lovely soda bread and scones. It was such a nice change from Navy food and accommodation, and I found the people of Belfast most hospitable and kind.

But only seven weeks after our arrival at Plymouth, I was taken to the R.N. Hospital suffering with quinsy. Rejoining R.N. Barracks, Devonport on 16th May 1940, I qualified for my 2nd class gunnery rate and picked up a draft on 9th July 1940 that took me to Scapa Flow to join an "F" Class destroyer, HMS *Fame*, spending my 21st birthday travelling on the train heading north. I managed to get a bottle of port wine to celebrate – my first venture towards alcohol, but there were no ill effects when I joined *Fame* in the late evening of the 10th.

One of the first jobs after we left harbour was to go to the aid of one of our submarines in difficulty off the Norwegian coast. Attacked by Stuka dive-bombers, the ship was hit, causing some damage and loss of life. After this we proceeded to Leith in Scotland to be refitted and have the damage repaired.

One morning I was awakened for the morning watch (4.00 to 8.00am) with a cupful of champagne from the sailor calling me. Three or four of the crew had broken into the wardroom and stolen a lot of drink, as well as a birthday cake intended for a party planned to celebrate the First Lieutenant's birthday. Later in the morning "Clear lower deck" was piped and we all assembled on the upper deck while our lockers were searched. Some of the champagne had been poured into sea-boots in the paint store for'ard. The guilty men admitted to the theft and were duly – but lightly – punished with stoppage of leave and pay.

Our first job after the refit at Leith was, along with several other destroyers, to escort the new battleship *King George V* from the Tyne. On the way our ship ran aground during the night on the notorious "Whitburn Steels", near Sunderland, along with another two destroyers. One got off almost immediately and the other a few days later, but we were well and truly stuck. A fire started in the boiler room and we had to work like mad to try and put it out while at the same time get the ammunition and torpedoes off the ship. This we finally managed to do. The coastguards rigged a breeches buoy to the ship and we were safely transferred.

We were put into an empty army billet on the cliff top and went down to work on the ship each day, ferrying stores and equipment to the shore. We got aboard by being transferred on a box worked by a pulley. We later learned that the ship had been several miles off course when she ran aground and our captain and navigating officer were court-martialled.

Our pay was not big in those days. One day, while playing football in our army billet, the ball was kicked through a window in one of the unused huts in which, lo and behold, we found 500 brand new army blankets! These were taken by some of the boys and sold to local inhabitants at five shillings each, but the theft was discovered and quite a few finished up being fined at a magistrate's court in Sunderland. Anything of value was stolen and sold. It was not unusual to see a sailor pushing a wheelbarrow full of eggs along the coast road after midnight trying to make a little extra money!

One day, at the height of tides, the empty shell of our ship was towed off the rocks and our days in the north east had come to an end, by which time, I believe, all that was left unsold on board was the after funnel and the White Ensign! I went by train back to R.N. Barracks at Devonport, arriving on 12th December 1940.

On 22nd June 1940 the French had signed an armistice with Germany. Britain wanted the French to sail their naval ships to British ports, thereby preventing them falling into German hands. The German/French armistice, though, had stipulated that France's navy should be transferred to German control. To prevent this, those French ships already in British ports were boarded and taken over.

Among the French warships in Devonport and Portsmouth were two old battleships – the *Paris* and the *Courbet*; two modern destroyers – the *Triumphant* and *Leopard*; two other destroyers; six torpedo boats; seven submarines; and several smaller units.

While in barracks I was put into a group called Party "A". We were called to the gymnasium on the evening of 2nd July 1940, issued with marching order equipment, and told we would have to sleep on the floor of the gymnasium that night. Rumours were rife ... we were going to France to cover a raiding party – all kinds of weird ideas were advanced. The following morning we were called at about 5.00am and marched down through the R.N. Barracks to the dockyard gates. We were split into groups and I, as a young leading seaman, was put in charge of a group of eight men and given a specific task. We had to board the French battleship Paris and along with other groups – all armed – we were to take over the battleship from the French officers and crew. Apparently there was a move afoot by the French to take all their ships from various British dockyards over to Vichy, France. This we had to stop.

I and my merry men had to go down to the stokers messdeck, turn all the men out at the point of a bayonet and, once they dressed, to escort them into the drill shed at R.N. Barracks. The giant French submarine *Surcouf* was tied up alongside *Paris*. She was a huge submarine for those days, having an 8" gun and carrying a seaplane. When a party tried to board the *Surcouf*, it's leader, Lieutenant Commander Dennis Sprague, commanding officer of HM Submarine *Thames*, was shot dead. Lt. Comdr. Griffiths, the son of Mr. W. A. Griffiths, secretary to the Admiral Superintendent, who had been appointed as liaison officer to the *Surcouf* when the submarine arrived at Plymouth on 20th June, was also killed as was a Royal Marine sergeant and a French submarine crew member. I could not resist taking the French Admiral's cocked hat as a souvenir, squashing it flat and tucking it down my jumper but eventually lost it when the cruiser *Exeter* went down.

All the Frenchmen were kept under guard in the drill shed for the rest of the day. Some volunteered to stay with the British Navy. The majority were entrained that evening at the railway station in the Royal Naval Barracks and sent back to France.

CHAPTER EIGHT

H.M.S. Exeter and the Road to Hell!

uring this time in R.N. Barracks, I had seen HMS *Exeter*, an 8" cruiser, being repaired in Devonport Dockyard after her epic battle with the German pocket battleship *Graf Spee*. Her scars received in the Battle of the River Plate were healed and she was once more ready for action. In March 1941, I got a draft chit to join her. During the first couple of weeks onboard, Plymouth was badly bombed and on several occasions we had to close up on our anti-aircraft guns to help repel the German bombers. Captain of the *Exeter* was Captain Joe Beckett. He told the ship's company one day at "Clear lower deck" that it was our task to seek out the enemy and destroy them in battle. Tragically, he dropped dead on the gangway on commissioning day and Captain O.L. Gordon took over command of *Exeter*.

We left Devonport on 24th March, 1941. Many of the ship's company had wives and families in Plymouth and had had to leave without many of them knowing their families' fate in the Plymouth blitz, but we were at war – total war.

We went to Scapa Flow and for the next month or so and operated with the 1st Cruiser Squadron doing gunnery and torpedo trials. While at Scapa Flow many of the ship's company heard about the loss of some of their families and their homes but they were not allowed to leave.

On 2nd May 1941, we left the Clyde with a large convoy in company with the 7th Destroyer Squadron and while running down the coast of West Africa heard that the giant battleship *Bismarck* was not too far from our convoy. Our destroyers left to seek the *Bismarck* and we were left to carry on with the convoy past Freetown and around the Cape to Durban and Aden.

This was our job for several months, doing convoy work between Durban and Aden. I must say I enjoyed those days sailing under the Southern Cross; the weather was always nice, a canvas bath was rigged up on the fo'c'sle and after spending four hours in an 8" gun turret closed up at cruising stations, it was lovely to get in the salt water bath and relax looking up at the starry heavens. I was promoted to Petty Officer in September 1941.

Whilst at Mombasa, my shipmate Fred Aindow and I went ashore together. While passing a native compound we heard the sound of beating drums. We had been drinking, were in a happy mood, and entered the compound. There was a ceremony going on – a native girl was choosing a husband, so Fred and I joined in the queue. The men were passing a sword from one to another and when they saw us at the end of the queue they got quite angry. Fred and I took to our heels across the fence followed by a number of irate natives, but we managed to elude them.

We called into Durban quite a few times and were always made most welcome by the South Africans. Many of the ship's company were invited to private houses and were entertained at parties on a lavish scale. I was no exception. I thoroughly enjoyed myself there, going surfing, horse riding, dancing, etc., but all this came to an end. In September we moved to Ceylon (The Pearl of the Orient). Japan was on the brink of entering the war. We visited the Maldive Islands and then Calcutta.

This was such a change from South Africa. The squalor and poverty of Calcutta had to be seen to be believed. We sailed down the River Hoogley after three or four days in Calcutta, taking a convoy to Rangoon in Burma. While escorting this convoy, we were ordered south to join the *Prince of Wales* and *Repulse*.

Going through the Malacca Straits we heard the grim news that the *Prince of Wales* and *Repulse* had been sunk. It was awfully hard to believe. I had many friends on both these ships. Evidently she was attacked by high level torpedo bombers shortly after 11.00am on 10th December 1942. The attack lasted some two hours. The *Repulse* sank at about 12.30pm and the *Prince of Wales* an hour later. There were about 2,000 survivors from the two ships, about 850 men were lost, which included Admiral Phillips and the captain of the *Prince of Wales*, Captain J C Leach, who had gone down with their ship. The survivors were picked up by three destroyers.

We arrived in Singapore on 10th December and were now one of the biggest ships in the area. In the evening the destroyers brought the survivors into Singapore. *Exeter* had made arrangements in the cold storage shed in the dockyard for the arrival of the survivors. They were quickly given a medical check, followed by hot drinks, cigarettes, and a good tot of Navy rum, and dispersed into the barracks for the evening. There was a huge cheer in the shed when the captain of *Repulse*, Captain W.G. Tenants, came in with his head bandaged – he was a very popular man.

On Christmas Eve 1941 we were convoying ships to Colombo in Ceylon. One of the ships in the convoy was the *Erinpura* which carried a lot of the survivors of the ill-fated *Prince of Wales* and *Repulse*. Then it was back to Singapore again. With the fall of Singapore in February 1942, we moved further south to Batavia and operated between this place and the Dutch Naval base of Surabaya in Java.

The story of the ensuing battles in which we took part in the Java Seas has already been told in several books, *Fight it Out* by our Captain O.L. Gordon, *No Surrender* by Chief O.A. Bill Johns, and one or two other books, so I will not bother giving details of the Java battles except to say I was in the funeral party which buried our dead from the first action on 27th February 1942. It was a beautiful day and the cemetery at

Kembang Koening in Surabaya was on a ridge overlooking the harbour. There was a slight breeze and the air was scented with spices. The bugler sounded the Last Post and it brought tears to many an eye thinking of these brave men being laid to rest many thousands of miles from home and their loved ones.

On the evening of the 28th, *Exeter* sailed from Surabaya after completing temporary repairs. In our company was the destroyer *Encounter* and the United States destroyer *Pope*. We were hoping to make our way through the Sunda Straits between Sumatra and Java and thence to Colombo for a well-earned rest, but this was not to be. Once more we encountered heavy Japanese naval forces and were hit in "A" boiler room and elsewhere. The Captain gave the order to "Sink the ship", then "Abandon ship". I thought about the half bottle of Navy rum in my locker and one of our CPO's actually went back to get some from his, but went down with the ship.

I tried to lower a 27 foot Whaler from the davits, but it was hopeless, so without much thought I jumped into the sea from the port side. My main concern was to get clear of the ship's screws as the ship was still going slightly ahead. The *Exeter* reluctantly sank with her Battle Ensign flying, wildly cheered by British sailors who were in the sea all around her. I managed to find a 16 foot oar and hung onto this for some two hours, then came across a flotta net with several men on it and changed to this. Several Japanese destroyers passed by but they did not stop and one could see the grinning Japanese faces lining the side. It was quite frightening as we did not know if they would shoot at us in the water.

During the late afternoon one of the men on the net from the destroyer *Encounter* suddenly said "Steer for the church, down the avenue in between the trees. They are bound to let us in." It was time to leave that net.

Prior to the battle, we had seen scores of sharks, but I did not think about these until the last hour or so. When I did, I lived a million deaths, especially when seaweed or flotsam touched my legs. Perhaps the gunfire or bombings had frightened them off – I will never know.

Many years later I learnt that the Japanese victor of the Battle of the Java Sea, a Vice-Admiral Nishimura, was some two and a half years later in command of the Japanese battleship *Yamashiro*. He was killed in the battle of Surigao Strait when the *Yamashiro* was torpedoed by the American destroyer *Newcombe*, and some eight minutes later rolled over and sank, taking Vice-Admiral Nishimura, and almost all of her crew with her. Retribution!

We were eventually picked up by a Japanese destroyer, but every so often they would kick their screws forward and move ahead. Quite a few men were lost in this way. They were obviously afraid of any lurking American submarines. We were so exhausted we just collapsed in a great heap on the after part of the destroyer, and lay there all night, too weak to do anything.

Late the following afternoon we sighted land. The place was Bandjarmasin in Borneo. On entering harbour we were transferred to a huge oil tanker, were ushered down below with shouts and hits, and the hatches were battened down on us. The atmosphere was terrible, with no food or water. We stayed there until brought up on deck the following evening. To our amazement, a hospital ship was in harbour. It was the Dutch hospital ship *Op-Ten-Noort*. We thought we were going to be repatriated, but unknown to us then, she had been captured by the Japanese who did not comply with the Geneva Convention.

I was informed many years later by 'Doc' Adrian Borstlap, a Dutch doctor at the Macassar POW Camp and a great friend to many POW's, that the *Op-Ten-Noort* of the *Koninlijke Paketvaart My* (the Royal Packet Company) was leased to the Dutch Royal Navy as a Red Cross ship (6,000 tons). On 21st February 1942, she was bombed in Surabaya, Java, by the Japanese, resulting in the death of one doctor and two nurses (Japan had never undersigned the Treaty of Geneva).

She was sent to pick up survivors after the Battle of Java Sea, but was seized by the Japanese and taken to Bandjarmasin, Borneo, and then to Macassar, Island of Celebes. There she was used for several weeks as a hospital for the survivors of the Java Sea Battle and as a transit point for POW's.

In June 1942, all the patients were transferred to the Macassar Camp and the Dutch doctors and nurses on board carried on providing a kind of out-patients clinic, mostly dental services.

On 23rd November 1942, she sailed to Yokohama, where she arrived on 5th December. The ship's crew and medical staff were interned on Formosa and later in Korea. The ship with a Japanese crew sailed from there to the Philippines and the Indies, partly as a hospital ship, but also as a transport for troops and war material such as ammunition, rubber, oil, etc. She sailed under the name of *Teno Maru*.

On 10th September 1944, she sailed for the last time from Maizuru in Japan and was, after a few days, lost at sea. The Royal Packet Company says she probably hit a mine, but it is more acceptable that she was sunk by a US submarine, as the US Navy had been hunting her!

We were put in boats and transferred over to the hospital ship. The seriously wounded were put into the hospital sector of the ship. The remainder of us were pushed into a limited space right up forward. We could hardly move. We were given one small ball of rice, the size of a meatball, and we queued for hours for a drink of water from a tap which had no more than a trickle coming from it. We were parched. After all, we were only about 5° south of the Equator.

I met up here with an American by the name of "Pony" Moore from the American submarine *Perch*. He asked if I fancied trying to escape, but one look over the side of the ship into the clear water put that idea out of our heads – there were two huge sharks. In any case, it would have been hopeless as we were to find out later.

The Japanese could not understand why no British officer or men had the honour to commit suicide rather than surrender. It was made clear that prisoners of war were so disgraceful that they did not deserve to live, but there were far too many of us to kill so we were to be used as coolie labourers by the Japanese army.

It was said that Japanese soldiers, when they parted before battle, would say to each other, "See you in Yasukuni Shrine." They all wanted to lay down their life for their emperor and country and to finish at the soldiers' shrine Yasukuni – one reason why they were found to be so fanatical.

The *Op-Ten-Noort* left Borneo and on the third day we arrived at Macassar on the Island of Celebes. After tying up we were shepherded off the ship by armed Japanese guards, who kicked and pushed and hit men with the butts of their rifles. They lined us up in rows of five and it took over an hour for them to count and check us. We eventually marched off with our captain at our head, paraded through the streets of Macassar and shown off to the local population who crowded the streets to get a glimpse of us. Most of us were barefoot and had hardly any clothes. The roads were red hot. Quite a few of the men were helped along with the butt of a rifle or a prod with a bayonet. The smell of stale fish pervaded the place – we could see it hung up outside the small shops and stores along the route. Flies were all over the place. We had to march about seven miles or so. Many men who marched with us that day were destined never to return but to be buried in the ant-infested soil of Macassar and many other places in the Celebes.

We eventually arrived at an army camp which had been used by Indonesian soldiers of the Dutch Army. They consisted of huts with bare walls and stone floors and were divided up into cubicles with about sixteen to twenty cubicles in each hut. We were pushed into these, six men to a cubicle. There was no bedding and no furniture of any description. We had no food that night and just lay exhausted on the stone floor and slept the sleep of sleeps.

Next morning a feeling of utter desolation descended on me. There was no contact with the outside world and no idea how the war was progressing. Food was not provided until the afternoon, when we were each given a ball of rice and some drinking water. This went on for several days. We were so weak that many who stood up blacked out and had to sit down again.

After a week we were moved into different huts inside barbed wire compounds – the Americans in one, the English in another, the Dutch in another, and the Indonesians another. One of the guards was a vicious character nicknamed "Gold Tooth", so-called because of his wide expanse of gold teeth. He had no culture or breeding; a small man with beady eyes and a great protruding jaw, just like an ape. He was feared, I believe, by the other Japanese guards and officers and was responsible for the deaths of many prisoners of war. He would beat up men whether sick or not on the least pretext, with the dreaded baseball bat. Gold Tooth was tried at the end of the war as a war criminal and shot.

I once saw him try to pull a man's moustache off with a pair of pliers. The *Exeter's* First Lieutenant who in those days was Lt. Comdr. Cooper (later Captain R.N.) tried to remonstrate with Gold Tooth only to have his shins badly kicked by him. He was a very brave man to even attempt to do this. The Japanese guards had no respect for our officers and they were physically abused the same as the rest of us.

One of the men in my cubicle, "Hugo", who had been an officers cook on the *Exeter* tried making soup from grass. He said it was full of vitamins but when I tried some I became quite ill afterwards.

The Dutchmen in Macassar with us were mainly soldiers, plus a few sailors. The soldiers had plenty of clothes and money whereas the English and American sailors had no money and very little clothing. Our boys used to trade for food with local natives over the fence at the back of the galley and charge the Dutchmen a little extra for doing it for them. They took an awful risk and quite a few of them were caught and savagely beaten.

Another Japanese punishment was to make two prisoners face each other and flick the end of each other's noses continuously. This resulted in one's sore and tender nose swelling up. I was caught trying to knock some coconuts down off a tree one day and had this punishment inflicted on me.

After about a month in the camp, the Japanese started organising working parties. We worked on various projects from gardening to working at the docks and emptying the luxurious bungalows of furniture and fittings which originally belonged to the former Dutch colonials. These were crated up and sent back to Japan. When out on working parties we were always searched on arrival back at camp. One day when working in the dock area I found an old tin of condensed milk. When marched back to the camp I carried it on my head under the hat I'd acquired. I was caught when the Jap guard searched me and was terrified thinking of the beating I would get. The guard called the sergeant out. The tin, which had been a bit battered and had one or two holes in, had started to melt and the condensed milk was running down my face. The Japs must have thought it quite funny and to my amazement, belted me a few times and let me go. This was most unusual. I took to my heels as fast as I could in case they changed their minds.

Another day I was in a working party allocated to work at the Japanese Headquarters. I was put with the Jap barber and had to clean up the barber's shop. He seemed quite pleased when I had finished and started talking to me in a mixture of Japanese, Malay and English. He said "Churchill *dame*, Roosevelt *dame*" (meaning no good), "Stalin number 1." I cottoned on to the fact that he was a communist and played it clever and agreed with him. I did not have much of a choice (the Communist Party was banned in Japan). He seemed quite pleased, especially when I

63

put up my arm with the clenched fist. He gave me ten cigarettes, two tablets of Palmolive soap, five Japanese Occupation guilders, and a drink of wine and a pair of patent leather shoes, size 10 – far too big for me as I only took size 7, but I put them on. When we were finished I marched back to the camp wearing only my loin cloth and a pair of patent leather shoes far too big for me. I must have looked a peculiar sight, but who cared – at least I had a pair of shoes on my feet.

Another method of smuggling was the "benjo men", "benjo" meaning lavatory. Food was brought into the camp by the benjo men who came about three times a week to empty the sewage pool. The pipes which they brought in to suck the sewage were loaded with food and the benjo men sold this to anyone who had the money to buy it. The price charged was quite high and the only people that could really afford it were the Dutch army men who had plenty of Dutch guilders. The natives preferred this currency to Japanese occupational guiders, not that there were any in the camp. These benjo men had quite a good innings at this racket before being found out and then it was a brutal beating for them.

It was amazing the rumours that went around in the camp. The Australians had supposedly attacked the northern end of the island; the Americans had attempted to recapture Singapore; and so they went on during the whole of the time I was a prisoner of war – perhaps it was good for morale.

The thought of escape was always there, but when one weighed it up it seemed almost impossible. Nevertheless, three very brave Dutchmen did try it. Their names were Lt.ii Haan (R.N.V.R.), Sgt. Knill (Royal Netherlands Ind. Army), and Seaman Pelletier (Aeroplace Techn. R.N. Entrop). They escaped on the night of 5th September 1942, managed to get into the hills, but were recaptured on 8th September due to the treachery of the local native population. They were brought back to the camp in a terrible state having been badly beaten up. All the men in the hut where the three escapees belonged were put in solitary confinement, beaten up by berserk guards, and kept there for about three weeks.

The whole camp was assembled and a Japanese naval officer by the name of Maroi came into the British compound and read the death penalty out for the three escapees. He could not speak very good English and said that the three of them would be 'shotted' to death. They were taken from the camp to the town prison and we learned later that they were made to dig their own graves and were beheaded on 15th September 1942 on the fairground in Macassar. We were told that if this happened again the room-mates of any escapee would also be put to death, so we put any thoughts of escape out of our minds – our only escape at that time seemed to be death.

Later, on 28th March 1945, a working party found the skeletons of the three brave men which were reburied in the cemetery at Macassar. After the war they were taken to Batavia in Java and laid to rest in the Military Cemetery.

About this time there was a directive from the Japanese asking for more prisoners of war to be sent to the mainland. Those in charge in our camp started to send out forms asking for specific tradesmen. One week they wanted welders and to try and get out of the camp one would try and outdo one s friends and put down more years experience than they may have done. The next week it would be carpenters, and the same thing would happen. Had they bothered to tot up the number of years experience any one person claimed, they would have found some men to be over one hundred years old with experience in ten different trades, but they didn t seem to catch on.

Eventually, a large group was formed and I was one of them. I had said on my last form that I was a draughtsman. I had just got over a very bad bout of some kind of tropical fever and was very weak indeed. On 14th October 1942, I was one of a thousand other POW's who were marched down to the dockyard in Macassar for shipment to Japan. I was so weak I could hardly walk and a couple of my shipmates had to half- carry me most of the way. Such was the comradeship among *Exeter*'s crew – I shall be forever grateful to them. We had spent some five or six months at Macassar and now were boarding the *Asama Maru* for our journey to Japan and the unknown.

Many POW's being transferred to Japan from places like Thailand and Singapore on Japanese ships lost their lives when the ships were torpedoed by American submarines who could not have known that these ships carried POW's. Ships like the *Chichi Maru, Kachidoki Maru, Rakuyo Maru* and possibly many more – so we on *Asama Maru* were rather fortunate (if one can call it that).

We were stowed in the holds of the troopship and were allowed up on deck for twenty minutes each day to breathe God's fresh air. During this time spent on deck we could see Japanese troops – they used to draw their hands across their throats as if to say – you are going to have your heads chopped off when you arrive in Japan. We loved them too!

At the port of Nagasaki we were put on a ferry boat and taken to an island called Koyagi in the bay of Nagasaki. We disembarked and, under Japanese army guards, were marched to the small village square. We were assembled in front of a dais and a Japanese civilian started to tell us that we were going to work on shipbuilding in the Kawaminomi Shipyard just down the road. He said if we worked hard it would only seem like fifteen years, but if we did not work hard we would be severely punished. No wonder so many men lacked the will to carry on living and died much more easily.

When all the speeches were over we marched about two miles to our new camp. It was between some hills, backing on to the sea. We were put into rooms, about fifty men to a room. I was in a room with all Navy men. Some were from the *Exeter*, some from the destroyer *Encounter* (which had been sunk with us) some from the American submarine *Perch*, and the remainder from an American destroyer, *Pope*. An American was detailed off to be the room 'chief' or 'hancho' as the Japanese called them.

I was in Room 5 at Camp 2 at the Fukuoka POW Camp, and my room mates with their POW numbers were as follows:-

POW No.	Name	Nationality
42	Vaneste	American
43	Carne	British
44	Formals	British
218	Bronson	American
219	Bartel	South African
220	Bayfield	British
221	Bryant	British
222	Bond	British
223	Cox	British
224	Delman	American
225	Dague	American
226	Dunlevey	British
227	Doyle	British
228	Erickson	American
229	Evans	British
230	Foley	American
231	Fairhurst	British
232	Goodwin	American
233	Greene	British
234	Goss	British
235	Gates	British
236	Hurden	American
237	Hyde	American
238	Hazel	British
239	Hendwood	British
240	Honeywell	British
241	Johnson	American
242	Jenkins	British
243	Jeffs	British
244	Clikey	American
245	Kirk	American
246	Kaye	British
247	Lembeck	American
248	Lamb	British
249	McCreary	American
250	McCray	American
251	Maxwell	American
252	Matthews	American
253	Munn	British

254	O Connel	British
255	Perry	British
256	Phillips	British
257	Roberts	British
258	Rasmussen	American
259	Roberts	British
260	Rogan	British
261	Stevenson	American
262	Shook	American
263	Strousse	American
264	Stywegg	Dutch
265	Soloman	British
266	Steel	British
267	Stone	British
268	Thompson	British
269	Walton	American
270	Willinger	Dutch
271	Westhuzen	South African
272	Wright	British

The following were the Allied Officers of Camp 2 Fukuoka Camp:-

Officer-in-Charge	Major Harrison	American Air Force
	Lt. Comdr. Chubb	Royal Navy
	Lt. Sloan	American Army
	Lt. Allan	American Army
	Lt. Mickey	American Air Force
	Lt. Strong	American Air Force
	Lt. Michells	American Navy
	Lt. Blane	Royal Navy
	S/Lt. Bond	Royal Navy
	S/Lt. Jenkins	R.N.R.
	Mr Naylor	R.F.R.
	Mr Egan	R.F.R.
	Mr Farran	W/O Royal Navy
	Mr Beckford	W/O Royal Navy
	Mr Harding	W/O Royal Navy
	Mr Hicks	civilian
	Mr Davis	Sgt. Major

I knew all these names and numbers because I kept a list and managed to keep it hidden from the Japanese guards.

Our rooms had double banked sleeping places either side and a long wooden table in the centre with wooden benches each side of it. The floor was concrete. The sleeping places, made of rough wood, had a type of matting covering the floor where each person slept. We had one blanket each and our pillow was made of straw material compacted in the shape and size of a building brick. The woodwork was rotten with fleas and lice, bedbugs abounded, together with a strange jumping flea called in Japanese "Shirami".

Our clothes consisted of a seaweed-type green suit and a pair of rubber-type shoes like sandals with the big toe in one section and the remaining toes in the other section. They were clipped around the ankle. These were about the only possessions we had. The first few weeks in the camp took it's toll. We had come from a tropical climate in the Celebes Islands to a cold Japanese climate – almost the same as in Great Britain. Many men died. We used to put them in a type of orange box coffin and they were taken to Nagasaki where they were cremated, after a fashion. One of the burial party was given a pair of large chopsticks to pick out one or two bones which were ground into ashes and put into a small urn. These were put in a church – St George's in Nagasaki – for eventual return if that ever came about. This never happened because the city was bombed. We must have lost about fifty to sixty men in the first few months in the camp due to pneumonia and other respiratory diseases. Our doctors did what they could, but without proper medication it was hopeless.

More men started to arrive in the camp: Australians, a few Canadians, more Dutch and Indonesians, and even civilians who had been captured at Guam and were treated just the same as prisoners of war. These men were older and did not fare so well. Also some civilians from Wake Island were interned. One of these men was eventually put in a confinement cell – a bamboo cage standing about 4'6" high and about 3' wide. He died after about three days in there.

Our food consisted of a bowl of rice for breakfast, a tin of rice for lunch with a strange concoction called "Digon". This was supposed to be a vegetable and was something like a cross between shredded turnip and cabbage and had a sour taste. Supper consisted of a bowl of rice and the head of a fish. The only part I never ate of this was its eyeballs. I knew every bone in a fish's head by the time I finished there.

After several days in the camp we were divided into different groups for working in the dockyard – draughtsmen, platers, welders, caulkers, gas cutters, etc. The routine was to be called at 5.00am, morning muster at 5.10 and breakfast at 6.00am. Then we mustered for work at 6.30am carrying with us our lunch – a small tin of rice about the same size as a herrings-in-tomato-sauce tin.

The Japanese army guards then counted us. It sometimes took them an hour. It was not unusual to see a sergeant of the guard hitting a Japanese private in front of all the POW's for not counting us right. We did not mind – it meant less time in the dreaded dockyard. When they had sorted this out we marched down to the square in the village where Japanese naval guards took over from the army. Once again we were checked and when all was well, were marched into the Kawaminami Dockyard and handed over to our civilian hancho who again checked us. There was one hancho for each group – he was usually a chargeman of a specific trade.

I well remember marching to work one winter's morning when it was very cold. We had stopped at the village square to wait for the naval guards to take over from our army guards. They were a little late so the Senior NCO from our army guards got up on to a dais and got us to do PT to keep warm. He egged us on with Japanese words and we responded, but what he didn't know was that we were shouting naval abuse at him! He thought we had entered into the spirit of the occasion. I think this was one of the few times I had a good laughing spell while a POW!

Marching from the square to the dockyard with the navy guards every prisoner had to march in step. If he was caught out of step he was beaten. This was difficult for those with swollen feet and ankles caused by beri-beri. Also, the step was called out in three different ways: the English called "left-right-left"; the Americans "up-two-three-four"; and the Dutch "links-lect-links-fier". The beating-up was a daily occurrence.

According to the Geneva Convention, POW's are not supposed to do war work. The Japanese ignored this. Anybody objecting would have been beheaded or shot – possibly both! Once the civilian hancho took us over from the naval guards, we were allocated our various jobs. I was in charge of the platers group, along with a Dutch sergeant. The plater's job was quite a dangerous one as most of the time he would be on narrow staging over the side of the ship. Quite a few had serious accidents. At 12.00 noon we stopped for half an hour for our tin of rice, then back to work until about 5.30pm. We were then mustered by our hancho and handed back to the naval guards, marched back to the square to our army guards, and then back to camp.

On arrival back at camp we washed, but it was too cold in the winter to strip for a wash down. I think in four years the Japanese took us down to the communal bath in the village about four or five times at the most. At 6.00pm the food was brought to the rooms, consisting of rice and fish heads. Each man in the room put his bowl on the table and we took it in turns daily to serve this rice out. One would see fifty hungry men all watching the server in case he put more rice in one bowl than another. They could tell almost to the grain and there were many arguments on this subject. The room chief would then look at the bowls and, once satisfied, we could take our bowl and sit on our bunks and eat.

One had to abide by the rules of the room to ensure that the small amount of food which came into the room daily was evenly distributed. Because we were always hungry as POW's it taught us to live together under stress as decently as we could.

The Japanese guards in the camp consisted of two different units. One of them were old Chinese war veterans who looked after administration, the galley and various other jobs. They were in the camp the whole of our stay there and we got to know each other well. The other guard was a unit of the Imperial Japanese Guard. This unit was changed roughly every month. They were real swines, constantly beating men upon the least pretext. They did not stay outside the perimeter, but were in and out of our rooms continuously.

At 8.00pm we were mustered in our rooms and when the Japanese guard came in to check us we had to call out our numbers in Japanese, depending on our position in the ranks. With fifty men in the room it was difficult to remember the Japanese numbers. Any man who made a mistake was beaten up. Within a few weeks we had learnt how to count perfectly in Japanese.

After 8.00pm and the muster we were not allowed out of our rooms except to go to the 'benjo' (toilet). We were not allowed to visit other rooms. With no books to read (a few were smuggled in from Macassar), no mail from home, no letters to write, life was indeed hard. I was always dreaming of home and food and wondering whether tomorrow could possibly be as bad as today. Lights were out at 9.00pm.

When men went to the toilet at night they had to put a "benjo" sign, written in Japanese, on the ends of their bunks. There were only three of these signs in each room and it was quite normal for five or six men to be out of the room at once. Often we could not wait for men to come back and so one had often to take a chance that the guard would not check their rooms at that particular time. Occasionally one got caught and as it was useless trying to explain to the guard that there were not sufficient "benjo" signs in the room, one accepted a working-over. Owing to the fact that we were eating only rice (which is grown in water) and drinking green water (supposed to be green tea) we had to go to the toilets four, five or even six time's a night, so one never really got a decent sleep. The "benjo" was outside the building and consisted of planks of thin wood with a space in the middle, where one squatted over the space. Apart from being very cold in the winter, the smell that permeated the place was so horrible that you spent as little time as was humanly possible there. Men who suffered from dysentery had to pay any number of visits to this awful place. The Japanese used the human excreta for their gardens and often, while one was squatting over the hole, a long bamboo pole with a container on the end was pushed underneath you by any Japanese civilian wanting to fertilize his garden! Nothing was sacred in these camps!

I was caught once having no "benjo" sign on my bunk and the Japanese guard took me out to the main guard room opposite the main gate. There sat another six guards on benches. He beat me with a baseball bat about eight times, then I was

70

made to climb into the branches of a tree and sit there all night. This was in the winter and all I had on was a linen loin cloth. Needless to say I went down with pneumonia several days later. This was in my last year of captivity and I was a little lucky as the doctor had managed to get a few M and B tablets, plus putting a huge needle into me to draw off fluid – so I managed to survive.

I spent a lot of time in the evenings day-dreaming on my bunk. I used to think about England and its green fields and the primroses growing in the hedgerows, about the Sussex Downs, about how my brothers were getting on (I had two in the army, and my next elder brother was in the merchant navy), about my girlfriend at home. I wondered how my fellow shipmates were faring who were still at Macassar, especially my old shipmate Baron Fred Aindow. But Baron was an astute man – I was sure if anybody survived he would – and I was glad to find this was the case when meeting up with him again in Formby, Lancashire, just after the war ended.

Our doctors at the camp did a wonderful job as far as was humanly possible. There was little or no medicine for them to work with and the Japanese insisted that sickness be kept to the minimum. We made things more difficult by trying all the usual dodges. One was required to have a temperature of 102° or 103° before going sick. We used to obtain a little bottle (the Japanese sometimes had small bottles which had contained chilli peppers) and just before going into the doctor would fill it full of boiling water and put it underneath the arm. The bottoms of our trousers would be tied and at the last minute we would let the bottle slip. The only way our temperatures were taken was by the under-arm method.

Another trick was when a man had been in a compartment in the ship where electric welders were working, he got what was called a "flash" where the eyes became sore and temporarily blinded for quite some time. Quite often chaps would put chilli peppers into the eyes which helped to create a "flash", but this made them very sore and there was no treatment available.

Another method was to get a tap with a 7 lb. hammer. This caused contusion of the joints depending on where the blow was delivered, and our hands would begin to swell up. I did not have to do this. I was hit on my right index finger by a Japanese shipwright while holding a punch. A few days later the finger swelled up and we had little or no vitamins in our bodies to help combat the swelling. I visited the Dutch doctor, Dr. Max Waisfisz, who got two men to hold my arms. He put a piece of cloth in my mouth so nobody would hear my screams, and proceeded to jab my finger with a blunt pair of scissors. This helped to release the pus, but the pain was terrible. Each morning I had to have the finger probed causing many a sleepless night just thinking about it. I was off work for two months, but the Japanese at this time decided that if a man did not work he did not require so much food, so instead of three bowls of rice per day I only got two. After about two weeks of getting this probing treatment, the doctor pushed the scissors into the hole in my finger underneath

71

the skin and out the other end. Several days later he cut the top of the finger between the two holes with a penknife dipped in boiling water and then put a piece of cellophane to act as a drain. All this was done without any anaesthetic. It was a really horrible two months for me. Dr Waisfisz was a regular medical officer of the Royal Netherlands Indies Army and Senior Medical Office at Nagasaki POW camp. He retired with the rank of major in 1950 after the independence of Indonesia. I still bear the scar to this day and possibly would not have been able to bend my finger if it had not been for an English doctor called Syrad. He gave me a wooden ball and told me to exercise with it each evening. I still cannot bend it fully, but at least I have the use of it. After the war, about 1978, I had to go to Birmingham for a medical regarding my finger. I was most annoyed when one of the two doctors interviewing me asked who had put me up to try and get a pension. He then told me to drop my trousers. I said I was there about my finger, but he replied that he had to go through the usual medical procedures, as most servicemen will know. I was awarded about £600 but no pension.

Back in the camp, if a man was sick he would lend his rice away until he thought he was going to be better; or if a man wanted to celebrate his wedding anniversary or birthday he would lend a bowl of rice away until that date. A character called Moses, who belonged to the American army and had been captured at Corrigidor in the Philippine Islands said to me one day, "If a man lends a bowl of rice away, borrow it, because he might be dead tomorrow." It seemed at the time a callous way of behaving, but I slept on it and decided that if a man died he would not need the rice anyway, so I started to borrow rice. Many months later Moses asked how I was doing. I told him I owed about 240 bowls of rice; he said he owed 320. Eventually we declared ourselves bankrupt and told the Dutch interpreter who took us around each room in turn and told the inmates. We had to pay one bowl of rice back per day to those still living and were eventually solvent again. One of the POW's who worked in the kitchen used to scrape the rice off the side of the copper in which the rice was cooked – it came off in sheets – he used to give me a little of this which I would chew to help kill the hunger pangs.

Another way of supplementing my diet was by stealing the Japanese workers lunches in the shipyard. They used to bring their food wrapped in large handkerchiefs. They would then bend a welding rod into an S shape and hang these on eyebolts under the ship or inside compartments of the ship. They would then go about their various tasks. There were about seven or eight slipways and I used to vary my visits to them: one day I would take No. 2 slipway and steal a couple of lunches; the next day I would taken No. 7 and do the same thing; then back to No. 1. I would throw the handkerchiefs, tins and chopsticks away and eat the rice and fish. This helped tide me over during the period I was bankrupt. It was a dangerous pursuit and I was lucky to get away with it.

The toilets in the shipyard were awful but that was the place to visit in order to learn any news – it was amazing the rumours that originated from that place. Women labourers used to come and use the same toilets. Life was basic.

There was a serious accident in the shipyard about this time. The Japanese were building a brand new dock to take the keels of two new ships. The inner or landward one had been finished and a ship was already being built in it. A caisson was put across separating it from the outer or seaward dock which had not been completed. The caisson dividing these two docks gave way one day and the sea poured in smashing the ship which was being built in the inner dock. Two of the POWs helped rescue some of the Japanese workers. The next day the bosses in charge of the dockwork were lined up and beaten by the Japanese naval guards. That same afternoon, all the POWs and Japanese workers were assembled in front of a dais and a Japanese admiral and his interpreter climbed onto the dais. The two POWs who had helped save several Japanese workers' lives were called up in front of the dais. The Japanese Admiral said, "Although enemy – very brave men", and proceeded to give them five cigarettes each, a small bottle of chili powder to use with their rice, and a parchment scroll written in Japanese which they obviously could not read. One of the POWs was Taff Phillips who was in the same room at the camp as me and we pulled his leg quite a lot about this.

We tried all kinds of tricks to try and sabotage some of their efforts at building ships. I well remember putting nuts and bolts into pieces of machinery waiting to be hoisted onboard ships. We had to be most careful – it would have been "off heads" if we had been caught.

By now the Japanese in the shipyard were busy as ants tunnelling under the hills in and around the shipyard. Huge caverns were drilled out and on completion lathes and machinery were moved into them. Electric lights were rigged up and whole machine shops went underground. This led us to believe that bombings were expected, indicating that the Allies were getting nearer to Japan. We also sensed that Japanese forces were taking a beating as the guards became even nastier and beat us up on the least pretext.

One of the Indonesians who was in the camp with us was found to have leprosy. The Japanese guards built a hut for him surrounded by a stockade. His rice and water were passed through the fencing as nobody would go near him. He had made a bamboo flute and when we returned to the camp after work, feeling tired and sometimes wet through, he would greet us with well-known melodies. The Japs would get mad and throw huge bricks at his hut to try and get him to shut up, but to no avail. He was the only one who dared to ignore the Japanese guards. Just before the war ended he was moved from the camp but we never did find out what happened to him.

I had learned the two Japanese alphabets "Katakana" (the phonetic version), and "Hirigana" (the written one), from the young Japanese lad I worked with, whose name was Mishoshiri. A young Chinese lad who had been captured in Singapore knew "Kanji", the Japanese written language, from old Japanese newspapers found in the dockyard. We gleaned the news that the German war was almost over, which meant that the war effort against the Japanese would be stepped up. Sure enough, for the first time we began to see the odd American bomber appear in the sky around the Nagasaki area. I remember one day being told by my Japanese civilian boss, Tsutsumi, that we would be going home soon. All signs were pointing to an early end to the war against Japan, but one always had the thought in mind as to how the military would react to the POWs. Would they go berserk and kill us all – especially if there was an invasion of the Japanese mainland? It really did not bear thinking about!

About this time the Japanese started releasing Red Cross parcels. They had been in the camp for years and so we got some sugar, butter, etc., and the luxury of a pair of American boots and socks. The Japanese did not want their workers to realise that such luxuries existed so did not distribute much.

We had lost many men in the camp – wonderful men – through dysentery, meningitis, beri-beri, pneumonia and all kinds of diseases. It was very sad to see a man start to go down with something, it being so difficult for him to tackle the uphill fight to recovery. Men lost the will to live after two or three years in captivity and just gave up hope. Once that happened it was a slow downward slide.

I was glad of my early beginnings at the orphanage and the tough environment in which I grew up. It certainly helped me in those difficult days – somehow or other I never gave up hope or lost my pride. One would say goodnight to one's close friends not knowing whether any of us would be dead in the morning, so we used to discuss among ourselves who to contact back home in the event of this happening.

One thing the Japanese never kept us short of was toilet paper and, as the Dutch and Indonesians never used it (they carried a small container of water) it was always in abundance. Occasionally we were given a packet of tooth powder, but no brushes. Soap was a rarity. When we went down to the dockyard we would go into a compartment with a rivet fire, take our trousers off and hang them over the fire in a bid to get rid of the lice.

Mail was almost non-existent. I received a card from my brother who was serving in Burma. I think all he was allowed to say was, "Hope you are alright". When the war ended I received about seven letters which had long been sent but never received. It wasn't known at the time but, thirteen weeks after the sinking of *Exeter*, we had been posted as "Missing, presumed dead".

In early August 1945, Misoshiri, the Japanese boy who worked with me, said that there had been a big bang, as he described, in Hiroshima. Many years later I was to learn that on 6th August 1945, Colonel Tibbets led the way to Japan from Tinian in the Mariana Islands with the *Little Boy* as the bomb was called, tucked in the bomb bay of his B29 aircraft called *Enola Gay* and at 8.15 and 17 seconds am the *Little Boy*, a black and orange shape weighing nearly 5 tons, was released on the 255,000 people of Hiroshima. At an altitude of 1,870 feet the nine and a half pounds of cordite drove the uranium chunks into each other and the equivalent of 13,500 tons of TNT exploded in the sky. That's what Misoshiri had meant by a big bang. We were really glad not to know at that time exactly what had happened at Hiroshima with it's huge loss of life, otherwise it would have worried us sick at the thought of what the Japanese would do to their prisoners by way of reprisals. It was then that a change in the attitude of the Japanese began to be noticed. Where once they had swaggered around arrogantly, they now seemed much more subdued.

CHAPTER NINE

The Nuclear Route to Freedom

On 9th August 1945, we went to work as usual in the Kawaminami shipyard at Nagasaki and went about our various tasks. Coming out of our little tool shed I noticed a silvery looking object in the sky above. This was about 8.50am. On closer look it was a huge bomber – a B29. About ten minutes later there was an intense and blinding flash, like the arc on an electric welding rod only far more powerful, and it seemed surprisingly long. Then the tremendous roar of the explosion and a terrific heat was felt, followed by an enormous mushroom cloud that blossomed out like a tree. There was a certain elegance about it and then a deadly stillness … something awful had happened.

Then all hell broke loose in our shipyard. Everybody started rushing for the air raid shelters including the Japanese guards. We were herded into a shelter under the hills with hardly any room to move. Many comments were advanced that morning in the shelter as to what had happened. Some thought an ammunition dump had gone up, but nobody even dreamed of an atomic bomb. We did not find this out until some weeks later.

We were kept in the shelter for quite a few hours and just after lunch time came out and were assembled. Bodies were being carried on stretchers – they had the most horrific burns imaginable. We were marched back to the camp.

Excitement was starting to build up at the thought that the war might be reaching it s climax. We sat and discussed it most of the evening. We were to learn a week or so later, when the Americans dropped a note on to the camp along with supplies, that an atomic bomb had been dropped. We were truly amazed. Years later I learned the true story of the bombing of Nagasaki. A B29 bomber called *Bocks Car* with a Major Chuck Sweeney in command was detailed for dropping the second atomic bomb on Japan. Minutes before take-off from Trinian in the Marianas, Sergeant Kuharek, the Flight Engineer, found a problem on *Bocks Car*. The lower rear bomb bay auxiliary transfer fuel pump was not operating properly and 600 gallons of gas fuel was isolated, but even with this problem (which was an acute one), the mission was ordered to proceed. The primary target was Kokura in the northern part of the island of Kyushu; the alternative target was Nagasaki on the western side of the same island. The bomb carried was called the *Fat Man*, ten feet eight inches long and five feet in diameter.

Behan, the bomb aimer, was told to drop the bomb visually when he saw the giant arsenal in Kokura which supplied arms to the Japanese army. Major Chuck Sweeney made several runs over the target area and each time the arsenal was covered by haze. Things were beginning to look desperate as fuel and time were running out. He made a decision and headed for the secondary target – Nagasaki, and they were not bothered too much by fighters. Kokura was reprieved, but another city substituted.

Bocks Car was in serious trouble. The B29 was facing a deteriorating fuel situation with just enough fuel for one pass over the city of Nagasaki before heading for safety. The bomb aimer, Kermit Behan, found a hole in the cloud layer and aimed for the stadium. Bocks Car lurched as the *Fat Man* bomb fell towards the ground. When the bomb left the B29, arming wires were extracted enabling the weapon to run on it s own power. Safe operation timing clocks held switches open so that the bomb could not detonate near the aircraft. As it fell nearer towards earth, additional switches were closed by barometric pressure, then radar fuses were actuated to sense the exact height above the ground. As the shiny black weapon reached an altitude of 1,540 feet, arming and firing switches closed and the high voltage already built up in massive condensers attached to a layer of high explosive. The detonators triggered a bursting forward, the resulting shock wave quickly pressed the separate sections of plutonium together, in turn the now dense plutonium sphere compressed a tiny initiator composed of beryllium and polonium. Alpha rays emitted by the polonium acted on the beryllium, which sent a shower of neutrons out into the surrounding dark grey metal. In a millisecond Nagasaki became a graveyard. *Bocks Car* did not make it back to Trinian but just made it to Yantan Field on the Island of Okinawa. These facts are from William Craig s book *The Fall of Japan.*

The day after the bombing of Nagasaki we went to work as usual, but very little was done. The Japanese seemed in a state of shock as many of them lived in Nagasaki. The next day we did not go to work and in the afternoon the room chiefs were called over to the camp administration office together with several men from each room. They came back with Red Cross parcels, one parcel between two men. Several hours later we each received another parcel, and before the evening was out our bunk space was almost filled up. These Red Cross parcels had been held by the Japanese for goodness knows how long without any attempt at distribution. We still did not know if the war had ended. At noon on 15th August, Emperor Hirohito broadcast to the people of Japan. The national anthem was played and the Emperor's voice was heard by the ordinary people for the first time:

"We declared war on America and British out of a sincere desire to ensure Japan's self-preservation and the stabilisation of East Asia." (This of course was a lie, it being far from our thoughts to infringe upon the sovereignty of other nations or to embark on territorial aggrandizements). *"The war has developed not to Japan's advantage, while the general trends of the world have all turned against her interests. The enemy, moreover, has begun to employ a most cruel bomb, the power of which to do damage is indeed incalculable, taking toll of many innocent lives. Should we continue to fight it would not only result in the ultimate collapse and obliteration of the Japanese nation, but would lead to the total extinction of civilisation."*

Hirohito expressed grief for the fallen, for the wounded and homeless, and pride in the role of the armed forces. The broadcast made no mention of unconditional surrender and gave no hint of what might happen in Japan. The whole Japanese nation was shocked. Many people believe that the Emperor should have been tried as a war criminal – after all he was on a par with Hitler – but the powers that be must have decided otherwise.

Word filtered through to us that the war had ended, but it was not until 20th August that we knew officially. An announcement was issued from the Camp Commandant's office which read as follows:-

Announcement
POW Camp Fukuoka 2 : August 20th 1945

'Both Japan and the Allies stopped the fighting under an agreement and a truce will be signed shortly. Then the war, which has lasted almost four long years, will be over. We know you are tired of the life in the war prisoner camp. We can imagine how happy you are now. Your long cherished hope to be with your loved ones will be fulfilled. We are not enemies now, we are friends with one another. We want to see you go back where your loved ones are and begin to enjoy your normal lives. At present we don't know exactly when you start for your homeward journey, we will let you know as soon as the date is announced by the army. Until then let us have an orderly and peaceful camp life. We will help you so that you may be able to start for home safely. On the other hand you are requested to keep orderly lives and observe the rules and regulations until then."

The Commander

So that was it, officially. We really could not believe it. Men clasped each other – some cried openly – one cannot put into words the emotional feelings ... we were so happy. Our days of humiliation and suffering were almost over. That night I lay on my bunk among all my Red Cross parcels and thought of my shipmates who would not make it back home.

Amongst all our joy, I felt very sad that evening as I thought of all those wonderful men who had died in the *Exeter* action. It seemed so very long ago. I also thought of the men who had died in captivity, some dying even now (two men died five days after the war was over). We who had the privilege of serving with them would never forget them.

Many men (after four years of just rice) became sick eating all the rich foods from their Red Cross parcels, but that didn't seem to worry them. They were free and that meant all the difference in the world.

The days rolled by, life was easy now and we pleased ourselves as to what we did while we waited to be liberated by the American army. All the Japanese guards had disappeared except the Camp Commandant and a Japanese sergeant nicknamed Bo-Ko-Go (Japanese for air raid shelter). Maybe it was just as well otherwise a few old scores might have been settled. The American air force dropped supplies to us almost daily: clothes, food, medical equipment. Sometimes they would drop huge containers full of fruit cocktail or juices. They would come crashing down, falling through the roofs of wooden Japanese houses in the near vicinity of the camp. One day, while picking up American parachutes, I found a note addressed to us. It read as follows:

Fukuoka Camp No. 2
Nagasaki
August 31st 1945
Allied Prisoners
The Japanese have surrendered. You will be evacuated by Allied National Forces as soon as possible. Until that time your present supplies will be augmented by airdrop of USA food, clothing and medical equipment. The first drop of these items will arrive in one or two hours. Clothing will be dropped in standard packs for units of fifty or five hundred men.

Bundle Marking	Contents	Quantity per man as follows
a 3	Drawers	2
a 1-2	Undershirts	2
b 21	Socks, pr	2
a 4-9	Fatigue I piece H.B.T.	1 piece
c 22-29	Jackets	1
a 10	Caps	1
b 11-20	Shoes, pr	1

a 102	Handkerchiefs	3
c 22-26	Towels, Bath	1
b 10	Laces, Shoe	1
c 27-29	Soap, all purposes	1
c 11-20	Powder Insecticide	

There will be instructions with the food and medicine for the use and distribution.

Underneath was a list of crewmen and their addresses. I still have this note today.

Saipan A.O. 52

"Lottie Sue Super Market"

We deliver. We do not answer the phone for complaints.

Captain J.J. Brown	S/Sgt. J.J. Penhallerick	Captain H.W. Connor
Route No. 2	25 Knox Avenue	1112 Ballad Avenue
Little Rock	Buffalo 16	Dallas
Arkansas	N.Y.	Texas
Lt. R.M. Gaither	S/Sgt. M.P. Mayer	
Ransom	Route 3	
Kansas	Boone. Iowa.	
Lt. J.R. Mitchell	S/Sgt. G.J. Jeppstron	S/Sgt. S.J. Smith
16110 32 Avenue South	325 East High Street	No. 6 Stafford Court
Seattle. Washington	Hastings, Michigan	Cochos. N.Y.
Captain C.H. Smith	S/Sgt. F.M. Hall	
Vashon	235 No. Lakeview Avenue	
Washington	Winter Garden. Florida.	
S/Sgt. J.W. Simms	Cpl. Earl. H. Wilson	Lt. R.P. Grant
Springhill	711 Cedar Street	18418 Cherry Lane Ave
Alabama	Detroit, 21. Michigan	Peomoke City, Maryland

Look for books and magazines in bundles of clothes.
Atomic bomb on Nagasaki. Yanks went into Tokyo August 30th 1945.
It won't be long now. Good luck and God speed back to the Golden Gates.
Write us when we are in good old USA.

80

This was the first indication that an atom bomb had fallen on Nagasaki and we were truly amazed. Many men wanted to go to Nagasaki town so they could try and get a train to Tokyo and be liberated quicker, but this was discouraged. There were several rumours that disease was rampant in Nagasaki – also the Americans had been informed of our numbers.

One day the President of the shipyard where we had worked sent news that he was giving the camp two pigs to eat. We had no butchers in the camp, but five of us went down to collect them. They were very reluctant to come with us and we had to pull them on ropes most of the way. The question then arose as to how to kill them. It was decided to hit them on the head with a 14 lb. hammer, the idea being to stun them. This was duly done and the pigs went berserk. I have never seen four sailors move so quickly out of the makeshift pen. When the pigs had quietened down a new plan was agreed upon. They were tied up and one of the lads got a knife from the kitchen and cut the pigs' throats. Somebody said the pigs might have TB so we called the doctor in to check them over and he said they were alright. The pigs were then cut up and boiled in a big rice copper. Needless to say I did not feel like eating pork – quite a few men were ill after eating that along with the American goodies.

Men were starting to get a little restless thinking that we should have been on our way home by now, but in early September a platoon of armed American Marines with automatic weapons suddenly appeared in the camp. They took the Camp Commandant away with them. The next day they appeared again and landing craft came into the small bay by the camp. We were told to board them and as we moved away the loudest cheer went up until gradually the place that had been our home for the last three and a half years disappeared out of sight. It was over.

We went alongside the quay in Nagasaki and disembarked. The place looked awful – it was like a wilderness. The Americans had rigged marquees on the jetty and we had to go into one and strip off completely. We were then de-liced by a DDT powder spray, after which we were medically examined. From there we went into another marquee and were given clean underwear and new jeans; then into another marquee where we were given writing paper, envelopes, toilet requisites, coffee and doughnuts; then up a gangway to go onboard the American aircraft carrier *Chenango*. The organisation was marvellous.

My thoughts suddenly dwelt on the fact that I was utterly alone. For almost four years a strong relationship had built up among the fellow prisoners of war and all this had, or was about to be, ended. In a flash I felt this great sense of loneliness. We were to part after all these years – Americans, Dutch, Indonesians, Australians, Chinese – all scattering like leaves in the wind to their different countries, homes and loved ones.

We proceeded to sea that evening. The Japanese islands were soon left behind as a very bad dream. The sea was blue, the sun shone, there was no anxiety about food – we headed for Okinawa and freedom. All the prisoners of war slept on folding beds in the hangar. There was hardly room to move, but it was lovely to be at sea again. When we arrived several days later in Okinawa, a typhoon had sprung up so the ship had to put to sea again and ride it out for several more days. Eventually we re-entered Okinawa Bay and anchored. We were then taken off by landing craft to the beach, where we stayed under canvas for a week or so and ate with the American service men.

Every so many hours, the occupants of a tent would be called out to board an aircraft to fly to Manilla in the Phillipine Islands. My turn came and about twenty of us boarded a C46 aircraft where we sat on benches and ate 'K' rations. At Clarke Field in the Philippines an airforce band played us in when we landed before being put on military buses and taken to a place near Manilla where we were allocated a marquee. There we were to stay for the next three weeks.

Whilst in this camp we were questioned by Ministry men and had to fill in numerous forms relating to our captivity. Gracie Fields came out to entertain us. We were beginning to get a little fed up at the delay in getting home, but realised that the necessary formalities took time. After three weeks we were taken by coach to the quayside in Manilla where we were ferried out by boat to the British aircraft carrier *Implacable* for the next stage of our journey home. On *Implacable* I met many old shipmates that I had served with prior to joining *Exeter*. It was nice to be brought up-to-date on all the things that had happened since the last time I stood on the deck of a British ship.

Our first port of call was Honolulu, where we stayed for several days. Then we set sail for Vancouver in Canada. On the journey over, the *Implacable* ship's company did everything in their power to make us comfortable: deck games were arranged and we even tasted beer for the first time. One of *Implacable*'s crew, slightly undersized, was taking the air on the flight deck when he was tapped on the shoulder by the Paymaster who was responsible for feeding the ship's company. Thinking he was addressing an ex-POW, the officer said, "Never mind, my good man, we will soon build you up and have you back to normal." The sailor turned round and replied, "It's about bloody time, Sir, I've been on this ship for two years and haven't had a decent meal yet!"

We arrived at Vancouver to a tremendous welcome. That afternoon the ship was open to visitors and any amount of fixtures and fittings were stolen by souvenir hunters. All the POW's were disembarked and taken to the railway station, where we were placed on board a train that was to take us three thousand miles across Canada from the west to the east coast. The date was now early October. Before entraining, we were given a 'welcome card' by the Government of the Province of British Columbia which read as follows:-

"British Columbia meets you with a cordial welcome and a deep appreciation of your sacrifice in defence of all that free men cherish and hold dear. We who were spared the actual physical impact of war give thanks, humbly and gratefully, for all the safety and security which we enjoyed in those years when you, and whole peoples, endured with grim patience the heel of the aggressor. You have come out of the Valley of the Shadow of Death to be with friends whose warm good wishes will follow you wherever you go – may good fortune attend you, and may you find the contentment in which to rebuild your lives and to go on in the peace and happiness which you have done so much to win for yourselves and for us all."

This was a very warm and touching welcome, the likes of which we were to experience the whole of the way across Canada.

From British Columbia the first stop was Calgary in Alberta, where we were welcomed by bands, flowers, the whole works. The journey was really wonderful. We had an observation car on the train from which could be viewed the magnificent scenery through which we travelled – and the food was excellent. Then on through the Rockies, Manitoba, Ontario, Quebec, with receptions the whole way, then to Nova Scotia – it took us five days crossing Canada. We were then taken by coach to No. 2 Transit Camp at Debert near Truro in Nova Scotia, where we were to stay for another two weeks.

It was while I was at Debert that I received a telegram from my girlfriend's parents telling me that she had married another fellow. I was quite upset, but thinking about all I'd been through and her not knowing whether or not I was still alive, I quite understood how it must have been for those who waited.

Early November 1945, almost three months since we had been released, we were taken to the docks and boarded the French liner-cum-troopship *Ile de France* for the last leg of the long journey home. We spent four days aboard this ship and everybody was deliriously happy. Soon we saw the shores of England. I could never describe my feelings – it was something I had dreamed about for the last five years.

On arrival at Southampton, wives, families and friends were waiting to greet their long-lost loved ones. I did not have anybody meeting me as my brothers were all in their different services so could not be there. I felt very lonely at this particular time. The captain of *Exeter*, Captain Gordon, introduced me to his wife and family so this helped to dull the ache.

A few of the POWs came home to find that their wives had remarried. We had been posted as missing presumed dead for almost four years and this must have been a shattering experience for them. Many of the POWs who returned from Macassar, Nagasaki, Sumatra, Pamella and Borneo were sick in mind and body, never forgetting the horrors of these camps, suffering with dysentery, malnutrition, beri-beri, tropical ulcers and various other diseases. These things, coupled with brutality, shipmates dying, no letters from home and the years of deprivation, had left it s mark. I look back and thank God that my early life had helped to pull me through. I have not enjoyed writing about my experiences as a Japanese POW because it has made me relive the horrors and traumas of those dark days – now I just want to try and forget.

I am asked by many people, even to this day, how I felt about the Americans dropping the atomic bomb on Hiroshima and Nagasaki. I can only speak for myself and my reply has always been the same. I thought it was right, the reason being that if the Allies had had to invade Japan, most of the POWs would have been killed by the Japanese, millions of lives would have been lost by both the Allies and the Japanese – far more than were lost in the two cities that were the recipients of the bomb. There were still many fanatical Japanese who would have carried on with the war if their country had been invaded. It is easy today for people who were not even old enough to take part in the Second World War to pass judgement.

I stayed two days in London, seeing the sights. Waiting in a barber's shop for the barber to try and fix my hair, as it had been shorn off while a POW, I read the *Daily Express* and it mentioned that several ratings from HMS *Exeter* had been awarded decorations for the Java Sea Battle. When finished at the barber's, I went to HM Stationery Office in Kingsway, bought a supplement to the London Gazette, and found to my surprise that I had been awarded the Distinguished Service Medal. I thought of many brave men on the *Exeter* who should have received it. The medal was later sent to me by post.

After several days I left London as it was far too busy for me and went to Sussex. My brother had just arrived back so I stayed with him and his wife at a little place called Billingshurst, near Petworth. I spent many weeks cycling around the country lanes, admiring wild primroses that I had not seen for so long, and savouring the delights of rural Sussex.

Approximately three months later I had to report back to the Royal Navy at Devonport and once again met up with old shipmates and acquaintances.

I had very mixed feelings about staying on in the Navy at this time. I was medically examined and found to be reasonably fit, so thought I would try to get out another way. My next visit was to the optician who said, "Put your right hand over your right eye and read the letters under the red line." I read, "Made in Great Britain." The optician looked at me in amazement. My next stop was the psychiatrist who also found me fit, so I stayed on in the Navy.

I was put on a gunnery course after a few weeks and, spending the next six months completing it, found it difficult to concentrate on the subjects, but managed to scrape through the examination by the skin of my teeth. My next move was to

HMS *Gosling*, a training establishment for National Service Men near Warrington, Lancashire. I was back in the Royal Navy proper. I spent a year and one month at this establishment as an instructor.

I left HMS *Gosling* in October 1947 and joined HMS Royal Arthur, the Petty Officers training school, on 9th October. This was a leadership school and all Naval Petty Officers had to do six weeks course there, consisting mainly of lectures and physical training. One of the instructors there was Prince Phillip, who at that time was a young lieutenant in the R.N. We contributed towards a Visitors Book as a wedding present for him as he was due to marry Princess Elizabeth, our present Queen. He used to referee our hockey matches and reached the final of the table tennis championship held at *Royal Arthur*.

I left *Royal Arthur* on 5th November 1947, staying at R.N. Barracks for two months before joining the aircraft carrier *Victorious* on 6th January 1948 as a seamanship and gunnery instructor. The *Victorious* belonged to the training squadron at Portland as did the *King George V* and *Anson*. We trained many young seamen on these ships.

While I was on this ship a picket boat capsized in Portland harbour. She was bringing liberty-men off shore one night when she went down and twenty or so sailors lost their lives. I had the job of helping the sailmaker put some of the bodies in canvas.

Whilst off the north west coast of Ireland we ran into terrible weather, causing huge mountainous seas. Most of the young fellows were sick and quite a lot of damage was done to the boats on the flight deck. We put into Belfast Lough for shelter, but were ordered by the Admiralty to proceed to Rosyth with a naval guard trained to take over the battleship HMS *Royal Sovereign* from the Russians, to whom we had lent the ship during the war. We arrived at Rosyth but had to wait nearly two weeks before the Russians finally turned up.

We then went back to Portland where I decided to leave the Royal Navy and try my luck outside. I left HMS *Victorious* on 2nd May 1949 and joined R.N. Barracks, Devonport, to do my release routine and finally left the Royal Navy for the first time on 12th July 1949.

I was still in the B Reserve and come the Korean War was recalled to R.N. Barracks, Devonport on 26th November 1952. During the intervening three years I worked on merchant navy ships but missed the Royal Navy quality of life.

From Devonport I fulfilled senior CPO duties on several ships and after eighteen months aboard HMS *Lochinvar* signed on for another ten years in February 1952.

In October 1954 I joined the frigate *Cardigan Bay* at Singapore and in early January 1955 we visited Japan. It was back to my land of horror and I wondered what my feelings would be. Strange to say time was a wonderful healer and this was ten years later. Although I found that I d forgiven them I can never forget what they did to us.

On 17th June 1956 I was drafted to HMS *Woolwich*, a submarine depot ship and promoted to Chief Petty Officer on 10th September 1956. Staying with *Woolwich* until March 1959, my next posting was a military prison in Malta. After four years of the worst possible form of prison life in Japan, this was a crazy posting for me and I got transferred to R.N. Sea and Air Transport Control at Luqa Airport, Malta.

Then came two years on a frigate, HMS *Eastbourne*, followed by a spell as instructor at an R.N. base near Edinburgh.

On 20th May 1964 came a posting to a tribal class frigate, HMS *Nubian*. Two years later, with most of it in the Far East, the ship developed prop trouble and the Captain asked if I could rig sail. "Certainly," I said, and I promptly started to do this along with my captain of the fo'c'sle, Petty Officer Jack Henry. We rigged the fo'c'sle awning on the foremast as a foresail and put the quarterdeck awning as the mainsail on a jury rig on the helicopter platform, and it proved quite successful. We had to push out the awning over the side on long staves, then had huge blocks and pulleys to control them. *Nubian* managed to make way through the water at a steady pace, but it must have been quite a sight – a modern gas turbine frigate under sail! A signal was sent to the Commander-in-Chief at Portsmouth requesting "permission to sail up harbour". "Not granted," was the reply. "Out oars and pull" – in other words, take a tug!

On 30th May 1966 I joined HMS *Condor*, a training base at Arbroath for Fleet Air Arm mechanics and fitters, where I was responsible for the cleanliness, maintenance and day-to-day running. At an Admiral's inspection I was asked by our Captain – in the absence of the responsible petty officer on a course – to take charge of the Canoe Club. Entering the club premises just before the Admiral entered and not knowing anything at all about it s activities I saluted him on arrival and reported, "Canoe Club correct and ready for your inspection, Sir". "How many canoes have you?" the great man asked. Wildly guessing I said, "Sixteen, Sir." "How many members do you have?" Still guessing I said, "Forty-five, Sir." "Where do you do your canoeing?", was the next question. With uncanny inspiration and dry throat I hazarded, "Glen Fiddock, Sir." He didn't bat an eyelid, thanked me, and carried on with his retinue out of my life.

The Commander spoke to me quietly afterwards, "Buffer, Glen Fiddock is a famous Scottish malt whisky and the Admiral is a Scotsman. I do hope for your sake he didn't think you were having him on!" But I never heard any more about it.

On 12th November 1968 I joined an advance party to the new leander-class frigate, HMS *Andromeda*, being built in Portsmouth Dockyard – the 48th warship to be built there this century and 182nd since shipbuilding began there in 1690.

At the end of January news arrived that I'd been awarded the British Empire Medal and on 18th April Admiral Sir John Bush, Commander-in-Chief, Western

Fleet, boarded *Andromeda* to present it in the presence of my wife, son and daughter. I was amazed at the number of congratulatory telegrams I received from old serving officers and men with whom I'd served during my career.

The commission took us mainly to the Persian Gulf and the Far East with my final nostalgic visit to Hong Kong. Returning via Port Elizabeth and the Cape, we arrived at Portsmouth in January 1971, when the daily traditional issue of rum in the Royal Navy came to an end. It's passing, after more than 200 years, drew many a tear and "A Matelot's Farewell to His Tot" from one of the many mourners is featured among the illustrations.

At the end of January 1971 I was drafted to the Polaris submarine base as Chief Boatswain's Mate. Polaris crews would do underwater patrols of two months at a time, so the base tried to provide them with every possible luxury between patrols. It had one of the finest swimming pools in the country, it's own ski slope, squash courts, tennis courts, a riding school, shops, discos, bars, etc. This also helped to keep them in the base, so relieving Helensburgh, the nearest town, from the strain of dealing with men who had spent a long time at sea, very often not in the best of circumstances and with quite a bit of money to spend.

On 24th May 1971, I was among the first twelve CPO's promoted to the new rank of Fleet Chief Petty Officer, which was a warrant rank. An Act of Parliament had been passed and we were given the Royal Warrant. We were then called 'Mr' by the officers and 'Sir' by the men.

The next day I was entertained by the Commodore and his senior officers at the Boat Club. They also presented me with a square plaque with a marlin spike and a rigging knife, all chromed, with the names of all the ships on which I d sailed inscribed on the blade – these were the tools of my trade. On 9th June I finally left the Polaris Submarine Base, had a month's leave then went to HMS *Cochrane* in Rosyth to do my demob routine.

On 10th July 1974 I left the Royal Navy.

To cover all my life in the Royal Navy would be impossible, but one thing is certain – I can look back with pride that I belonged to the finest service in the world and had the privilege of serving with wonderful officers and men.

I think today, more than anything, I miss the comradeship. I am often asked if I had my time over again would I do the same thing. My answer is "most certainly".

To the best of my knowledge, apart from HMS *Andromeda* (which, at the time of writing, is in the Persian Gulf) all the ships I served on have gone. I feel a certain sadness about it all, but the memories of all those ships, shipmates, POW friends, establishments and far away places will always be with me. They will never fade because once they pulsated with life, laughter, sadness and fun.

YES, life was simply great under that 'GREAT UMBRELLA'!

PART THREE

THEY FOUND ME A SHIP – TWICE!

Sam Morley

CHAPTER TEN

A Mariner in the Making

*I*t was April 1930. With an appetite whetted by seven years of naval stories from the local library came the decision, one Friday afternoon, that running away to sea was the only means of escape from a fate worse than death. I was thirteen at the time.

Fate, at that time and if I remember correctly, was embodied by a sinister physics master radiating icy malevolence at my failure to produce a backlog of written-up exercises based on his lectures and the puerile excuses offered each week for their absence. Unless the paperwork presenting my version of his teachings over the past ten weeks was on his desk by Monday, the consequences, I was informed, would be dire. Very dire.

There was a Royal Navy recruiting office in our High Street, into the windows of which I would often gaze on my way home from school, fascinated by the quality of seafaring life portrayed. On that fateful Friday it seemed to offer sanctuary from the impending wrath of Mr. Andrews. I walked in and asked if they could find me a ship – quick!

But it was not to be. The Chief Petty Officer in charge explained that the days of running away to sea to escape the punishment awaiting a procrastinating schoolboy had long since passed. Before one could enter the modern Navy, there were forms to be filled out and parental signatures obtained. Even then, he explained as I put the forms in my pocket, it could take months before the Admiralty decided if and when they thought I was worth training for a life afloat.

There followed a somewhat traumatic scene at home, with a furious father tossing torn-up forms on the fire and a tearful mother making a silent resolve to visit the school to learn what was bugging her little darling.

Came Monday, while standing out front undergoing a harrowing cross-examination by a cynical and nit-picking 'Sir' over the unpresented work, came a welcome respite. The classroom door opened to admit the duty Hall-boy, who told my persecutor I was wanted immediately in the Headmaster's study. Relief, followed by apprehension, gave way to shock at the sight of Mum – in her best coat – sitting at her ease across the desk from the omnipotent 'Sir of Sirs'!

Having delivered a kindly homily in her presence – once he d finished questioning me on my reasons on wanting to depart suddenly for the wide blue yonder – there followed more searching questions in the presence of the physics 'Sir' summoned to the study once she had left. Then, once he'd left, came the Head s decision to award me six-of-the-best ("If you flinch, boy, it doesn't count") bent over the chair on which my Mum had so recently sat. Three, he patiently explained while selecting the instrument of his choice from the dozen or so in the corner, for not attempting the work I'd been set; and three for causing my parents unnecessary alarm in a stupid attempt to evade the consequences. I finished up with special studies during games periods and after school, and was allowed one month's grace to get that homework up-to-date.

Whether I ever did or not has long been irrelevant, but I do remember that pressure of homework certainly eased up on all and sundry after that. No doubt the Old Man put the word around the staff room that desperate pupils running away to sea to escape the taskmaster's wrath was not the kind of publicity sought by a school needing all the funds and scholarships it could get.

There ended my first attempt at entering the Senior Service.

Nine years later, Hitler marched into Poland and the British nation was instructed to register for National Service. Many of my pals in the Stepney Electricity Board, where I worked, chose to follow their trade in the Corps of Signals or the Royal Army Service Corps. But here at last was the big chance to fulfill those boyhood dreams of intrepid adventure on the high seas. Without hesitation I wrote "Royal Navy" on the form asking which of His Majesty's forces would I prefer.

Army, Navy or Air Force was equally bad news to my newly-wedded wife, but she reckoned I'd chosen well when many destined for other services were called away for training early in 1940.

It wasn't until the end of May, with evacuation from Dunkirk due to start in a week, that I was summoned to attend a Royal Navy examination centre at Romford, Essex. I remember a sense of privilege as many of those electing to join the Navy had their preferences over-ridden with a brief communiqué and a railway warrant to report to some God-forsaken Army camp or another in a remote northern fastness.

At Romford I was first asked if I could swim and if I wanted to be a seaman, stoker or marine. A friend had gone in as an Electrical Artificer, and showed up in a petty officer's uniform when on leave only a couple of months after he'd joined. I couldn't see him getting there via a training session as a stoker or marine, so figured it could only have followed on from a seaman's course. I did not know at that time that tradesmen, or artificers to give them their service title, were chosen from qualifications listed when registering, and sent to a naval trade college for both basic and specialist training. Having failed to list skills and diplomas (mainly through modesty about the former and sheer lack of the latter) that resplendent petty officer's uniform was never to be mine. Later, when I knew all these things – and more – right glad was I that Dame Fortune had me enter the Senior Service through the 'Seaman's door'. Not many of the colourful friends and equally colourful experiences over the ensuing five and a half years would have had their equivalents in a 'tiffy's' mess.

With papers marked up for examination as prospective Seaman's branch material, came a series of medical and mental fitness tests. Being almost fifty years ago, there's very little remembered of them except that the eyes almost let me down. Not that there was any difficulty in reading down to the printer's name on the sight chart with either optic (there certainly would be today) but then they put some kind of large booklet in front of me with lots of multi-coloured dots scattered about at random against each matt black page and I was asked to read what could be made of the dot pattern. In some cases a numeral or letter was distinguished, but as it went on the pattern became progressively complicated, until I gazed and gazed at one page with blank bewilderment.

"If you can't see the figures '84' picked out in green dots against the red ones," said the young man testing me, "it means I'll have to write you down as red/green colourblind. And that, I'm afraid, will bar you from the Seaman's branch. To know the difference between a port and starboard light on a ship or the buoys marking a safe channel is considered rather important in the Royal Navy. Otherwise you could be responsible for sinking as many of our ships as Hitler. But colour isn't that important when pumping oil or shovelling coal into a ship's boiler, so you can still wear a nice blue sailor-suit as a physically-fit stoker."

But all my dreams over the years had revolved around the upper-deck activities of a seaman. I was almost in tears as I blurted desperately, "Oh, I saw the figures 84 just as soon as you turned the page over, but thought there was something else you were wanting me to notice."

"Yes, I thought that's what it might have been," he said solemnly and turning over the next page, asked, "Now can you see this 37 I'm tracing around with the point of my pencil?" I stared long and hard, and then asked hesitantly, "Are you sure it's not 57?"

He clapped me on the shoulder and said, "Well done! Although you're not all that hot in distinguishing some shades of red from some shades of green. Slightly red/green colourblind, I'd say. Should you ever be responsible for one of our ships running into the middle of a convoy, the harbour wall, or on to a minefield, let's hope it'll only be an old unimportant ship with all the crew accounted for!"

I knew nothing of this aberration before, and completed my time at sea without ever once sinking my ship – or anybody else's come to that – for the reasons stated, but still have difficulty finding a dark red peg against the green turf on a golf tee and am inclined to answer my wife, "What red flower?" when, following her pointing finger through the window over breakfast, I try to make out a dark red bloom backed by a dark green conifer.

Checking out from Romford I was told they'd be in touch soon. Sure enough, ten days later came a letter and a railway warrant to take me from Paddington to Plymouth where, having reported to the Regulating Petty Officer meeting the train, I was taken by truck with other ex-civilians coming in on the same train, to HMS *Raleigh* – an ex-holiday camp at Torpoint, on the south coast of Cornwall.

It was staffed by a team of Royal Navy 'workhorses' – mainly non-commissioned officers in their fifties, called out of retirement after a lifetime of regular service and whose duty it was to convert a motley throng of young men from all parts of the country into trained seamen fit to serve on a modern man-of-war. And all over a period of ten weeks! From what can be remembered they made a pretty good job of it.

Those ten weeks of indoctrination into the Senior Service were halcyon days, with lots of swimming, football, cricket and boxing crammed in among needs to digest the mysteries of echo-sounding gear, deep sea diving, ropes, cables, how to strike topmast, Morse Code, Semaphore flags, Rules of the Road at Sea, gunnery control, messdeck procedures, Beaufort's wind scale, how to sling and lash up a hammock, how to remove one's cap when appearing at the pay or defaulters table, how to salute an officer and how to hold a paint brush – whereby the first rule of good order and naval discipline could be effectively obeyed. "If it moves salute it, if it doesn't, paint it."

Most of the routine instructions were based on procedures laid down in our 'bible', the Manual of Seamanship Vol. 1, a 440 page hardback printed about 20 years earlier. We each were issued with a copy and expected to know it almost by heart when it came to seeking promotion.

With nearly fifty-five years intervening and little occasion for a refresher during that period there's not much remembered of the day-to-day scene while at Torpoint, but one or two highlights are ever-fresh.

I had done a bit of amateur boxing in my late teens – until going out with girls offered a more exciting way of exchanging body blows! But with little feminine distraction at Torpoint and a pretty young wife back home I'd spend time working out in the gym and a round or two with other young enthusiasts similarly inclined. I'd been selected for a representative Navy team in the 11st 6 class and during a PT session was in the ring with another young hopeful, when a lucky punch just below the sternum had him winded on the deck. There was a 'two-and-a-half ringer' (Lt. Comm.) in the group watching and he called out, "You're drawing back your arm and signalling your punches – hit straight from the shoulder!"

Looking sideways at my opponent just struggling to his feet and still in some distress, I replied, "Well I didn't think I'd done too badly, sir."

'No, you didn't," he said, "but that could very easily have been you lying there! Look, I'll show you."

Stunned, I watched him peel off his gold-encrusted jacket and loosen his tie, after which one of the PT instructors fastened a pair of gloves on his hands. He then went on conversationally, "In case you don't know, I happen to be the senior physical training officer of this establishment. I also gained a full boxing Blue when at Cambridge!"

Motioning me to the centre of the ring he stood opposite me with his arms hanging loosely down his sides. "Now," he said, "hit me as hard as you like above the neck!"

Horrified, I explained. "I can't do that! I haven't been in the Navy very long but know that striking an officer is about the most heinous crime in the book!"

"Hit me!" he repeated. "And that's an order, and deliberately disobeying an officer's order is almost as heinous as striking him. Remember, I doubt if your blow will land and you cannot be charged as these gentlemen around will testify that you were obeying an order! Now stop wasting my time, and HIT ME!"

Without further ado I let one go, but still somewhat carefully. My glove slid harmlessly over his shoulder as he swayed to the side.

"Now have another try, but don't hold back from impact."

He was beginning to irritate me so I really launched a big one – with the same result.

"You have already failed twice to obey an order. I'll give you one more chance. If you disobey yet again you'll qualify for Captain's report. Or would you accept my punishment?"

"I'll accept your punishment, sir," I muttered, launching a pile-driving left at his chin. As it grazed his ear I was hit by what seemed a double decker bus in about the same place I'd just hit my man, and sagged against the ropes.

"You're getting better," he said, "and your last two attempts helped me decide where to administer punishment if you failed again. And you will fail against a good boxer if you insist on telling him beforehand when you're about to hit out. Also your mental point of impact should be six inches behind the one you're aiming at. In other words, the back of the neck if you're going for the chin. That way your fist is still travelling at maximum power when the blow lands."

Advice that stood me in good stead when getting to the final in that competition and losing on points to a professional boxer doing his National Service at the time. But I've still got the silver medal!

When my joining papers revealed to the powers-that-be that I'd been educated at a secondary school up to Matriculation standard (albeit with very few passes) I was called before the Commanding Officer of the camp about half-way through the course. I didn't know what the interview was about and just answered his questions. It then transpired that he was checking if I was worth sending off to an Officer Training School; but, if nothing else, my unmistakeable cockney accent put paid to that idea, for which I've always been grateful. I'm sure to have made a lousy officer. Instead, keen interest was shown in my record as a qualified electrician, and it was arranged that I'd attend a course at Torpedo School once basic training was over.

In those days the torpedo division was responsible for not only torpedoes, but matters concerning mines, depth charges, explosives, gunnery control instruments, and all the electrics aboard a ship other than wireless telegraphy, asdics and radar. In modern times, with so much more specialised equipment about, the different kinds of expertise needed is handled by men trained in only one or two concentrated fields instead of cheerfully dabbling with the lot.

At the end of basic training at Torpoint, and carrying a stiff new canvas kit bag and hammock – both a sailor's personal property and responsibility throughout his naval career – I was part of a draft of newly-qualified ordinary seamen en route to their appointed home depot. British naval ships, personnel, and shore establishments throughout the world were classified as belonging to one of three home depots. HMS *Drake* at Devonport, HMS *Victory* at Portsmouth, or HMS *Pembroke* at Chatham. The fact that *Drake, Victory* and *Pembroke* were each the size of a small city – a brick and concrete walled-enclosure sprawling over a number of acres with a maze of roads, barrack blocks, admin offices, medical and dental hospitals, laundries, canteens, restaurants, sporting facilities, jailhouse, schools, etc, didn't detract from the fact that every naval establishment – ashore or afloat – had (and still has) it's own commanding officer, proper name, and bears the prefix 'His (or Her) Majesty's Ship'. It is to his designated home depot that a sailor is attached at the start of his naval career, and to which he returns for further training, or for another ship or shore station at the end of each spell of duty, until discharged from it when his service days are over.

I was assigned to HMS *Pembroke* at Chatham, Kent, only about 40 miles from my home, and many's the time over the ensuing five years that I rejoiced in not being sentenced to Portsmouth or Devonport – respectively 75 and 215 miles way. In fact, within an hour of arriving and completing the joining routine, I was out the gate again and learning the mysteries of how some of the 'barrack-stanchions' got to London and back for free by trimming an old green Woodbine cigarette packet to the size and shape of a Southern Railway train ticket!

The joining routine to which I referred earlier, was a standard practice where one's entry into depot is registered and a set procedure followed through various regulating offices and medical examinations. One is registered as port or starboard watch and the latter, to which I was assigned, allowed overnight leave from 4.00pm on the day of my arrival at Chatham.

Returning from that welcome surprise I quickly found that after twelve weeks of gentle indoctrination into Navy ways on the bracing Cornish coast, life in Chatham depot was a rude awakening to the real thing. The barracks were grossly overcrowded, and peopled by draft-dodging old hands sleeping it off in scruffy-looking hammocks that festooned the dormitory ceiling, with the result that we new entries had great difficulty in finding a site to practice slinging our pristine new ones. At Torpoint we had slept in the original holiday-camp chalets with four bunks to each chalet and plenty of room to stow possessions. At Chatham, kitbags served as combined wardrobe, chest of drawers, dressing table and laundry basket, and one was continually foraging around in them for a pair of socks, an envelope or a white front.

Depressing-looking kitchens occupied the basements of each of the three main five-storey barrack blocks – named Anson, Nelson, and Duncan – with a sour, slept-in odour pervading overall. Most of the barrack occupants were in transit, having come in from a ship as a survivor, or on transfer, or waiting to go on a course, but there were nevertheless quite a few of what were known as 'barrack-stanchions' who knew all the ropes – especially those to be pulled to avoid an unwelcome draft to a seagoing ship or distant station.

But within 48 hours of arrival at Chatham came my first draft chit. It was to report to HMS *Actaeon* for training as a seaman-torpedoman. Well, it wasn't much of a draft as far as physical movement was concerned, *Actaeon* being part of the Chatham complex. At *Actaeon*, the mysteries of torpedoes, mines, depth charges and explosives in general were taught. And taught pretty thoroughly, I should imagine, because even now – 50 years later – it s surprising how much I still remember of the drills and component parts connected with those deadly toys.

During instruction on how to deal with our own or enemy mines that might come my way on the high seas, I learned of the small intrepid team from R.N. Torpedo School that made history some six months earlier. At that time we were suffering colossal shipping losses in coastal waters from an unknown non-contact type of mine.

Conventional mines had detonating horns that caused the thing to blow up when one of it s horns knocked against a passing vessel. Filled with TNT and air, a mine tends to float to the surface, but is prevented from doing so by a wire rope securing it to its weighted cradle lying on the bottom. As an integral unit, each mine and cradle is dropped at night by enemy surface ships or planes and lies on the sea bed until a 6, 12 or 24 hour soluble plug dissolves – whereby the roller on which the wire rope is wound is then free to rotate. Tending to float, the mine rises to its predetermined depth below the surface, until the calculated pressure of water at that depth locks the roller again. And there Nemesis lurks patiently until a passing vessel obligingly bangs into one of the projecting horns. The idea of the soluble plug is for the mine not to rise and allow itself to be swept up too soon after laying, but to rise and do its stuff in what was thought to be a safely-swept channel.

Coastal shipping lanes and harbour entrances were swept by minesweeping trawlers every morning, and sometimes twice a day if it were a vital channel subject to suspected further enemy harassment since the early morning sweep of that day. Each trawler would tow a pair of long, thick serrated wires on the ends of which was a paravane – a porpoise-shaped contraption with vanes and planes whereby it could be set to run at a predetermined depth and angled out from the towing ship. The object being for the taut serrated wire to engage the anchoring cable of a hidden mine, the serrations on the wire plus the teeth on the coupling where it joined the paravane cutting through the cable and causing the mine to float to the surface. The next trawler in line on the sweeping flotilla would then sink or explode it harmlessly with rifle fire. All nice and matey 'point-and-counterpoint' stuff.

But early in the war we started losing ships in harbour entrances known to have been swept clean of conventional mines. A new and unknown type of mine was suspected. Fortunately, in November 1939, two were dropped by air in the Thames estuary and seen to lie exposed on the mud flats at low tide. The same night, the said intrepid team located them in pitch darkness with the aid of a single torch about 500 yards off Southend. The tide was beginning to turn and there was only time to attach a buoy and wait for low water the following afternoon.

After much heroic effort and skill, both mines were rendered safe before being shipped by road and under strong security escort to the Torpedo School for inspection and analysis of counter-measures. They were found to operate on an electromagnetic principle, whereby the steel hull of a ship passing over and through the magnetic field of the mine's detonating circuit would induce sufficient current to set the thing off.

Working night and day, the combined Brains Trust of the Royal Navy and a research team from Cambridge University came up with the solution. Surround the hull of each and every ship that ploughed our waters with a number of turns of cable and pass a constant DC current through them while the ship was in dangerous waters, the number of turns and strengths of charge passed through them to be calculated for each specific ship. The vessel's ironwork would thereby be polarised sufficiently to neutralise any effect it might otherwise have had on any lurking magnetic mine it happened to sail over – and it worked.

The unit of magnetic induction is a gauss – named in 1833 after a German scientist, Karl Friedrich Gauss. It took three months, thousands of miles of cable, thousands of DC generators, and a short period in dry dock, for each of the 5,000-odd Allied warships and merchant ships using Home waters to be de-gaussed, using the proven calculations of one eminent German to undo the machinations of his countrymen 107 years later.

My training at HMS *Actaeon* being over, I was sent to HMS *St Vincent* at Gosport, near Portsmouth, for high power and low power electrical courses; high power being the sort of thing I was used to – lighting, motors, heating, switchboards and the like – and I quite enjoyed learning naval procedures on these familiar subjects, although with unfamiliar appliances, accessories and circuitry. But low power was a fascinating subject, using just a few volts and insignificant currents to control the movement of mighty guns, load and fire them synchronously, plot the movement of ships 20 miles away, and several other ingenious functions long since forgotten – by me, that is. And this was all long before microchips and computers as known today.

During those six weeks at *St Vincent* I found some digs for my wife to come and stay in the vicinity, where I was able to join her from about 6.00pm until 7.00am the next morning when not required for duty. We had a charming landlady, who would give us the run of the house when she went to stay with her daughter.

On those evenings we'd sometimes invite one or two of my messmates to join us for tea or a drink. They'd show their appreciation by leaving a No. 1 suit for my wife to widen the trouser-bottoms, or take in the side seams of the jumper to achieve a skin-tight effect, two requirements for standard-issue sailor suits to make the new boy look a little more dashing, or 'tiddley' to use naval vernacular, whereby the wearer stood a better chance of impressing the girls at the dance as a seasoned, globetrotting 'Jack-me-hearty'!

Never mind that once Jack got back aboard, having worked himself up into a lather with the dancing and the beer, it needed a couple of his messmates tugging with might and main to help get that skin-tight jumper back over his head, with his body bent at right angles from the waist and arms at full stretch close to his ears. If he ever did get lucky at one of those dances, love's young dream might well have been a nightmare by the time his new romance had finished helping him out of that jumper!

Then came the day I passed out at *St Vincent* as a fully-fledged seaman-torpedo-man. Once back at Chatham I was put on an overnight Care-and-Maintenance party aboard two of our cruisers undergoing extensive repairs in the dockyard – HMS *London* and HMS *Euraylus*. Both ships had been stripped of their crews and were in dockyard hands. Once the workers had left the ship for the day, the C&M party went aboard to patrol the decks, guard the gangways, and stand by firewatching equipment in the event of air raids. There were plenty of them, with bombs dropping and guns firing all around, but our two ships remained silent and aloof from it all. It was all very eerie and I remember nothing of those two shadowy shapes. Well, I never really saw them – our C&M party would have to muster in the barracks to march into the dockyard about 5.30pm and assemble by HMS *London*'s gangway at 7.00am next morning ready to march back into the barracks. It being early November there was never any daylight whereby I could gaze with awe at the very first warships encountered close up.

This form of watchkeeping, one night on and one off, gave me leave from noon-till-noon on alternate days, and little time was wasted on those days before setting out on a 'run up the Smoke' and an overnight reunion with the family.

But it was too good to last. On returning from my third or fourth overnight leave there was a message at the gate to report to the Drafting Office, where I was given instructions to be at the Main Gate in two hours, complete with bag and hammock, ready to leave Chatham Barracks for HMS *Verdun*. The draft chit gave no indication whether *Verdun* was a ship or shore establishment, nor whether it was in Southend, Sydney or Somaliland. It took 24 hours to find out.

First came a trip in the back of a truck with about a dozen others also on draft, but to different ships and places. We discussed respective destinations and speculation was rife, but mainly guesswork, on what and where our next home would be. Only the regulating petty officer in charge of our draft knew the answers to that one. We were dropped at Chatham Station, from which a train took us to Waterloo. Then by truck across London to King's Cross, to await the overnight train to Edinburgh, followed by the local train across the Forth Bridge to Inverkeithing and finally by truck to the destroyer pens of Rosyth dockyard. Something like 24 hours had now elapsed since leaving Chatham and of our original number there were now but two, both bound for the same ship.

CHAPTER ELEVEN

'Before the Mast' on a V&W

H MS *Verdun* turned out to be the outboard ship of three scruffy, weary-looking destroyers tied up alongside the jetty wall. Not a bit like the sleek, smart men-of-war featured in peace-time news reels and magazines. Large patches of red-lead paint showed up between camouflaged sections of hull and superstructure and a jumble of ropes, fenders and loose gear littered the decks of the three ships as we scrambled warily over the pitching gangways that linked them.

Carrying bags and hammocks, we threaded our way through working parties getting in stores, water, oil and ammunition, and reported to the coxswain in his office (or 'caboosh', to use the navalese for any cramped personal or private quarters that went as 'perks' with a particular duty). In this case, the coxswain's caboosh seemed about the size of a telephone kiosk.

It was on the starboard side of the midships superstructure, the roof of which supported two sets of four-barrelled 0.5" machine guns. Standing in its doorway and surrounded by the nauseating stench of hot diesel fumes from the hissing salt-encrusted funnels, we went through the brief formalities of joining ship.

This consisted of being given an identification number in the Ship's Register and an allocation to a mess, a watch, a part-of-ship, a cruising-station, and an action-station. In my case it was respectively no. 1 mess, starboard and red watch, EA's mate, telegraphsman, and for'ard magazine. Which meant that no. 1 mess would be where I was to eat, sleep, write home, wash my clothes, store personal possessions, and keep myself generally amused when not working ship or on watch throughout the ensuing nineteen months aboard *Verdun*; that I belonged to starboard watch when it came to work or leave being assigned to half the ship's company – starboard or port watches – and to red watch when duties could be split three ways – red, white and blue; that because I was now considered trained in naval electrics I would work ship as required as assistant to the ship's electrical artificer instead of mustering with deck-working parties; that when starboard or red watch was called at sea my place was in the wheelhouse assisting the quartermaster; and that when alarms sounded for 'Action Stations' I was to drop whatever I was at and belt like the clappers to the for'ard magazine, via a descending succession of decks and watertight steel hatches – each of which, once I'd passed through, would be locked shut behind me by the damage-repair party stationed on each deck – until an enclosure about eight feet square down in the very bowels of the ship and racked all around like a wine bar's bottle store was reached.

Only instead of a fine array of Chardonnays, Pinot Noirs and sparkling Moselles, one was surrounded by straw-coloured, high explosive shells, each 4" in diameter, 30" long and weighing half-a-hundredweight, for feeding up by hoist to the twin-barrelled HA gun abaft the fo'c'sle – about six decks immediately above the magazine. But more of all that later, when the strident clamour of the alarm bells first introduced me to that claustrophobic chamber.

Threading my way through knots of working (and loafing) parties, none of whom showed the slightest interest in the arrival of the latest addition to their ranks, No. 1 mess was eventually reached.

Reporting to it's leading hand, I was given a locker for my kit bag and shown where to stow my hammock, before looking around and taking stock of my new surroundings.

The term 'open-planning' was not in general use in those days, but it might well have been applied to the seamen's messdeck on HMS *Verdun* – with some reservations. Imagine a trapezoid (a triangle with the top off) measuring approximately 40' from lobby entrance at the after end to the paint store/cable locker at the for'ard one, 25' wide at the lobby entrance, 12" at the paint store/cable locker bulkhead, and 7'6" from mastic-coated deck to painted steel deckhead. In that space about sixty seamen lived, slept, breathed, prepared and ate their food, cleaned and stored clothes, wrote long letters to loved ones about exhilarating life on the ocean blue, and practised new dance steps for the next run ashore! True, what with watchkeeping at sea and leave arrangements when in harbour it wasn't that often when all sixty were eating or dancing at one and the same time – but life was pretty much an open book to those who saw service on the likes of HMS *Verdun*.

There were many fixtures and fittings on that main messdeck. First and foremost the 'fish-frier', as the capstan engine was (un)affectionately known. The capstan was on the centre-line of the fo'c'sle, and the 'Heath Robinson' mechanism that motivated it was a massive steam-driven awesome contraption immediately below it, occupying about thirty square feet of our messdeck, and connected by heavily-lagged steam pipes and the like to the engine room.

Usually the first knowledge one had that the ship was about to lower or raise the anchor or moor to a buoy or leave it, was awareness of a ghostly stoker or two clanking spanners in the bowels of the 'fish-frier', causing evil-smelling oil fumes and steam to hiss and leak from tired valves, while exchanging hoarse comments with colleagues through voicepipes to the fo'c'sle or the engine room. Then would come the rumbling stop/start of the capstan taking up or letting out hawsers or anchor

101

chain, accompanied by the thunderous din of chain entering or leaving the cable-locker for'ard of the messdeck. And it always seemed to happen during the long watches of the night. The noise would be accompanied by gobbets of condensed steam issuing from leaky joints in the systems and dripping in hot smelly droplets off the surrounding steelwork on to those below. As No. 1 mess was cleverly slotted fore-and-aft between the fish-frier' and the cable locker, I must have acquired a lot of the pithy Naval epithets that stood me in good stead over the years from first hearing them hurled by messmates as those capstan-engine operators disturbed hard-earned slumbers.

There were four separate seamen's messes on the main messdeck of HMS *Verdun*. Nos. 1 and 3 on the starboard side and 2 and 4 on the port. Each consisted of a wooden table top about 12' long x 3' wide, with hinged steel legs bolted to sockets in the deck. The table-top had an upstand about $1^1/2$" high around all four sides to prevent anything like a mug of rum, a fannyful of pusser's peas or a plate of hot 'burgoo' (porridge) sliding on to the deck or over some unsuspecting messmate sleeping off a spell of watchkeeping on the lockers. The lockers were in a continuous row lining the ship's side, each with individual lift-up lids and loose flat plastic cushions on them allowing ratings to sit up to the table to write, eat, or chat. While on the inboard side of each table were a pair of 6' loose forms or benches for similar seating purposes. Overhead were rows of steel bars from which those who could find space slung their hammocks.

Mess traps – plates, cups, cutlery – in addition to tea, sugar, tins of evaporated milk, condiments and staple provisions – were housed in a tin-plated steel dresser bolted to the forward bulkhead in line with the mess table. Below it was a small space for mess kettle, tea pot, bucket, all-purpose 'fanny' (a cylindrical stainless steel cooking pot with hooped bucket-style wire handle) and cleaning materials. Each of the four messes so described comprised the self-contained home for about 20 ratings.

Beside the 'fish-frier', Nos. 1 and 2 messes were separated by a couple of stanchions supporting the fo'c'sle deck, capstan and anchor gear.

On the centre line between 3 and 4 messes were two hatch covers in the deck, each about 2'6" in diameter, from which a vertical ladder led down to the stokers' messdeck through the after one and to the watchkeeper and communications personal home-from-home in the case of the for'ard one. I still remember my early bewilderment seeing those hatch covers spring open and shut with ratings popping up and down through holes, for all the world like chipmunks in a Walt Disney film!

Nor was it unknown for a couple of blokes finishing up as hospital-cases through one of those hatch covers being up and a good sea running. One man would fail to notice it was open as he lurched for'ard from the galley carrying the piping hot dish laden with his messmates' piping hot dinner, and the other would be halfway up the ladder from the lower messdecks in time to receive a flying boot and part of the other's 'food parcel' on his unsuspecting 'crust', the former being lucky to escape with a lacerated or broken leg and the other a multiplicity of gravy burns and bruises, never mind verbal abuse from hungry messmates obliged to wait and scrounge alternative cold 'tack' from the pusser on finding their original '*plat du jour*' had lost its piquant appeal after being scraped off decks, hatch-combings and boots!

This might be a good time to explain what can be remembered of how the Navy fed its seagoing forces in those days. On big ships – battleship, cruiser, aircraft carrier and the like – it was 'general mess' – much the same as in most shoregoing establishments of the armed forces, and needing little or no explanation from me. So-called trained cooks prepared and often ruined perfectly good food and served it up at meal times in specified areas furnished for that purpose. But 'canteen-messing' was the practice in small ships – and destroyers with crews of 140 to 200 were about the largest of the small ships. The pusser (generic navalese for all forms of Admiralty officialdom, pronounced to rhyme with 'fusser' and derived from 'purser' [controller of the ship's purse]) would run a 'general store' on each ship in the charge of a supply petty officer, referred to as 'Jack-in-the-Dust', or 'Jack Dusty', a name going back hundreds of years when packaging was in coarse-weave sacks with deliveries of flour, bread, potatoes, meat, vegetables and non-foods like paint, coal, timber, canvas, ropes and cleaning materials leaving their marks on the bloke responsible for checking, stowing, and entering in it all up.

The Jack Dusty inventory on a V&W destroyer would run into several thousand items – all cross-referenced, priced and stowed. Each mess appointed its own caterer, usually a senior hand with a sound experience of pusser's food and procedures; often the 'killick' or leading-hand of the mess ('killick' is navalese for a small stern anchor on a ship and when made leading-seaman-stoker-signalman, etc, one would sew an anchor to the upper left sleeve on one's uniform). Mess housekeeping was the responsibility of two ratings referred to as 'cooks-of-the-mess', delegated in pairs on a 24-hour rota basis. Everybody below leading-hand took their turn, hence the time-honoured maxim 'Pick up the hook and you don't take cook!'

The mess caterer would decide on the meals for his mess each day and issue a requisition for the cook-of-the-mess to draw the stock of food needed from Jack Dusty early in the forenoon watch. Dinner had to be prepared and sent up to the galley for cooking in time for those with the noon-to-4.00pm watch to comply with the 11.30am pipe, 'Afternoon watchmen to dinner!' In the unpretentious Navy, it's always been dinner at the middle of the day and supper in the evening.

The cooks-of-the-mess, in pairs, took over from the previous two at 8.00am each day, and for the ensuing 24 hours had to combine their watchkeeping duties with those of housekeeping. They would keep the mess clean, stow away accumulated mess traps and loose clothing, wash up crockery and utensils, prepare meals for the galley to roast, fry, boil or burn, from which they would collect and serve to their messmates at the recognised times. All under the experienced and watchful eye of the mess killick. Now when the members of a mess had been together for some time there'd be a professional flair about it all, irrespective of who was duty cook-of-the-day, but not everybody went to sea for the first time with inbuilt expertise to prepare *nouveau cuisine* presentations from the raw material stage for twenty hungry sailors. Yes, talking with some of those who served in those old V&W's it shouldn't be difficult to put together a fairly novel form of 'Weird Food Guide'.

Back to the financial aspects of canteen-messing. At the end of each calendar month, Jack Dusty did his sums from the requisition chits received, and calculated what each mess had spent in his store, before equating it with what the pusser had authorised on the basis of 1s 8d per man per day. His figures were passed to the acting paymaster of the ship. If the mess had not spent all in its allowance then the difference was paid in cash to the mess-caterer, who shared it equally with the members of his mess. If they'd been doing themselves proud and were overspent, then the difference was billed to the caterer, who was then obliged to collect the necessary contribution from all whereby the pusser was not out-of-pocket.

Everybody liked the idea of a little share-out but not everybody wanted it at the expense of frugal feeding, especially when the adjoining mess seemed to be forever stuffing themselves with figgy-duff and yet still avoiding mess bills at the end of the month.

But everything was bewildering on that first day as I sat drinking the cup of strong, over-sweet tea, kindly offered by one of my new messmates.

Over that first 'cuppa', I was told that, with the exception of a four day boiler-cleaning break every four or five weeks, we spent most of our time at sea, guarding convoys of merchant ships entering or leaving home waters. There were many of the nation's older destroyers and newer corvettes forever escorting and patrolling the 'dicey' and icy waters around these sceptred isles, and our patch was mainly the stretch between the Forth and Thames estuaries. It was a seventy-two hour run – give or take a bit – depending on convoy speed, tides, what sort of zig-zag course we steered and just how much unfriendliness we had to contend with from enemy aircraft, mines, U-boats, E-boats, etc.

Over that first cuppa I learned a lot about my first ship, supplemented since by much research for the sake of this book. She was one of sixty-eight V&W destroyers built between 1916 and 1925 and all given names beginning with the letters 'V' or 'W'.

Verdun was launched in August 1917, eight months after the keel was laid in January of that year. Her displacement is given as 1,090 tons, she was 300 feet long on the waterline, 29'6" beam and needed a minimum of 8'0" of water to keep her keel off the bottom. Her twin-shaft, oil-fired, geared turbine engines developed 27,000 horsepower and she could knock up 34 knots on a good 'downhill' run – and many's the time every one of those 'horses' was needed to get us to or from some bit of bother or the other! In peace time she carried a crew of 134 but by the time I joined there were about 170 of us. Originally her main armament was four single 4.7" guns, also two sets of triple 21" torpedo tubes amidships. But with hostile aircraft the main hazard, and little or no involvement anticipated with large enemy surface craft, a number of V&W's – including Verdun – had been altered for escort duty with their guns changed to one twin-barrel, high-angle 4" gun on 'A' gundeck and another on 'X' gundeck. The removal of 'Y' gun gave a greater area on the quarterdeck for stowing and firing depth charges, the principal weapon against U-boats, but there was not much need for them in the North Sea, a stretch of water considered by the enemy as too shallow for emergency crash dives when detected and attacked.

Verdun, like so many of our warships, had been laid up in Rosyth with the 9th flotilla in 1921, remaining there for the next 17 years dreaming of the one great, glorious honour that came her way in November 1920, and best described as follows:

After World War I, the body of an unknown soldier was brought home from the battlefields of France and 'buried among the kings' in Westminster Abbey on 11th November 1920. Part of the inscription on his tomb reads:

"Thus are commemorated the many multitudes who gave the most that man can give."

HMS *Verdun*, one of His Majesty's newest and most powerful destroyers of the day, was given the honour of conveying the selected warrior from Boulogne to Dover, fully encapsulated and secured on a raised bier between the two sets of torpedo tubes.

Great publicity and ceremony was given to the occasion and research has provided the following descriptive matter:

The Unknown Warrior was laid to rest in Westminster Abbey on Armistice Day, 11th November 1920, in a comprehensive ceremony which included unveiling the newly-built Cenotaph in Whitehall. The casket in which the body lay was borne on a gun carriage covered with a Union Jack, on which were spread a steel trench helmet, a khaki belt and a Crusader's sword. As the procession reached the Cenotaph it was joined by King George V, who became Chief Mourner. At the memorial service held in the Abbey the coffin was presided over by a guard of honour made up of Victoria Cross holders. The King scattered French soil – specially brought from France – over the coffin as it was laid to rest.

Great care had been taken to ensure the complete anonymity of the Unknown Warrior and there are many versions of how he came to be selected from the countless thousands of unrecognizable bodies in the battlefields of France. To get the facts right I spent a morning at the Imperial War Museum, London, going through press cuttings, magazine articles, books and other literary data with Mary Wilkinson, of the museum library, who herself has made a study of the subject. She warned not to take it all too literally, as some of the data had since been proved inaccurate, but thanks to talking about it to some pals, one sent me a *Daily Telegraph* press cutting of November 1939 and I think what follows is the correct version. It's a letter to the newspaper from Brigadier General L J Wyatt, General Officer Commanding British Troops, France & Flanders, 1920, and Director of the War Graves Commission:

To the Editor of the Daily Telegraph
Sir,
From time to time accounts have been published purporting to relate how and by whom the Unknown Warrior s body was selected in France for burial in Westminster Abbey on Nov. 11, 19 years ago. I should like to give here the authentic account of what took place.

In October I received a notification from the War Office that King George V had approved the suggestion and the proposal that the burial should be in Westminster Abbey on Nov.11. I issued instructions that the body of a British soldier, one that would be impossible to identify, should be brought in from each of the four battle areas – the Aisne, the Somme, Arras and Ypres, on the night of Nov. 7 and placed in the chapel of St. Pol. The party bringing each body was to return at once to its area, so that there should be no chance of their knowing on which the choice fell.

Reporting to my headquarters office at St. Pol at midnight on Nov. 7, Col. Gell, one of my staff, announced that the bodies were in the chapel and the men who had brought them had gone ... The four bodies lay on stretchers, each covered by a Union Jack; in front of the altar was the shell of the coffin which had been sent from England to receive the remains. I selected one, and with the assistance of Col. Gell, placed it in the shell; we screwed down the lid. The other bodies were removed and reburied in the military cemetery outside my headquarters at St. Pol.

I had no idea even of the area from which the body I selected had come; no one else can know it ... The shell, under escort was sent to Boulogne ... The next morning, carried by the pall-bearers who were selected from NCOs of the British and Dominion troops it was placed on a French military wagon and taken to Boulogne Quay where a British destroyer was waiting ... Six barrels of earth from the Ypres Salient were put on board to be placed in the tomb at Westminster Abbey so that the body should rest in the soil on which so many of our troops gave up their lives...

Then HMS *Verdun* moved off, a guard of honour of Bluejackets at 'the Present', carrying that symbol which for so many years, and especially during the last few months, has meant so much to us all.

Yours Etc.
L.J. Wyatt.

Kirkby Lonsdale, Nov. 1939.

The first two paragraphs of the letter leave no doubt about the care taken to ensure that no living person could claim a positive link with the official Unknown Warrior, but as the Press reports in the War Museum presented a more impressive word-picture than that implied by the final two paragraphs of the good General's letter, I've condensed them into the following:

The coffin into which the General and his aide had placed the stretchered body was a massive oak casket made from a tree that had grown in the Royal Park at Hampton Court Palace. The casket was bound with heavy wrought iron bands and in the centre of the lid the following was inscribed in Gothic characters:

A BRITISH WARRIOR
WHO FELL IN THE GREAT WAR
1914 – 1919
FOR KING AND COUNTRY

Below the lettering rested a fine sword of antique design selected by King George V from his private collection.

On the morning of the 10th November 1920, the casket, swathed in Union Jacks and floral tributes, was placed on a French military wagon drawn by six black horses at St. Pol and taken to the Quai Carnot at Boulogne followed by a procession over a mile long. Awaiting its arrival at the dockside was one of His Majesty's newest destroyers, HMS *Verdun*. *Verdun* had been chosen having been named after the French battlefield that had withstood the German onslaught and remained in French hands throughout World War I, with the heroic slogan of Marechal Petain as its watchword – "*Ils ne passeront pas!*" (They shall not pass!)

At the quayside Marechal Foch paid an eloquent tribute to the Unknown Warrior, before *Verdun* steamed out of the harbour with the casket, enshrouded with flags and flowers, secured on a special platform rigged between the two sets of torpedo tubes. At each corner stood a member of *Verdun*'s crew in full uniform with head bowed and rifle held in the reversed salute position throughout the journey to Dover. A convoy of six destroyers met her in mid-Channel to escort her into harbour, accompanied by a sixteen-gun salute from Dover Castle. At 3.00pm the casket was borne ashore by six warrant officers representing the Navy, Army, Marines and the Air Force. It was then placed in a funeral coach and taken by train to Victoria Station, London, from where it was transferred by horse-drawn gun carriage to the Cenotaph and finally Westminster Abbey.

* * *

A year later, 1921, HMS *Verdun* went into mothballs for 16 years, but her 'illustrious passenger' of November 11th 1920 is still drawing mourners and sightseers to Westminster Abbey from all over the world – nearly seventy-five years after the inaugural scenes just described.

Many who served on *Verdun* in World War II will swear on a stack of Bibles that the ghost of that illustrious passenger still haunted the upper deck during the 'graveyard' watch. "How silly!" you will say, but certainly not so when she'd be wallowing through the Stygian gloom with a 40-knot gale howling through the rigging. Clinging to a lifeline from the jackstay stretched fore and aft, you'd be trying to make your way along the iron deck when a shapeless mass, shrouded and unrecognizable, would loom up coming the other way, accompanied by unearthly clanking and rattling. "It's the Unknown Warrior come for me!" was the first terror-stricken reaction – until finding it was the 'kye bosun' wrapped in half a dozen 'lammy-coats' distributing hot cocoa to those on watch and ready to jump over the side in a flat panic himself at first sight or sound of YOUR approach!

Verdun had brought a convoy north that morning and was under orders to break away when reaching the Forth, collect essential supplies (including Sam Morley) from Rosyth, and waste no time in getting back before dark to Methil, about 25 miles east of Rosyth, where a southbound convoy was assembling. At first light the following morning that convoy was due to start its hazardous voyage down the swept channels of the east coast.

I'd hardly stowed my gear when a burly seaman – the duty bosun's mate – came stalking through the messdeck blowing his bosun's call and shouting the time-honoured command, "Secure for sea. Close all 'X' doors and openings. Special-sea-duty men to your stations. Hands to stations for leaving harbour!" Followed shortly after by the cry, "Blue watch close up!" We were off to war.

Scuttles (R.N. equivalent to portholes) were closed and screwed down – shutting out the last lungful of fresh air the messdeck would receive for the next three days; miscellaneous cups, seaboots, ditty boxes, etc, were swept off the all-purpose table and stowed safely to avoid a shambles if the ship should suddenly lurch – as ships have been known to do through the years; and various crew members hurried away to their various duties.

Other than giving a hand with closing scuttles and shifting loose gear onto racks, I would remain a passenger until red watch was called in about another two hours. So I wandered out on deck as the 'fish-frier' johnnies arrived to prepare the capstan for action. A tug had loomed up alongside and taken one of our wire ropes to help pull us away from the two inboard ships. Underfoot I could feel the deck vibrating as *Verdun*'s twin turbine engines flexed their muscles. Once clear of the destroyer pens the tug cast off our rope, to be hauled in by the capstan, before we proceeded down river under our own steam.

Passing under the Forth Bridge, I looked up at the massive array of steelwork far above. My first sight of that 50 year old feat of British engineering was when passing over it in the train that brought me up from London – and now, here I was with patriotic pride re-awakened just two hours later, passing under it in a destroyer, and both passages were 'freebies' with the compliments of H.M. Government!

There were about sixty merchant ships of varying size, colour and nationality anchored off Methil when we reached them at dusk, just as the nightly cry of "Darken ship!" was being piped. Most had been convoyed round the north coast of Scotland from the Atlantic seaboard, but a number sought protection with the convoy while trading between coastal ports. A cold but thankfully dry night at sea was spent prowling around the 'flock', watching and listening for marauders on our Asdic and RDF (later known as Radar) equipment. Being red watch, I spent the first dog watch – 4.00 to 6.00pm – and the middle, or 'graveyard watch' – midnight to 4.00am – in the wheelhouse seated on a stool at the engine room telegraph control. Beside me at the wheel stood the quartermaster, a seasoned A.B. named 'Greasey' Gough (everybody named Gough in the R.N. was 'Greasey' just as all Taylors were 'Buck', Adams were 'Daisy', Whites were 'Knocker', etc).

When the Officer of the Watch from his control position on the bridge wanted to alter course or change speed, he'd give the necessary instruction through the brass voicepipe to the enclosed wheelhouse on the deck below. The quartermaster, with the other end of the voicepipe 6" from his ear, would repeat the instruction, turn the wheel for a course change and instruct the telegraphsman to ring the speed change, in propeller-shaft rpm, down to the engine room. It was just a sit-and-wait job for the telegraphsman, but the quartermaster could never take his hands from the wheel, his ear from the bridge voicepipe, or his eyes from the ever-dancing and ticking gyro compass repeater. Although he was in charge, it was about half way through that four-hour middle watch that Greasey asked if I'd like a go at the wheel to give him a break. Official permission had to be sought from the officer on the bridge before I could do so but I remember thinking the gentleman in question must have 'lost his marbles' when it was promptly given.

Here I was, just a few hours after joining my first ship, being allowed to drive it! But no query was raised except to ask my name and to repeat the course I was about to steer.

We slowly circled the anchored ships throughout the night, which meant a never-ending succession of course changes and calls of "Up 1", or "Down 2", in relation to revs. Greasey had wasted no time in dropping his head on his folded arms over the telegraph handle once he'd given a little guidance on how to anticipate rudder movement by a counter touch on the wheel. It was a cold night but I remember how the sweat ran down my back when the first call came from the bridge, "Up 2 – steer 223". I almost screamed to the recumbent figure in the dark wheelhouse, "Greasey, he wants up 2 and steer 223!" "Well, at least you won't have to repeat the instruction," mumbled Greasey – roused from his snooze as his hand automatically shifted the lever on the rev. indicator. "I reckon everybody in the ****ing convoy heard you! Now just gently slide the wheel a couple of spokes to starboard and as the gyro compass shows she's begun to turn, slide her just as gently a couple the other way, and then bring the wheel back to midships – keep adjusting slightly until the gyro stops 'hunting'. Then when you're nicely on the new course just call up the voicepipe "Revs 35 Course 223" – and not so ****ing loud this time!"

Sometime during the watch, the wheelhouse door slid open and in stalked the shadowy shape of one of the gun's crew, wrapped in a couple of 'lammy' (duffel) coats, a thick woollen balaclava covering most of his face and head, and carrying a steaming hot fannyful of bitter cocoa – or pusser's 'kye', as universally known by all that sail the wintry sea; and many's the wintry night at sea when a frozen watchkeeper in some exposed part of the ship would be tempted to pour that cupful of kye among the frozen toes in his seaboots instead of scalding his larynx and internal organs with it! It was standing practise in each of the three 4-hour night watches for one of the gun's crew on watch to be detailed off to boil up a fannyful of kye on the galley stove. Armed with a quantity of clean cups he'd then take his concoction through the Stygian gloom to all upper-deck watchkeeping positions. As the clatter of crockery heralded his approach to each station there would come a welcoming cry of "Here comes the kye bosun!", or, "About time too – thought you'd fallen over the side!" And then more bitter recriminations if it was found he hadn't kept it stirred enough on the stove, whereby 'orrible unmelted lumps of hot unsweetened chocolate were encountered while trying to sup the nourishing brew.

Finally came that long awaited eight bells (4.00am) when my relief came through the wheelhouse door still half asleep. After a brief word I left and staggered down vertical ladders to No. 1 mess, stripped off watchkeeping coat, seaboots, trousers and other superfluous clothing, found my hammock in the feeble rays of one coloured security light and wasted no further time in wedging myself in among the log-jam of snoring bodies.

At around 7.00am came the duty bosun's mate, piping and shouting "Wakey, wakey, lash up and stow", and all sorts of oh-so-witty observations to announce the start of another day – wit that was hardly appreciated by one not long abed after the graveyard watch. A hoarse unknown voice close to my ear accompanied by a violent shake of my hammock confided that it was about to be cut down unless I got it lashed up and stowed by the time he counted three. Then some kind soul protested "Leave him alone, he's just come off his first middle!", but I still had to get out – having slung it over the table, access to which was sought by those planning to get breakfast under way.

110

Breakfast would mean the first available member of the mess taking the tea kettle out on to the iron deck and while exposed to wind, waves and wintry weather all around, filling it with fresh water pumped up by hand from a standpipe close to the guard-rails. The contents of the laden kettle would be taken half-a-dozen paces and poured into a galvanised open-topped tank abaft the galley bulkhead three parts full of superheated water, thanks to a steam pipe coil running through it for all the world like an immersion heater. The kettle would be filled again from the hot tap near the bottom of the tank. This was the cookie's version of the heat-exchange principle. Nobody draws off hot water from his tank until an equivalent quantity of cold water has been pumped up and added. Not, that is, if a blasphemous tirade from our aggrieved 'galley-slave' was to be avoided.

Then there was the problem of finding somewhere to stand your tea kettle among those of other messes that got there before you, plus the bubbling fry-ups, porridge ('burgoo'), and laden skillets of kippers ('split-head pheasants') that some of the more self-indulgent lads brought along to the galley and left under the tender care of the ship's cook (laughingly referred to on sea-going 'small-boats' as 'chef').

Once back in the mess with the tea kettle full of boiling water, the usual routine was for a couple of handfuls of leaf tea to be tossed into the cylindrical full-length strainer that fitted snugly through the top of the kettle, pour in a tin of evaporated milk, add two or three handfuls of dark brown Demerara sugar, give a few twirls of the strainer, and 'Jack's gut varnish' was ready to pour.

Meanwhile, those so inclined would be carving nice thick slices off a loaf of bread and toasting them against the spiral elements of the Creda bars that heated the mess-deck, before spreading each slice with the best part of a week's civilian butter ration.

If you happened to be one of those who didn't take sugar or preferred your tea black, you'd need to dive at the tea kettle and pour off your own cupful before the additives went in.

And even after 50 years, the all-pervading aroma of a morning messdeck at sea – created by burnt toast, carbonized heater spirals, condensing steam droplets impregnated with hot crude oil, stale tobacco, the fug of well-used hammocks combined with that of sour watchkeeping clobber lying in sodden heaps – is what comes to mind when John Masefield tells of:

> "The call of the morning tide
> Is a wild call and a clear call
> That may not be denied! "

Old V&W destroyer ratings have no difficulty at all in denying it!

At 8.00am the next pair of duty cooks on the rota took over the job of housekeeping in the mess once those who had the forenoon had left to relieve their opposite numbers on the four-hour morning watch. As the morning watchkeepers got stuck into their breakfast, the cooks started tidying up the mess. One would get a bucket of

111

hot water for washing up the cups, etc, using the same routine as those who had 'wet the tea' earlier, but without waiting around the galley to bring it to the boil. Then, wielding broom, brushes and cleaning cloths, every last crumb and unwanted clutter would be winkled out and consigned to the 'gash' bucket – an all-purpose open refuse bin in each mess into which anything unwanted, unpleasant or unsavoury was tipped by all and sundry until, slopping over, it was carried through and out to the upper deck and ditched into the ocean through a canvas chute secured to the lee-side rails. And such paint as still remained on the ship's side was inclined to suffer a little further maltreatment on a wild night when a change of course turned the lee-side into the weather one, and rather than search for the head of the chute in the Stygian gloom, a desperate sailor would fling the contents of his gash bucket over the rail – only to find himself clawing old tea-leaves and potato peelings out of his hair on his dash back to the shelter of the messdeck lobby due to another 'misplonk' on wind direction! Quite often he would finish up trying to scrounge another bucket out of Jack Dusty, having lost hold of the handle of the last one in mid-fling!

More hot water would be drawn in a clean bucket and with the help of a bar of pusser's hard – a coarse cleaning soap – tables, lockers, stools and deck would be scrubbed, rinsed, and protectively covered until dry. Dinner was the next consideration. The two cooks-to-be would no doubt have peeled and left potatoes in soak overnight, as they would the dried marrowfat peas if stocks of fresh vegetables had been exhausted. Whether it was to be a roast, an 'oosh', a 'clackered' meat pie, or a pot-mess, depended on what joint of animal had been dissected by Tanky's cleaver that morning *(Tanky was Navalese for Jack Dusty's assistant)*. 'Oosh' was usually from scrag or shin, chopped up, smothered in onions, heavily seasoned, and left to simmer slowly on the galley stove, swimming in its own RBG (Rich Brown Gravy – the cynical messdeck term for any viscous additive to one's dinner irrespective of the colour, consistency or flavour acquired during its preparation).

The flour-and-water pie-crust that one so enterprisingly prepared and rolled out on the mess table, before bringing the partially cooked meat back from the galley in order to spread it lovingly over the dish like an awning, was known as 'clacker', and many a handsome-looking meat pie would be found to have its 'clacker' heavily impregnated with splinters off the mess table when finally brought down from the galley and served – the duty cook of the mess having learned belatedly that his venturesome attempt at *cordon bleu* pie crust should have had liberal sprinklings of flour under it during the rolling sequence if it was ever to be prised free of the table!

A pot-mess was a five-star 'oosh' left simmering on the galley stove in a large pot forever, with everything that was potable or edible tossed in to thicken it up – and in inclement weather it was everybody's favourite, being brought down from the galley and taken back for re-heating as each group of watchkeepers hungrily ladled it on to plates from where the pot hung at meal times swaying safely from the hammock rails above the tables. As the levels went down so more thickers and water were added, and 'thickers' would be anything a fellow messmate could find on the shelves to chuck into the depleting pot rather than have the contents thinned-down through just adding water. Handfuls of porridge, barley, beans, lentils, stale bread, etc, come immediately to mind, and rumour has it that a pair of well-seasoned old seaboots, complete with equally well-worn seaboot stockings, may well improve flavour and add consistency to the nourishing mix if left to simmer long enough!

At first light the assembled merchant vessels had started raising anchor and moving into position in the convoy as it slowly took shape heading out of the Forth and towards the open sea. The previous evening there would no doubt have been a summons from the Commodore for all Captains to attend a meeting on his selected flag-ship when final decisions on sailing time, course, signals, zig-zag pattern, convoy speed and expected time of arrival in the Thames Estuary would be established. Each captain would give an account of his ship's best speed and convoy experience, from which would be calculated what position it was to take up in relation to other ships in company, matters like what to do if attacked, not to panic, and to avoid firing on each other in the event of a night attack. Most sea-going merchant ships by this time had some form of gun on the stern manned by trained personnel from a branch of the Royal Navy known as D.E.M.S. (Defensively Equipped Merchant Ships), but being without sophisticated gunnery control systems or discipline, the general opinion was that they were a greater source of danger to their friends than ever to the enemy!

Like a crocodile of school children, the ships formed into parallel lines in accordance with the sailing plan laid down by the Commodore in one of the lead ships. He would usually have been a retired naval officer called back into service to take charge of the movement of designated groups of merchant ships and would liaise with the R.N. escort vessels appointed to protect them. Signal lamps would be constantly flashing and signal flags fluttering up and down the halliards as we circled the lines of ships – exhorting this one to increase speed, that one to stop making smoke, another that it was out of station, etc, and many the pithy or unintelligible roar through a loud hailer from an irate skipper on his bridge taking exception to whatever he was being told by – in his opinion – some self-important whippersnapper on the bridge of a tinpot warship!

We hadn't been at sea more than a couple of hours when the alarm bells sounded for 'Action Stations!' Everybody charged about at breakneck speed and I remember asking in bewilderment my way to the for'ard magazine – Sam's action station! It was down the messdeck hatch to the stokers mess, with hordes of stokers fighting their way up the ladder to get to their designated stations, then down another hatch to another small enclosure and then down another hatch into the magazine itself.

Each time the repair party on each deck would bang those watertight hatch lids down ominously as I went through and – even more ominously – hammer the clips home real hard. I felt entombed forever.

There were three of us in the magazine and we had a good quick instructional council of war on which racks held which shells; how to set the nose-cone fuses on D.A. (delayed action) shells, and how to signal for the loaded hoists to be pulled up. It wasn't long before the ship shuddered with a deafening bang. "We've been hit!" I cried. Trying not to show my terror I asked if the damage and repair party above would knock the clips off to allow us to get out before she sunk. "Shouldn't think so," calmly said the leading hand in charge. "What you heard was just 'A' gun firing, and hurry up and get another couple of H.A. 'prodgies' on the hoist to help keep her firing. You ll soon know when the bombs start dropping, even when they're the other side of the convoy; the explosion is magnified under water and is about five times louder than what you just heard!" He was right too!

Not that any bombs dropped this time. That first panic was only a reconnaissance plane that kept well out of range while their spotter did his sums and reported our size, course and speed back to Hitler. My colleague said when they come out looking this early it'll probably mean dive bombers this afternoon if it's sunny, or torpedo-bombers at dusk. He was right again, on both counts!

So twice more that day we were summoned to action stations. The first time soon after the start of my afternoon watch in the wheelhouse when I heard the shout on the bridge 'Enemy aircraft approaching Red 150' followed immediately by the strident bell for 'Action Stations!', but I had to wait till the coxswain came up to take the wheel from the quartermaster on watch and the chief q.m. (my old friend Greasey Gough from the middle) arrived to take the telegraphs from me. Then it was helter-skelter down ladders and ducking like mad as everything in the convoy that could shoot banged away at JU87's screaming out of the sky.

The magazine was like the inside of a big drum with half a dozen top tympanists knocking out *The Anvil Chorus* on its hull, but it was all quiet again in about 15 minutes, although I believe one ship in the convoy was hit.

Then just before the end of my watch came a wave of Dornier torpedo bombers hugging the top of the waves. They didn't hit anything that time.

Down there in the magazine, one had to rely on what the gun-deck captain remembered to shout down the voicepipe in the heat of battle, and he didn't have much time to stop and stare with trying to keep his gun aimed and firing at rapidly moving targets.

It was only when it was all over and we returned to cruising stations, with those off watch round the tea kettle on the messdeck and taking it in turns to toast a slice of bread in front of the electric heater's spiral elements, that everybody released their own version of what had taken place.

114

Time after time we had gone into a crazy 30 degree turn at full speed to take avoiding action from whatever the enemy was aiming at us, accompanied by the roar of our main and secondary armament hammering away and the clatter of things being thrown around the messdeck, with the result that there was always crockery, and whatever had been left unattended when the alarm bells went off, to be cleaned up off the deck before the mess could be made habitable again. "A fine introduction to life afloat", I remember thinking as my first 24 hours at sea drew to a close.

Luxuriating in a middle and morning stretch in my hammock I was fully charged when entering the wheelhouse for the forenoon – 8.00am to 12 noon. During that period those off watch worked 'part of ship' – care and maintenance of designated areas and equipment, so it wasn't until the following morning that I reported to the chief electrical artificer and proceeded to learn a great deal of the extensive range of electrical equipment there was on a modern man-of-war. And even if a twenty-six year old ship wasn't all that modern there was much to learn despite having earned a living as a qualified electrician up until four months earlier.

For instance, every morning we'd descend into the bowels of the fo'c'sle, boiler rooms, and engine room to perform routine maintenance on the three vital motor generators that energised the ship's de-gaussing coils – thousands of yards of cable around the internal bulkhead below the water-line that turned the vessel into a polarised magnet and neutralised it against lurking magnetic mines.

There was the master gyro compass to be checked over, gunnery control relays to be kept clean, the searchlight carbons to be examined and adjusted if it had been used during the night, and a number of other duties I wouldn't have a clue on how to start if asked to do so now; but the old country would need to be in a pretty bad mess if obliged to approach me on that score.

Sailing south there were a number of alarms to enliven the day and ensuing night but nothing very momentous happened to the best of my memory until we approached the shores of East Anglia. The swept channel for our ships was kept to about five to ten miles off the east coast and involved constant course variations. A considerable turn out to sea was necessary off Sheringham where low tide would expose miles of beaches. I think we lost far more shipping in the six years of war through running aground in those waters than ever through enemy action. One dirty night, with driving rain and gale force winds blowing ships in every direction, I remember the Officer of the Watch gazing into the murk frantically trying to flash course instructions with the shaded Aldis to some of the wanderers. Wiping the lenses of his night glasses he said, "They'll be waking up at first light in Norwich to stare at some of those stupid bastards steaming down the High Street!"

The swept channel around that part of the coast was known as E-boat Alley. German motor torpedo boats would lie in wait for the approaching convoy under cover of darkness, often tied up to one of our buoys so that their presence would not be picked up easily on our radar screens. Then all hell would break loose as powerful engines roared into life, star shells burst overhead, and mighty explosions rent the air as torpedoes struck home on one or more unlucky ships. By this time the sea and sky above was a huge network of star shells and tracer bullets with everybody firing every which way as the E-boats roared off into the night at 45 miles per hour. Should the target ship, or ships, be mortally wounded, then would come the cry of 'Away lifeboat s crew!' in an attempt to find and pick up survivors. 'Lifeboat's crew' meant volunteers nearest to the ship's whaler. Hurling themselves into it they would grab an oar apiece while others would unlash it, turn the davits out over the side and lower away until the boat was hanging just above the wave-tops. The self-appointed coxswain would wait for the best moment to trip the patent release gear and the boat would drop the last two (or ten!) feet with a sickening thud or lurch. Assuming it hadn't turned over or smashed against the ship's side, the makeshift crew would start pulling like mad in search of the stricken ship and crew. There were times we actually found and picked up people from the water and got them back aboard, but instinctive volunteering for lifeboat's crew was always a dicey business, and getting back to the ship in the dark, hooking up the falls and waiting for the ship's company to answer the cry of 'Clear lower deck!' and pull the boat and its contents out of the water and on to 'decka-firma', was even dicier. Especially with a captain who considered his ship a 'sitting duck' all the time it was hove-to on its errand of mercy and would ring down 'half-speed ahead', starboard 20° while the whaler was still swaying its way up to the davit-heads!

At the approach to the Thames Estuary we'd leave the convoy and moor in the harbour of Sheerness, where supply vessels would tie-up alongside and replenish our water, food, oil and ammunition stocks. *Verdun*'s return trip with a northbound convoy would have already been planned by Shore Command and within the ensuing 24 hours we'd be out there once again emulating sheep dog trials – midst a mixed bag of ships whose safe journey up to the Forth Estuary was the objective for the next two and a half days.

One soon got used to the routine. Invariably those rotten Germans would come seeking trouble when about to have my dinner, or my supper, or just off watch; and once back in the mess after a succession of ear-piercing guns, bombs and high speed turns there would be the task of deciding just whose were the meals that had spread themselves over the deck midst an assortment of broken crockery during the spell at 'Action Stations!'

Highlights included a 96-hour boiler clean back in Rosyth every four to six weeks, when almost everybody had a lay off watchkeeping and a bit of local leave, except the poor old duty-watch stokers who – wrapped in rags from head to foot – would crawl between the still warm boiler tubes de-coking as they went, with the object of maintaining efficiency of hard-worked boilers. Efficient boilers are not only essential for providing steam needed to turn the ship's engines, but where else in bad weather was one to hang a blanket, shirt, collar or pair of socks after a spell of 'dhobeying', other than on the guard rails around that huge cylinder in No. 1 boiler room? Or No. 2 if all rails were taken up in the for'ard one by some enterprising 'dhobey-firm'.

That would be a couple of lads who'd set up a little business offering to do any-body's laundry for a fixed tariff, but there'd always be one pair going out of business and another brace of optimists starting up, as most of us preferred to do our own rather than part with a hard-earned sixpence for a shirt, say. Even when raised to A.B. soon after joining *Verdun* the extra 15 pence (6 new pence) per day did little to improve my lifestyle. With a further 18 pence a day a year or so later when passing for leading seaman came a far reaching decision that was to change my destiny.

Realising what a big colourful world there was out there, I decided that returning to the local council as a happy-go-lucky electrician when it was all over would not do at all. There was now a burning need for sufficient knowledge to control my own affairs, and with this in mind I enrolled with a correspondence school for a course in advanced electrical engineering, as advertised in one of the magazines that came to the ship. Many hours off watch over the ensuing Naval years were spent swotting text books and writing exam papers, and then following examiner's instructions on weak-nesses that showed through when the marked-up sheets were returned. Much of what was learned in that fashion stood me in good stead in the years to come when building up a business that went on to make and market its own range of lighting, switchboards and busduct systems. The seeds of that enterprise were no doubt sown in those dog-watches spent poring over text books on the messdeck of HMS *Verdun* on the North Sea, and irrigated by condensation dripping off the cold steel deck-head on to foolscap sheets of ruled examination paper featuring Sam's calculations and theses. And drops were still falling three years later – this time from a perspiring forehead – when completing the course during dog-watches aboard HMS *Redoubt*, in the warmer waters of the Indian Ocean and Burma Sea. Only at that stage it was tak-ing a lot longer for mail carrying my homework or teacher s comments to reach their respective destinations than it did while aboard *Verdun*. Yet, in all those years and despite the perils of the war, I don't remember one of those postal packages ever going adrift.

Those dog-watch activities between decks round the mess table had all the hall-marks of a happy domestic scene. While engaged in my own 'self-raising' studies another would be writing home, there'd be this one busy ripping up and re-sewing the seams of his shore-going jumper to give it a more 'tiddley' look, and that one "crashing out" his smalls in a bucket of suds. One man seeking advancement would be studying his seamanship manual and asking his 'oppo' to test him on Morse Code or 'Rules of the Road at Sea'; a cook-of-the-mess would be peeling spuds or getting pusser's peas into soak for tomorrow's dinner; a bitter squabble would be in progress near the messdeck loudspeaker with one starry-eyed matelot drooling over the latest Vera Lynn being played, while another vented unfavourable opinions on the lady in question.

'Uckers' was ever a popular past-time on the messdeck. Possibly better known by its lay title of Ludo, the matelot's version bore little resemblance to that respectable nursery or parlour game when Jack roared, "Uckers, you !*ckers, take six!" on throwing a double six, thereby removing his opponent's 'blob' that was holding up the advance of his own counters. There'd be an 'Uckers' knock-out competition organised through the ship with the final played-off on the fo'c'sle when in harbour. That would be a grand affair.

For the HMS *Verdun* 1941 Uckers Final, once we'd moored up at Sheerness after a southbound run, the chief boatswain's mate had rigged up a Ludo board about eight feet square made of painted canvas. The squares, home bases and 6" diameter counters would be painted the appropriate colours, and a pair of 6" dice fabricated by the ship's carpenter. An old hand at shipboard carpentry and 'Uckers' would probably knock up and secrete a spare pair of dice for such time as an over-energetic heave of the giant dice-cup – a suitably decorated messdeck bucket – had one or both disappear over the side and float away with the tide.

With the scene set on the fo'c'sle for the final round of the tournament each of the competitors would make his entrance separately, dressed in the weirdest and most outlandish clobber he could muster and go to his appointed corner attended by seconds and messmates. Every throw of the dice would bring roars of support and derision from the crowd gathered around the scene and after the counters were moved the thrower returned exhausted to his corner where his seconds would revive him with a brisk towelling and muscle pummelling, plus a swig from the tot saved from that forenoon's rum issue. Good harmless fun improvised to relieve the monotony of weeks at sea, and it's amazing the ingenuity a bunch of sailors can dream up to relieve boredom!

Similar knockout tournaments were planned with draughts, chess and cribbage but nothing compared to those wild Uckers finals.

The BBC wireless programmes – nobody referred to it as radio in those halcyon days – were a great source of entertainment, especially those devoted to playing requests. 'Forces Favourites' was the regular one with a lady s 'cut-glass' voice linking each record with the family members or friend that called for it. Half listening one day I remember hearing the well modulated announcement, "And now we have Bing Crosby singing "You are my Sunshine", for Able Seaman Sam Morley on HMS *Verdun* somewhere at sea. It comes at the request of his wife, Patricia." I remember having written to her sometime previous about a dream in which we'd been separated and the haunting music of that lovely ballad brought us back together again. She'd written to the BBC and asked them to play it for me, and how fortunate I was somewhere down on the messdeck when they did. Even if it did mean that for the rest of my time on *Verdun* I was 'Sunshine' Morley!

Some of the names were ingeniously funny. Once again, only half listening, the wireless got full attention when 'sweet and lovely' announced, "We've had a little trouble tracing this next request from Able-Seaman McHammock-Lashin of 'Rose Cottage' aboard HMS *Suffolk*. Well, Able-Seaman McHammock-Lashin", she went on, "You asked for 'A Woman is No Good', but having gone through our record library without success it has been suggested you may mean 'Blues in the Night', in which 'A woman is no good' features in the lyric." What she didn't know was that the name of the said Able-Seaman is a fictitious one used in jest among old-timers when referring to an anonymous third party; and that 'Rose Cottage' is the messroom set aside and isolated on big ships and shore establishments to which poor Jack is temporarily transferred should he have been unlucky enough to have contracted 'a social disease' from a female companion during his last run ashore. A very shrewd and heartfelt choice of song-titling by old 'Mac' that had our messdeck in an uproar!

CHAPTER TWELVE

Alarums and Excursions

*I*n January 1941 I went home to London for 4 days boiler-cleaning leave – well, discounting the nightly bombing blitz it got me away from war – and brought my wife away from it back to Scotland to stay at digs I'd found in Dunfermline, about 4 miles from Rosyth. By this time it seemed that me and the war had settled down to a predictable pattern – at least while aboard *Verdun* and as predictable as anything could claim to be during those 'orrible years. Three days away on a south-bound convoy, half a day at Sheerness, two and a half days on a northbound convoy and a day in Rosyth. During that day we'd stock up with water, oil, provisions and ammunition, especially the latter if there'd been more than our fair share of unfriendly activity en route. While in Rosyth those with permanent or temporary homes within ten miles were granted all-night leave, so by coming back with me my wife and I would see a little more of each other than had otherwise been the case, and it would also provide her with a well-earned break from the shattering dusk-to-dawn rain of bombs on London every night.

We started out with some rotten luck when the lady (for want of a better word) sharing our unlit compartment on the overnight train from King's Cross, alighted at Darlington in the Stygyan gloom with Pat's suitcase. It wasn't until approaching the dawn's early light in Edinburgh that we first noticed the luggage rack was empty. Empty, that is, except for a battered old attaché case containing some pack-ets of tea, sugar and miscellaneous groceries. Pat's case has been laden with suffi-cient personal clothing and toiletries to cater for a long stay away from home, including the pretty blue outfit she'd had made especially for our wedding day a year earlier. She was heartbroken and, I think, is still inclined to look a bit misty-eyed whenever conversation veers to that subject today. Especially that within a few hours of reaching the digs in Dunfermline we were engaged in sad farewells when I left to rejoin my ship and she to face a lonely stay in a strange environment – an environment where some of the local Anglophobes were inclined to cheer when the morning news gave out that London had once again been heavily bombed through the night!

She spent a year up there, mostly a lonely and depressing year, during which she changed digs two or three times. It was around Christmas 1941 that I qualified for a couple of weeks leave, while *Verdun* underwent a spell in dry dock and a major refit. During this time my spouse decided to shake the dust of Dunfermline off her heels and return to live in London – bombs and all – happily clutching me by the arm and the beginnings of our 'made in Scotland' offspring under her coat. It wasn't until June 23rd 1942 that the said offspring first saw the light of day in a Surrey nursing home and was christened Susan Virginia.

Through most of 1941 life aboard *Verdun* had continued as described earlier – each voyage terminating with a hasty change into tiddley No. 1's and a mad dash through Rosyth dockyard for the Dunfermline bus. There were, however, times when an unforeseen emergency interrupted the sequence of escorts riding 'shotgun' with the next southbound convoy. Enemy action or engine failure (or both) being responsible for a sudden change of plan. In such cases we'd get the signal from Base, as we steamed up the Forth after seeing our northbound convoy safely into the anchorage at Methil, to race into Rosyth, spend three or four hours getting in essential supplies, and then back to Methil to head south for another six day stint. In such cases leave to 'natives' might be conceded during the time spent re-stocking ship, and how we that qualified would double through the dockyard to catch the Dunfermline bus in time to meet-'n'-greet our loved ones – and then reverse the procedure to get back on board before leave expired. I believe Susan Virginia owes her very existence to one of those emergency '*noon-to-3.30-leave-to-natives*' sessions back in September 1941!

On 24th May 1941 came a break from the southbound/northbound convoy routine. All day the messdeck radio had dispensed shock news of how the German battleship *Bismarck* had sunk HMS *Hood* and damaged HMS *Prince of Wales*, two of the greatest and most loved ships in the British Navy. *Bismarck*, 43,000 tons with a crew of over 2,000, and her heavy cruiser escort, *Prince Eugen*, were now free to go on and roam the North Atlantic destroying such of our shipping that had escaped the U-boats. Two of our county-class 8" cruisers, HMS *Norfolk* and HMS *Suffolk*, were trying to keep their distance and report positions as they shadowed the two enemy ships by radar in the sub-Arctic waters, but in the awful weather that prevailed that was easier said than done. In other words, both *Bismarck* and *Prince Eugen* had given our cruisers the slip. The Admiralty then signalled to every available warship, "To all Naval vessels in Atlantic waters, drop whatever you re doing and find the *Bismarck*!" Well, that may not have been the exact wording but it was certainly the gist of what each ship was told to do.

Verdun was instructed to get back to Rosyth at full speed, fill up with oil-fuel, load up with plenty of S.A.P. (semi-armour piercing) ammo, and take on fresh water and essential food. One or two suggested that a hundredweight of large Kind Edward potatoes wouldn't come amiss, in the belief that if we got close enough to the

Bismarck undetected, we could probably do as much damage to her chucking spuds as we would popping off our 4" H.A. guns at her heavily armour-plated sides and decks!

Then in company with two other V&W's whose names I forget, and the old 6" cruiser HMS *Emerald*, we were one of several groups sent out hurriedly to seek and destroy the enemy. Well, not so much destroy, but certainly seek and try to get a signal away giving her position, course and speed before being blasted out of the water!

Hurtling through a most vicious and unfriendly ocean at twenty-six knots, with sometimes just the top of the funnel showing above the turbulent seas – judging by what we could see of our fellow V&W's as they breasted the waves – was no picnic, especially when on watch as quartermaster and trying to steer the stated course, as time after time the ship came to a juddering halt when piling into yet another mountain of bile-green water. Talking of which, even the most hardened salt-water sailor among us was the colour of that water as hour after hour the ship corkscrewed her way toward the North Pole. Time after time I'd send down for more ship's biscuits to chew and swallow before throwing up into a bucket lashed to the binnacle. There was an urgent need for food of any sort to avoid being retched inside-out if there was nothing there – at least, that's the way it felt.

The contents of the messdecks clattered, crashed and shattered in all directions with every pitch and roll; many prayed that *Bismarck* would show up soon to put us out of our misery but, thankfully, it wasn't to be. She never did get to meet us, for after two and a half days came the glorious news that she'd been spotted about 700 miles north of Brest and had slowed down considerably due to damage inflicted by our ships and aircraft, especially a torpedo attack by Swordfish off HMS *Ark Royal*, one of which scored a fortuitous hit on *Bismarck*'s rudder thereby putting her steering out of control. She wandered over the ocean seeking the safety of the Brittany coast, at times heading back unwillingly toward the Home Fleet ships pursuing her. Before she could get close enough to Brest and protective air cover, the battleships HMS *King George V* and HMS *Rodney* were within sufficient range to open fire with their 14" and 16" main armament respectively on the morning of 27th May 1941. By 10.30am it was all over, when HMS *Dorsetshire* fired the final torpedoes into what was left of the *Bismarck* and put her under the waves with her battle ensign still flying.

Verdun, still about a thousand miles from the scene, then got the signal to return to base and carry on whatever it was she was doing before the panic. All aboard breathed freely again and proceeded to enjoy the luxury of an ocean cruise as we steamed back to the Forth at a steady fifteen knots in the spring sunshine with a following wind and sea.

Many books have been written on the *Bismarck* story, but to those wanting to know more I would recommend Ludovic Kennedy's *Pursuit*, published by Collins in 1974.

He was a watchkeeping lieutenant on HMS *Tartar* – one of our illustrious tribal-class fleet destroyers – and *Tartar* played a somewhat far greater part in that exercise than did *Verdun!*

Just five and half weeks after the outbreak of war on September 3rd 1939, the battle-ship HMS *Royal Oak* returned from a search for enemy warships and anchored in the northern section of Scapa Flow. At a little after 1.00am on the 14th, she was struck by three torpedoes fired by a U-boat that had penetrated the channel of Kirk Sound, and sunk in 13 minutes with the loss of eight hundred and thirty-three of her crew. This was just one of the great naval losses we suffered at a time we could so ill afford to do so, with major ships needed to guard convoy routes against surface raiders at sea and a deterrent to potential raiders lurking in enemy waters waiting to attack our ships whenever possible.

As First Sea Lord, Winston Churchill was well aware of the need for more capital ships and, with the outbreak of war, proceeded to bridge the gap by building a 'Phantom Fleet' of dummy capital ships with which to fool the enemy while waiting for the shipyards to produce the genuine articles.

Three old merchant ships of the required dimensions were requisitioned from their owners and sent to the Belfast shipyards of Harland & Wolff to be made over with timber, plywood, sheet metal and grey paint to resemble the battleships HMS *Resolution* and HMS *Revenge*, and the aircraft carrier HMS *Hermes*. Decks, superstructures, masts, gun turrets and guns were fabricated in wood and when finished were an uncanny replica of the ships they were meant to represent. However, they needed to be heavily ballasted to make them sit deep enough in the water and, with all that dead weight, their coal-fired boilers needed a far larger complement of stokers than could be spared from depot for the job.

When it came to drafting their crews from naval barracks, the dummy *Resolution* was named Fleet Tender A, dummy *Revenge* Fleet Tender B, and the dummy *Hermes* was Fleet Tender C. But as the subject of these dummy warships is only included in this book whereby they enter into the affairs of HMS *Verdun* we'll leave Fleet Tenders A & B and continue with the tale of Fleet Tender C – the dummy HMS *Hermes*, except to say that once commissioned and put to sea, all three were sent to join the Home Fleet in Scapa Flow.

Being far too slow and vulnerable to join in Fleet exercises and patrols, they were anchored in various parts of the semi land-locked waters of Scapa in the hope of fooling the enemy, but after taking a good look the enemy reconnaissance aircraft and bombers were neither impressed nor amused and ignored the dummies completely. As Commander-in-Chief Home Fleet found that having 'pantomime-policemen' around cramped his style, he sent them down to anchor in the Forth, close to Rosyth. Then it was decided they weren't such a good idea after all and, as we needed replacement merchant ships badly, Fleet Tender C was sent to join a southbound convoy at Methil bound for the Thames, with the purpose of ending her imitation-warship career at Chatham dockyard, where she would be re-converted for respectable mercantile purposes.

On Sunday, June 1st 1941, fresh from her 'Find the *Bismarck*' expedition, HMS *Verdun*, in company with her sister ship, HMS *Versatile*, had finished replenishing her food, fuel, water and ammunition stocks and headed down river to pick up the southbound convoy. Dominating the skyline above the assembled ships and awaiting arrival of the escorting destroyers, was the massive superstructure of Fleet Tender C. She took up station in the centre of the convoy as we moved off and the surrounding merchantmen were no doubt delighted to have what seemed to be such a powerful source of protection in their midst. Needless to say, we, the real guardians of the convoy, knew otherwise.

But it wasn't long before both escorts and escorted hated Fleet Tender C with deep loathing. As soon as we hit open waters after leaving the Forth Estuary, she was wallowing, wandering, and losing station in that turbulent North Sea, and it wasn't long before all other ships in the convoy were giving her as wide a berth as possible.

We rarely had trouble with enemy attacks during the first 24 hours of a southbound run, other than the occasional reconnaissance Focke-Wolff that would stay out of range and log our course, size and position for the fun-and-frolic Herrenfolk to come, but when the news got back that we had a Fleet aircraft carrier in our midst, half the German Luftwaffe came out to see and throw things while we, of course, threw everything we had at them. Of course, Fleet Tender C had no real guns, but to give the effect of reality, she'd been equipped with a single Lewis machine gun which one of the skeleton crew put to work every time an attack took place. But despite everybody s aggressive action, by the time night had fallen not only had we not yet damaged any of their planes but neither had they hit any of our ships.

The next day, the attacks started soon after dawn and continued through the day. During one of the rare moments when one could admire the afternoon spring sunshine without an enemy plane in sight Fleet Tender C suddenly stopped. The convoy 'lifted up its skirts' and carefully edged round her while *Verdun* steamed back to find what was wrong. She'd run aground! Well not exactly aground, but had got herself impaled upon the wreck of a ship that had hit a German mine and sunk there about three weeks earlier. We were just a couple of miles off the Lincolnshire coast at the mouth of the River Humber.

Verdun waited for high water with the hope of towing off '*Hermes-Two*' but she'd been badly holed below the water-line and if any undue force was used in trying to pull her away there was every chance of ripping the bottom right out of her against the superstructure of the ship on which she was currently perched. So her crew being instructed to abandon ship, we sent over our motor boat and whaler to bring

124

them away, and our scrambling net was rigged over the starboard quarter awaiting their arrival. And what a pantomime crew they turned out to be!

Singing, waving, standing up in the boats and shouting as they approached the ship s side, and dropping personal possessions while trying to pull themselves up the netting. The fact that most of them were also clutching flagons of pusser's rum among those personal possessions probably accounted for the fact that a number fell off the boat or netting and had to be fished out of the North Sea by *Verdun*-ites diving in after them! Anyway, everybody finished up safely aboard, the boats were hoisted back to the davits and secured, and – a signal having been made for HMS *Kittiwake*, a Harwich-based sloop, to come out and guard Fleet Tender C from the anticipated overnight E-boat attacks – *Verdun* sped off to rejoin the convoy. On the way some of us were regaled by those '*Hermes-Two*' survivors that had sobered up and were reasonably coherent on just what it was like being the main object of attention of Germany's war effort for the best part of 36 hours with nothing to fight back with but a Lewis gun and a few firkins of pusser's bubbly!

Sure enough the E-boats arrived that night and scored several hits on the stationary ship while *Kittiwake* did her best to fend them off. The damage done by their torpedoes caused Fleet Tender C to sink deeper on to the ship upon which she was impaled, but when we passed her a couple of days later with a northbound convoy there was her superstructure and flight deck still sticking out of the water!

As she was considered a danger to shipping and a protective base for E-boats waiting to pounce on passing convoys, every effort was made to destroy what was left of her – but without avail. In September 1941, a Canadian bomber squadron from Coastal Command went out with instructions to blow it out of the water, but after ten direct hits and twice that number of near misses her tripod masts continued to project out of the North Sea defiantly for the ensuing years until the Royal Navy wreck-disposal vessels got to work on the 'pick-a-back' ships in 1949. But it still took another eight years before the marker buoys of Trinity House could be lifted from the area.

I'm indebted to 'The Phantom Fleet' by A Cecil Hampshire for the information in the preceding paragraph.

Anybody putting in lots of seatime perks up at the magic word 'refit', when a ship would spend a month or more in dockyard hands and get a thorough going-over from top to toe – or masthead to keel, to keep it nice and nautical. During this time vital equipment would be added, exchanged or modified to conform with the latest state of the art; bruised and battered parts would be repaired or replaced, and as the ship stood all propped up and vulnerable in dry dock, underwater areas would be scraped free of barnacles and marine growth accumulated while at sea. But the magic word 'refit' was magic only because it introduced visions of an even more magic word – "Leave!"

125

For the dockyard to have as clear a run as possible to work about a ship the less of its crew remaining aboard the better. So 50% are sent on leave for 50% of the anticipated period she'll be in dockyard hands, and the other 50% go once the first lot returned. And of the 50% on board, half of them take turn and turn about with the other half in 24-hour spells ashore locally. So when *Verdun* started a minor refit in August 1941 Pat and I headed south to the old folks at home for a week and on return, I managed to get most of my time ashore with her over the next two weeks when not on duty watch. At the end of that lovely refit interval there was still a lot to do to get the ship ready for work with all the new equipment aboard, but by the end of September *Verdun* was once again heading down river to pick up a southbound convoy run at Methil in the established pattern.

But I think that was the run when we stopped heading south and turned west from the normal channel in order to escort ships into the Tyne Estuary for some reason, after which *Verdun* and our fellow escorting destroyer, HMS *Walpole*, tied up alongside a jetty in the harbour at North Shields before going to sea again later that day.

It was a pleasant warm afternoon as most of the two ships' companies basked in a blissful make-and-mend with just a few watchkeepers visible on deck. Being quartermaster I was on duty at the gangway between the two ships, idly admiring the 'mini art gallery' on the shield of *Walpole*'s X gun. There must have been a polished artist in her crew to judge by the high quality paintings of E-boats, Dorniers, Heinkels, etc, displayed – each, with a date underneath, supposedly registering a claim of destroying yet another enemy raider while going about her normal business.

Behind that gunshield their conscientious Chief Gunner's Mate was instructing a small party of seamen on some of the finer arts of 4" H.A. gun drill, instead of letting the poor devils get their heads down or dhobeying done. But on second thoughts they were more likely to have been men-under-punishment being put to work by the duty P.O.

Suddenly a terrific explosion rent the air, and through the hatches and gangways on both ships rushed hordes of bleary-eyed sailors blowing up lifebelts as they ran, while all the seabirds in north east England fled screeching to the horizon. It was not until the ships had closed up at action stations and people had stopped training binoculars and guns every which-way, to see from where and by whom we were being attacked, that the panic slowly subsided and the mystery clarified.

When at sea with little or no warning before enemy attacks, it was customary to keep a 'bullet up the spout' in readiness – well, a 4" shell in the breech. It would be returned to the ready-use locker when approaching harbour and the danger of being surprised had passed. *Walpole*'s gun crew had forgotten she still had one 'up the spout' when coming off duty from the morning's convoy run and during the general activity I'd seen around X-gun somebody had obviously decided to lean on the wrong button. Checking back on the angle and elevation of the gun at the time it was fired, it was calculated that the half-hundredweight projectile had passed between a couple of dockyard electricity pylons before proceeding in the general direction of the City of Newcastle!

Later that day, while making ready to part company and go back to sea, our First Lieutenant with a megaphone to his lips was calling instructions from the bridge to the deck parties who were singling-up and disengaging ropes holding the ships together, while from the bridge of the *Walpole* their No. 1 was doing something similar. Turning toward the latter and calling across the slowly widening gap between the two ships, 'Jimmy' bawled, "I say, *Walpole*, any truth in the story that your tame artist will be painting a Corporation tramcar on that X-gun of yours?!"

It was to be another fifty years before I met anybody else who had served on HMS *Verdun*, and that meeting provided an ideal story with which to finish off these colourful memories of that gallant old ship.

In September 1942, one Peter Down commissioned HMS *Redoubt*, a brand new fleet destroyer, the same time as I joined her in Brown's yard at Glasgow. But as my *Redoubt* memories will take up most of the rest of this book, I'll say no more about her now – except that forty-seven years later a few who had served on her decided to form an Old Redoubtian Association, with you-know-who in the chair. Soon after, and seeing a notice in Navy News of a *Redoubt* reunion, Peter got in touch and joined up with those of us living within 30 miles of London who meet three or four times a year at the Victory Services Club, Marble Arch, for a drink, a bite and a yarn. Especially a yarn!

His was quite an eye-opener – to me at least – on learning that after the best part of two and a half years in the Far East aboard *Redoubt*, he'd hardly paid her off and returned to Chatham barracks in January 1945 when he was sent off to the wars again with another sea-going draft chit. This time to – yes, HMS *Verdun*! She was still doing those east coast convoys and some of the characters whose names I could remember from 1942 were still on board when Peter joined her in 1945.

In answer to my question he said the barnacle-encrusted top section of the mast of Fleet Tender C was still sticking out of the Humber estuary when they passed it on the way back to Methil on the morning before V.E. Day, with the last northbound convoy of World War II. He described the carnival-like atmosphere on board the following morning as *Verdun* turned up the Forth and headed for Rosyth and home for the last time. On approaching harbour it was customary to hoist the ship's pennant numbers close up to the yardarm, where they'd remain throughout the 20-mile run up-river, until acknowledged with an answering pennant from Commander-in-Chief Rosyth s signal station on the hillside above the Forth Bridge. But nobody wanted to do anything customary on that festive day. Rummaging around in the flag lockers they came up with a German battle ensign taken from an E-boat sunk on a previous convoy action, and a 'Guinness is Good for You' flag picked up elsewhere. These were proudly sent fluttering up the halliards with Guinness in the superior position!

But good order and naval discipline – the guiding principles of our Navy – frown on departure from time-honoured procedures. Up went the following hoist from Commander-in-Chief as *Verdun* approached the Bridge, "Do not recognise your hoist. Return to sea and seek permission to re-enter harbour displaying your correct identification!"

When preparing this for the book I phoned Peter at his home and asked how long were they kept out before permission to re-enter was given. He thought a bit before replying "I don't really remember now, Sam, but it couldn't have been long because I was pissed as a newt in Edinburgh by 3 o'clock that afternoon!"

CHAPTER THIRTEEN

Roedean School –
The Class of '42!

T he early pages of Chapter Ten described how I came to be directed into the torpedo division of the Navy after basic training. In May 1942, after nearly two years at sea, a signal came to the ship recalling me for a Leading Torpedo Operator (L.T.O.) course. Once back into Rosyth after my fortieth North Sea convoy, I left *Verdun* and, with all my worldly possessions, took the train to Chatham via Edinburgh and London. Then came much-appreciated in-from-sea-leave before reporting to Torpedo School.

Originally HMS *Vernon* was a complex of buildings at Portsmouth, but a number of those buildings had been badly knocked about by enemy bombing whereby activities normally carried out there had to be transferred elsewhere for the duration.

Fifty-odd miles east of Portsmouth was the empty Roedean School for Girls, sitting atop the rolling Sussex Downs on the Channel coast between Brighton and Rottingdean. Its female pupils and staff had been evacuated to Cumbria at the outbreak of war and the school loaned to H.M. Government for the duration. After inspection with regard to suitability, HMS *Vernon* moved in to help solve its shortfall in accommodation and classrooms. In May 1941 Roedean School for Girls became the training establishment for the *Vernon* torpedo school, and about a mile further east the hitherto unused and newly-built St Dunstan's Home for the War-blinded was requisitioned for V*ernon*'s High-Power School.

I spent two weeks at St Dunstan's on the high-power course, before transfer to the prestigious Roedean. One clear memory is the 4-bed dormitories (not a bit like the hammock-strewn Duncan Block 'scran-bag' of Chatham Barracks, nor the 'fish-fryer' messdeck of HMS *Verdun*!) every bunk in which once supported shapes far more interesting than some of those around when I was there (interesting, that is, to 25 year old sailors – not 77 year old authors!)

In 1986, Jeremy Greenwood of Quiller Press phoned to say he'd been commissioned to produce a book called *Stories Out of School* for the late Arthur Marshall, a well-known writer and Radio/TV personality. It was to be an anthology of personal school experiences by celebrities of the day. As Jeremy had published a couple of my early books he asked for a contribution (must have been short of celebrities!) and was sent the following: (I believe that's another Old Roedeanian whose one-liner they used to finish off the bottom of their page).

Sailors at school

I was a boarder at Roedean, on the Sussex coast near Brighton – still one of the foremost public schools for girls in the country.

Unfortunately, at that time there wasn't a girl in the place – just 200-odd sailors in from sea and undergoing an 8-week course in the use of low power electrics in the remote control of guns and torpedoes. It was the summer of 1942, I'd already done nearly two years on destroyers, and had been recalled to do this advanced course amidst delightful surroundings.

The fair and female peacetime pupils had been evacuated to Wales, or somewhere safer than the South Coast, and the classrooms modified to suit the requirements of a naval Torpedo School for the duration. Its only link with the former occupants was that we slept in the same dormitories and on the same bunks that once supported more graceful shapes than ours. And many's the night a restless sailor may have wondered whether there might still be a flimsily-clad prefect or two still lurking around the building, daringly seeking adventure with the present occupants.

So much so, that the said restless sailor, his passions inflamed by a canteen pint and a Hedy Lamarr film, could not resist leaning out and pressing the bell-push, one of which was fixed on the wall immediately above each bunk. Below each push was an engraved ivorine label reading: 'Press the button if you need a mistress for any reason during the night.'

After a short pause, stealthy footsteps would be heard heading towards the dormitory, the door would open quietly, and a form approach to sit gently on the edge of it.

In a low voice the duty Chief Petty Officer would breathe softly into the restless sailor's ear just what would happen to him, health-wise, if he ever again laid a blankety-blank finger on that blankety-blank-blank bell push during the rest of his blankety-blank-blank-blank stay at Roedean!

Sam Morley

From a school essay

All people should be gentlemen except ladies, but it puts a lot of variety in life if some are not.

Jilly Cooper

My wife's sister lived at Southwick, about 12 miles along the coast road from Roedean, with an interconnecting bus service between the two front doors. Over the first weekend after my arrival at St. Dunstan's I returned to London and brought her back with our infant Susan to stay with her sister, whereby the ensuing six or eight weeks we shared a little more family life than might otherwise have been the case.

I was duty watch on board one night in four, when one patrolled the boundaries of the school armed with a Sten gun and did an hour or two alone outside the front gates. Lurid thoughts and fears would crowd the imagination during those long and lonely spells on that vulnerable post – like nervously anticipating a boatload of Germans to scale the cliffs and surge across the road in search of prisoners to take back for questioning via their U-boat lurking below! Many's the night the duty guard would rush out of the guardhouse at the staccato roar caused by a hyped-up sentry letting fly at a rustling gorse bush on the cliff-top that had failed to respond to his hysterical scream of "Halt! Who goes there?"

The threat of invasion had receded but the bombers came over nightly on their way to and from London. Not only nightly, because there were always the hit-and-run day raiders who would hop across the Channel spraying machine-gun bullets in all directions and be half way home before the air raid sirens on the school roof could start wailing. I don't remember them doing any damage other than killing some harmless farm labourer working in a field adjoining the school.

Fifty two years later – stricken with an attack of nostalgia brought on by writing this book – I wondered if a courtesy visit to the old 'alma mater' might be on the cards. In 1947 Roedean had returned to its original status as the country's leading girls' school and in 1994 housed 440 boarders at fees of around £12,000 a year. My telephone enquiry on whether a group of septuagenarian sailors who had once boarded there would be welcome was greeted with delight, and lunch with a conducted tour was arranged for July 20th 1994. In answer to an announcement to this effect in *Navy News* and *Sunday Express* I found myself with 54 old matelots re-living our memories of Roedean. A plaque from the Roedean Old Boys Association was presented on the appointed day, and after lunch we left for tea at St Dunstan's on the neighbouring cliff top. Those who had shown interest were told that the plan had arisen through writing this book and were asked for anecdotes that might be considered for use in the text, similar to mine of the bell-pushes. Fred Riley, ex P.O/L.T.O. of Ilford, kindly sent the following:

"When the Navy occupied Roedean School in 1941, all the girls had been evacuated except the sixth formers, who were not due to leave until a few days after the Navy arrived. The naval captain in charge of the operation insisted that the girls moved out before the sailors moved in. I don't know what you are so worried about, captain," said the school principal. "My girls have got it up here, you know", tapping her forehead. "Madam," said the captain, "it matters not where your girls have it, I assure you my lads will find it"!"

131

While at St Dunstan's that day I was introduced to one of the Governors, Ken Revis, a blind ex-Army captain trained in bomb disposal who had spent many months at Roedean during the years preceding the D-day landings. His job was to work with the Navy in getting our coastal defence mines out of the way ready for our offensive shipping to head out across the Channel when the time came. To use his words – "The Navy swept them up and I blew them up!" Until his party found one trapped under the bottom timbers of Palace Pier, Hove – it blew up before he could free it, blinding him in the process. A brave man, over six feet tall with a fine military bearing and a helpful wife constantly in attendance.

Mention of D-day landings takes me back to the so-called rehearsal witnessed from the cliff tops in 1942 while at Roedean. On August 14th a number of us stood wondering and hazarding guesses on the flashing skies and distant rumbling – like a massive thunderstorm – from across the Channel, with high-flying aircraft zipping about in all directions. Only it wasn't a thunderstorm – it was the all-powerful German artillery dominating the day during our ill-fated Commando raid on Dieppe. The powers-that-be who conducted the war (but took care not to become too personally involved in it themselves) claimed it to be a successful exercise from which they learned a lot to stand them in good stead when it came to launching the Second Front. All I know is that it was about as successful as the Dardenelles, or the Somme, or the Bridge at Arnhem, or the Crete campaign, or the Charge of the Light Brigade, to name but a few phenomenal cock-ups that prove all too well how expendable we're all considered by those conducting a campaign.

My very good friend, Paul McGrath, was a 19-year-old Royal Marine Commando who took part in the Dieppe raid. We played a lot of golf together before he went to live in North Berwick ten years ago. Dieppe would sometimes crop up in conversation. One day I suggested he write his version of what took place at that awful shambles, and over the years he produced two detailed accounts. These he then condensed into a fascinating 24-page booklet with illustrations and maps. Believing it to be a saga of indomitable courage and comradeship I've reproduced it as a Supplement at the end of this book. From it the following statistics are extracted:

The assault group consisted of 5,000 Canadian troops, 1,000 British Marine and Army Commandos, and 50 US Rangers. Of these 3,560 were killed, wounded or taken prisoner. 90% of them Canadian. The German army lost 339 killed and wounded.

The RAF lost 106 aircraft and 67 pilots killed. The Luftwaffe lost 48 aircraft and 13 pilots killed.

The Royal Navy had 75 men killed and 269 missing or taken prisoner. Five tank landing craft, 28 assault landing craft and the destroyer, HMS *Berkeley*, were sunk by enemy action. The German Navy lost 78 men dead and missing, 28 were taken prisoner and one of their submarine-chasers was sunk.

The Calgary Tank Regiment of Canada tried to land 29 Churchill tanks on the main beach. Two drowned attempting to land; there were serious problems trying to get the remainder to move as the tank tracks couldn't grip the potato-sized stones; 15 managed to reach the promenade but not one penetrated the town. All were eventually disabled or captured. Of the 172 men making up the tank crews, 12 were killed and 159 taken prisoner. Only 3 were rescued from the beach to return to England.

"The overall objective," wrote Paul, "was for the attacking forces to capture Dieppe and the high ground on both flanks and hold their positions before withdrawing at the next tide. But the bulk of the attacking forces were overwhelmed by the German superior weapons and fire power. In broad daylight, without the element of surprise, it was a horrifying disaster. The German General Haase, who commanded the Dieppe area said, "The British seriously underestimated the quantity of weapons required for such an attack." "He was right," writes Paul.

Yet British Combined Ops HQ gave the news to the nation the next morning as though it were a great victory. The front page banner headline of the *Daily Sketch* claimed "COMMANDOS WRECK ENEMY BATTERIES AT DIEPPE." A quarter-truth. One German battery was destroyed by one Commando assault party, but the remaining three batteries destroyed our raiding forces. On the next day the front page of the *Daily Mail* claimed "TANKS ARE HOME FROM DIEPPE – BROUGHT HOME BY CANADIAN CREWS." (*Those particular tanks had never been unloaded from the vessels that had carried them from home*).

Paul's book ends with the following statement from Lord Louis Mountbatten, Commander-in-Chief Combined Ops:

"Dieppe ... gave the Allies the priceless secret of Victory

...If I had the same decision to make again I would do as I did before." !!!

(*The exclamation marks are mine.*)

* * *

I completed the course at Roedean with reasonable success and, with a pair of crossed torpedoes sewn on the sleeve of my left arm, returned to Chatham Barracks qualifying for another nine pence a day (3 ½p) as a leading torpedoman.

CHAPTER FOURTEEN

'Abaft the Mast'
on an R-boat!

O nce back at Chatham little time was wasted in getting me back to sea, for which I was truly grateful. Not that I was all that anxious for medals and cita-tions, but Chatham depot was a grotty overcrowded establishment where any that were not on duty watch on board had to spend the night in a claustrophobic sys-tem of bomb-proof tunnels that honeycombed the perimeter hills. It was a depressing experience joining queues carrying hammocks and trudging from the daytime accommodation blocks, like refugees, into the depths of the tunnel system until space was found in which to sling the said hammock. Come morning, the procedure would be reversed, while powerful blasts of much-needed fresh air were sent roaring through the labyrinth to overcome the stale pong-laden overnight atmosphere that could be cut with a blunt knife. And whereas the crowded messdeck on *Verdun* after a night at sea was no fragrant bed of roses, it was never as vile as that Chatham tunnel.

Very few ever slept down there of their own free will, but with nightly bombing raids the Admiralty ruled that as bomb-damaged matelots were of little use to the war effort it was anxious for as many as possible to survive should the depot suffer a direct hit. That being the case, it devised various forms of punishment and inconve-nience for any caught trying to turn-in elsewhere than in the tunnel built for the spe-cific safety of all.

Reporting to the Drafting Office after hearing my name called over the public address system with instructions to report, I learned my next ship was to be HMS *Redoubt*, a brand new R-class destroyer currently commissioning at John Brown's yard on the Clyde. Quite a number from Chatham came up with me on the train from Euston and, whereas in joining *Verdun* two years earlier I found myself one of a very small number of H.O.'s (Hostilities Only) ratings on the messdeck getting a first spell of sea-time among a crowd of seasoned 'salts', a large proportion of those join-ing *Redoubt* were new entries fresh from Civvy Street *en route* to their first ship after a couple of months basic training.

Redoubt proved to be a fine-looking destroyer and quite a lot larger than *Verdun*. Dockyard mates were everywhere in various stages of fitting her out in readiness for Lt. Comm. Nigel Roper, our captain, to carry out his final inspection. If satisfied he'd sign for her on behalf of the Royal Navy whereby John Brown and Co. could get paid and we could sail her out into the wide blue yonder. But there was lots to be done before any sailing-out could be considered.

In addition to the traditional fo'c'sle messdeck, *Redoubt* had one at the after end as well, whereby in an emergency the ship could stay reasonably operational even if the front half had been knocked for six. Seventeen of the torpedo division were housed in 14 mess down aft, and when it came to being delegated for responsibilities and duties, the recommends from Roedean and *Verdun* must have flattered me somewhat as I was put in charge of the ship's high-power network. That not only meant all the high power electrics from stem to stern and from keel to masthead, but it gave me the high-power switchroom as my own 'caboosh', and although meant to be on call for any electrical emergency anywhere, anytime, it also meant that I did no watches and – except for a call to Action Stations or an electrical breakdown – enjoyed all night undisturbed at sea; something every sailor longs for but few experience.

Being an 'old sweat' I'd learned by this time that privilege never came ready-packaged – it had to be recognised, grasped and moulded to suit in its early stages. With a heavy sea running slinging a hammock in the only crack of a gap left between 17 of them and trying to swing into it was no picnic. Many would just 'crash down' on lockers or mess table rather than sling up among the swaying 'sacks' of those who had collared the best positions first. So very early in the commission I recognised and made good use of a privilege by transferring my sleeping quarters from among the hoi polloi of 14 mess to the splendid isolation of the high-power switchroom. The problem of getting my hammock up in its confined space was solved by a round turn and two half hitches to the rung of the vertical iron ladder leading up to the after lobby and a rolling hitch to the safety rail protecting the switchboard. That way, the said 'mick' was lashed up and stowed behind the ebonite panel in 30 seconds flat every morning for the next 18 months. That particular memory is ever-fresh, because the same two hitches are still used today on a fine afternoon when slinging my garden hammock between a branch of an old apple tree and a convenient pool house stanchion nearby; and although there's a couple more stones of Sam these days, causing the tree to bend a little, those two basic bends from the old seamanship manual have never been known to fail over these past forty years.

Lower deck was cleared soon after joining the ship and the crew assembled on the jetty alongside – about two hundred officers and men. We were addressed by the captain standing on an empty cable drum, who in turn introduced his officers before giving the usual pep talk on how we were going to work this ship up into an efficient fighting unit of which all would feel justifiably proud. Looking around, nobody seemed unduly impressed but the word 'work' was no idle promise. There was any amount of cleaning necessary once the ship was free of the dockyard element, and never-ending deliveries of stores and spares to be carried aboard, recorded and stowed, whereby there would be a reasonable chance of tracking them down if ever needed later in the commission.

The next two weeks were spent getting acquainted and working up a routine in our respective duties. Those new to shipboard life soon learned how to roll out a 'clacker' without ending up with it irrevocably welded to the mess table and how to get the most out of an 'oosh' from a bit of scrag-end. One luxury was having cold taps on the bulkhead and a few feet from the end of the mess table. But there was still necessity to pump up on the iron deck and put a bucketful through the galley's 'heat exchanger' when needing hot water. The galley was in the after lobby and 14 mess was one deck below, whereby floundering around with a mess-kettle of near-boiling water on a murky night was still one big 'health hazard'. And there was still the need to struggle up top to ditch the 'gash' over the side. No main-drainage on the R-boats, despite being 25 years advanced on those old V&W's.

On the same note, *Redoubt*'s main armament indicated how they must have scoured the breaker's yard for our four 4.7" single guns, each of which carried the maker's name and the date 1917 on the breech mechanism. But as a Fleet destroyer we did at least have two sets of four 21" torpedo tubes which, during those weeks of preparing the ship for war, the members of 14 mess spent untold working hours cleaning and greasing, besides testing the firing and running mechanism in preparation for the real thing. Right glad I was just having to concern myself with electrical matters instead of being delegated to take charge of and do watches on those mammoth 'fish'.

It was the same with the weighty depth charges which, by ingenious manipulation of derricks, ropes and pulleys, we'd need to unload from the jetty and transfer to the explosives store two decks down, through hatches and into racks immediately below our own 14 mess. We must have taken about fifty of them aboard like that after commissioning and another twenty on the ready-use rails on the quarter-deck. A finger-crushing, shin-busting exercise but comparatively safe, needing primers and detonators in position before they could do any real harm.

A depth charge is a steel cylinder about two-thirds the size of a 40 gallon oil drum and packed solid with about 500 lbs of TNT. There s a 4" diameter hole through the centre line into which a primer is fittied from one end and the pistol with amatol detonator from the other. The detonator envelope (about the size of a Churchman cigarette) projects from the end of the pistol and sleeves snugly into an aperture at the end of the primer. The pistol has an adjustable hydrostatic valve which fires the detonator when reaching a pre-set depth after being rolled over the ship s side. When in harbour, depth charges were kept in the 'safe' position, by withdrawing the primer to the end of the central hole whereby an exploding detonator would not set off the main charge. Bringing it to the firing position was by pushing the primer back down the tube over the detonator. I was always nervous when priming a rack of charges after leaving harbour in case a detonator envelope was off line, causing it to break when pushing the primer over it. Don't suppose I'd have heard the bang if that had happened!

Preparing a ship for sea for the first time after being commissioned is a time-honoured procedure that has changed little since Woody commissioned HMS *Bellerophon* back in 1909, as described on page 14. I don't say we had a procession of horse-drawn wagons and sailor-drawn handcarts bringing our stores to the jetty alongside, as was the case with the mighty *Bellerophon*, nor did we take aboard 1600 tons of coal, and although many of the Evolutions wished on the ship's company by a capricious Commander-in-Chief are still practised, we were at least spared the physical perils and exhaustion of rigging and gathering in torpedo nets. But although *Bellerophon* displaced 20,000 tons with a crew of 900, against 1,800 tons and 200 crew on the part of *Redoubt*, with a 33 year gap between two commissioning dates there wasn't all that much difference in procedure and range of items necessary to stock up a man of war. Our range of headings must have been far more extensive than hers, taking account of the sophisticated needs for radar, Asdics, depth charges, gunnery control and modern radio, navigational aids, etc.

To find its way around the waters of the world a ship needs a compass – a magnetic needle that when freely pivoted or suspended and without outside influence, will always align itself parallel to the north-to-south axis of the Earth. Now everybody knows that – as they also know that the needle doesn't point to true north, but to the magnetic north – about 22 degrees west of true north as far as this country is concerned, but varies in different parts of the globe as indicated in a series of Admiralty magnetic charts. But what charts do not show is compass deviations caused by the ironwork built into each ship – decks, frames, bulkheads, guns, etc, and the proximity of anything ferrous to the master compass itself. This was usually mounted in the wheelhouse on a timber and brass pedestal – called a binnacle – with a projecting bracket to right and to left on each of which a hollow iron ball is fixed. Inside the binnacle is a long hollow vertical box, called the Flinders Bar. As compass deviation varies ship to ship, no vessel can steer an accurate magnetic course without its built-in compass deviation being known and minimised as best as possible.

The very first voyage undertaken by a new ship is to a nearby stretch of open water for the purpose of 'swinging compasses', where she heads in a countless variety of directions while Admiralty experts in the wheelhouse calibrate the known courses against the compass readings and adjust as necessary by adding small magnets to the hollow balls or Flinders Bar. Once they're satisfied, the Flinders Bar and hollow balls are locked and the experts present the Navigating Officer with the keys and a deviation schedule for every point on the compass. Having partaken of a couple of pink gins in the wardroom, everybody proceeds on their way, rejoicing in the knowledge that HMS *Redoubt*, with her newly-swung compass, should have little difficulty in finding her way back to the shipyard without having to stop and ask somebody.

Of course, the magnetic compass was really for emergency purposes, as all ships were fitted with gyroscopic compasses, where electricity kept a wheel spinning in a vacuum at 8,000 rpm. But come mechanical or electrical breakdown, like a torpedo through the main switchboard, the magnetic compass would come into its own.

When passing me out for Leading Seaman the first Lieutenant asked if I knew where the Flinders Bar was and what was its purpose. My answer could have been that it was in the C.P.O's mess where the gunner's mate invited his cronies for a 'wet' when they came off an extra-trying watch – a standard type of stump reply on the messdeck among those seeking promotion and throwing questions at each other in preparation for forthcoming exams – but I'd have been pushing my luck trying it out with our 'Jimmy' so giving him the right reply I got a growled, "Been doing your homework, have you?" instead.

It took two days to complete the compass routine before heading down river to Greenock to ammunition ship. This was done at a buoy with ammunition lighters alongside. Two days again with everybody pressed into the physical torture of handling – and I mean handling – 1,000 rounds of 4.7" shells, each weighing about half a hundredweight. They came to the ship packed in cases to be broken open in the lighter. Each shell was then handed from the lighter-hold to a man on the deck, then to another on *Redoubt*'s deck for a relay team of handlers to move half the quantity to the for'ard messdeck and down two decks to the shell-room racks serving 'A' and 'B' guns. The other half were humped aft, down two decks and into the racks of 'X' and 'Y' guns shell room. In addition there were a thousand rounds of cordite each to the after and for'ard magazines, not to mention 7,200 rounds of pom-pom ammunition in 40 lb cases of 20 rounds, 14,400 rounds of Oerlikon, plus a plethora of star-shells, rockets, flares, demolition charges and small arms ammunition boxes. All moved, lifted and lowered by means of old-established 'handraulic' equipment – like backs, arms, shoulders and thighs. By sunset each day the messdecks echoed with creaks and groans usually associated with a hospital geriatric ward.

Loch Long is a 'compass needle' of a parallel-sided lake – twenty five miles long, quarter of a mile wide for most of its length, with the pretty little village of Arrochar balanced on its northern tip. The southern end finished in the Firth of Clyde. The banks were beautifully wooded, and mountains rising to 3,000 feet, like Ben Lomond, Ben Arthur and Ben Donich, looked down on the loch from both sides. The scenic beauty was hard to believe as *Redoubt* slid gently along the placid water to Arrochar, with the grime and hustle of Glasgow left thirty miles away. But Arrochar was also the home of the Whitehead Torpedo Factory and the next few days were spent on torpedo trials and calibrations. As a member of the ship's torpedo party I must have been involved, but don't remember much, except that we seemed to be forever running up and down that loch firing torpedoes with dummy heads, steaming after them until they were out of fuel with buoyant yellow heads bobbing vertically on the surface, then spending hours out in the boats snaring them in with wire ropes to be hauled up on deck, scrubbed clean of oil, grease and loch detritus, before preparing the eight one-ton projectiles for another test-run.

This went on for four days with everybody too whacked at the end of each day to think of going ashore, even if there was anywhere to go. But Saturday night was party-night in Arrochar, when the boys in blue were invited by the villagers – most of whom worked in the torpedo factory – to a hoe-down-like festival and barn dance. The music was of the homespun variety, with the caller singing out to take your partner for a 'Strathspey', a 'Dashing White Sergeant' or a 'Sir Roger de Coverley'! It was a great evening of rustic merriment with a strong Highland flavour and many warm friendships developed therefrom with the local people.

Then it was off to war – well, not exactly war, but a four week period of speed trials, gunnery and torpedo shoots, evolutions, boat drills and Lord knows what else needed to try and convert a bunch of half-baked sailors and a brand new ship without any war record into a deadly fighting unit, honed to the peak of efficiency. But the country had been at war for three years and the Navy had lost half its tried and tested personnel and ships. Although new ships were being built faster than ever to replace our staggering losses, only time could train and build up the quality crews they needed. People were being sent to sea in fighting ships months before they were capable of fulfilling a useful function, in the desperate hope that the handful of experienced men with whom they were to sail would help guide them through the strange ways and words of a new environment.

There was the time when the guns crews closed up for cruising stations for the first time on the forty-eight hour run up from Greenock to Scapa Flow. The captain of the port side pom-poms delegated one of his crew to do a trick on the bridge as a lookout. "When you get up there", he was told, "Report to the Officer of the Watch and he'll detail you off on what bearing you are to keep your eyes skinned and how to report any movement or object." Off went the youth and arriving on the bridge wandered around staring at all the strange people and items of equipment until the irate Office of the Watch sang out, "You there – who are you and what do you want?" "I've been sent up, Sir, to be a lookout." "Where have you come from?" barked the officer. "Oldham," was the guileless reply!

Come the day we did an H.A. 'shoot' with an R.N.A.S. plane towing a wind-sock, or drogue, past the ship on a very long wire, and our main armament 4.7 guns firing independently at the drogue. But despite the long wire the H.A. shells were bursting far closer to the towing plane that to the towed drogue, until over the R.T. came the somewhat panicky voice of the pilot with, "Hey down there, tell that bunch of cowboys on your guns that I'm pulling this bastard, not pushing it!"

The less said about Scapa Flow the better. It's got to be the most dreary, God-forsaken, treeless, windswept landfall known to Jolly Jack, but by the time we got back in from exercises each day – usually after three or four vain attempts at mooring to a buoy – everybody was too tired to fancy a run ashore just for a beer and an old film at the canteen. It would involve half an hour in the 'trot-boat' across the black forbidding waters to the distant landing stage, and then back again a few hours later with a drunken crowd of matelots singing out of tune.

Mooring ship is something most readers will know about, but mooring *Redoubt* was forever a disaster. It meant the ship being coaxed carefully under difficult wind and tide conditions while approaching the buoy, and then dropping its whaler from the davits on to the turbulent ocean while still some distance away, to be pulled round to the buoy. One of the whaler's crew – the buoy-jumper – would scramble on to the flat top of the wave-tossed buoy and with a light-line pull a picking-up wire from the ship to be shackled to the buoy. The other end of the picking-up wire is then attached to the capstan for winching the ship up close enough so the anchor chain can be lowered through the hawse pipe for the buoy-jumper to shackle to the buoy ring. The ship capstan lets out or takes up the slack in the chain, the buoy-jumper collects his bits and pieces and climbs back in the whaler, the boat's crew pull round to the davits, lower deck is cleared to hoist 'em all back inboard, and the ship rides on the waves – securely moored.

That's how it's supposed to happen according to the book. But with half a gale blowing and the ship slewing, starting and stopping either or both engines in efforts to creep up and keep station with the wildly tossing whaler or buoy-jumper without doing either of them too much injury, and the fact that most of the people involved (including the captain) are still learning, the buoy-jumper falls in the water three or four times, the ship misses the buoy and has to go round again – and again – the picking-up wire gets lost over the side, and everybody's weary, wet through, and 'in the rattle' for incompetence!

After four weeks of endless evolution and effort there must have been some improvement because Rear-Admiral/Destroyers, 'Nutty' Burnett, came aboard one morning with his retinue and lower deck was cleared. He delivered a pep-talk on how fortunate we were to be considered competent enough to be sent to join the Fleet on a brand new and powerful destroyer as part of the 11th Destroyer Flotilla at a most crucial stage of the war. And although he didn't actually say as much, the look on his face brought to mind the Duke of Wellington's words to his aide when surveying the latest bunch of replacement troops sent out from England in the Napoleonic Wars:

"Whether they'll ever frighten the enemy remains to be seen but, by God, they certainly scare the wits out of me!"

Nobody had yet given out just where and when we were to join up with the Fleet but conjecture was rife. Hopefully, it wouldn't be the Home Fleet as its base was Scapa Flow and we'd all had enough of that. Slipping its Scapa moorings for the last time, *Redoubt* crossed the storm-ridden Pentland Firth and headed south down the west coast of Scotland. Next evening we were at Dalmuir Basin on the Clyde doing our first boiler clean, all done rather hurriedly before filling up with oil, water and provisions, besides replacing what was used up ammunition-wise during the trials at Scapa. Heading back down the Clyde we anchored in the dark off Gourock. The ship was now really charged up and ready for the fray.

During the night came the customary sound of getting under way and the prop shafts turning in their tunnel just a few feet below my hammock in the switchroom. Venturing out on the upper deck once there was enough visibility – not a lot bearing in mind it was a dreary late-November morning with daylight running from about 9.00am to 3.00pm in that latitude. But there was quite enough to see that *Redoubt* was out of sight of land and in the middle of a vast acreage of water full of troopships, fast merchant ships and warships all steaming south at about sixteen knots, and – as was learned later – on their way to Algiers in support of the first Army landings in North Africa. In our midst was a battleship, an aircraft carrier, three cruisers and about ten destroyers – a formidable escort, but well justified as there were over 60,000 troops in 23 large liners among us, not to mention the cargo vessels and their contents.

It bore no relationship to those east coast convoys I'd known. Although we had often escorted large groups of fast ships in *Verdun*, due to the restricted width of the swept channel they could only steam in pairs like a 'crocodile' of school children, and the escort vessels were no larger than sloops, frigates and H.A. destroyers like *Verdun*. But this Algiers convoy was spread over all the visible ocean with planes landing and taking off from the aircraft carrier to keep a watchful eye for submarines in the surrounding waters. On 30th November we were two days out of the Clyde and approaching Gibraltar. The sun shone, a balmy spice-laden breeze wafted off the coast of Spain, and the giant convoy made a majestic sight on a gently heaving ocean, with *Redoubt* and an Australian destroyer, *Quickmatch,* riding 'shotgun' on its north-western flank. It was late morning when our radar scanner picked up a blip on its screen where no blip ought to have been. Take *Quickmatch,* said the senior escort officer when signalled, "And go check it out!" It meant steaming away at high speed for several hours in a north-westerly direction, but the search was rewarded when sighting a single merchant ship of some 10,000 tons. When questioned, she claimed to be the Swedish ship *Nanking.* This message was transmitted to our senior ship in the convoy with details of course, speed and position when intercepted. It was wirelessed to Admiralty at 1635 seeking instructions. At 1726 the Admiralty replied, 'Ship is not, repeat NOT, Swedish *Nanking*. Italian blockade runner *Cortellazzo* is estimated to be in about this position.' (It must have been tea time in Whitehall for them to take 50 minutes to provide this information!)

We immediately stopped circling the *Cortellazzo*, told them the game was up and to abandon ship immediately. Their Capitano Palidini said the weather was too bad to take to the boats, but a short "Get on with it – you've got five minutes!", through the loud hailer from Lt. Comm. Rhoades in *Quickmatch*, and a couple of 4.7" shells across the bows from *Redoubt*, had a white flag fluttering up their signal halliards in double quick time. Pandemonium set in as their boats were lowered and rapidly filled in efforts to escape before the ultimatum expired. One boats' crew pulled like mad in a rowing style seldom seen at Henley, and about thirty of them struggled up the scrambling net we'd draped over the port side aft.

One was impressed by the quality of self-discipline shown as deckhands, officers and what turned out to be German intelligence agents scrambled desperately over each other to reach the outstretched hands of those of us trying to pull them aboard. They were housed under guard in the watchkeeper's mess up for'ard – the 'residents' being forced to find temporary accommodation elsewhere – and the half dozen or so Germans that were aboard the *Cortellazzo* were kept in the bo'sun's store down the tiller flat. This was considered advisable as little love was lost between the two sets of prisoners, and two Germans had already been shot and tipped over the side under mysterious circumstances during the boat ride across to our ships. Capitano Palidini made it clear that Italians had no quarrel with England and that they were sailing under orders from their German masters in transporting 2,000 tons of aircraft machinery from Bordeaux to Japan. He also made no secret of the fact that our German friends were believed to be Gestapo agents.

The senior officer of the convoy was asked by W.T. signal what he would have us do with the now abandoned *Cortellazzo*. Put a prize crew aboard? Put the Italians back and have her sail with us after the convoy? Or just sink her and get back to protecting our valuable ships and men? Light was failing and the wind rising when we were told to get rid of her and come back to work on the job we were meant to do.

"Right," said Lt. Comm. Roper, "we can do with some gunnery practice", and our 4.7's proceeded to poke her full of holes, but she didn't seem to mind and still rode the waves effortlessly; so he said, "We can't hang about and we can't leave her floating around in the dark as a menace to shipping, so let's put a torpedo into her." There's a faded photograph from a *Redoubt* shipmate on one of the illustrated pages showing the *Cortellazzo* on the receiving end of that torpedo at the moment of impact. In his covering letter he said he was on the bridge signalling to *Quickmatch* with an Aldis lamp when he stopped to take that photo – quite illegal as it happens –

and suggests it was me that sunk the *Cortellazzo*. Much as I would love to bask in the glory, Eric, it was another L.T.O. in charge of that operation, but sink her he certainly did. With the result that once she started dropping deeper into the water we left the scene and steamed like mad towards Gibraltar and the convoy.

By this time there was quite a sea running and our miserable passengers had a rough time of it as we hurtled through the waves. They were all physically sick, especially the Germans, who being down aft in the tiller flat had every bit of arrogance bounced out of their haggard, yellow features. Reaching Gibraltar in the small hours *Redoubt* tied up alongside the wall – without hitting anything (I think) – and the prisoners marched off blindfolded in the tender care of a well-armed military guard.

From Gibraltar we went into Algiers, which had only recently been prised free of Axis and Vichy French rule. Our First Army was in command although there were any amount of unfriendly people about, but as it was currently our 'bat and ball', leave was given to half the ship's company from 1.00 to 5.00pm. The Captain said a few words at the gangway to those about to go ashore, reminding them that there were still plenty of people in Algiers who did not like us or our country, and we all would be judged by individual behaviour in Algiers. In short, we were 'ambassadors' of Britain!

Special Allied Army of Occupation money had to be drawn to spend ashore, at the exchange rate of 300 francs to £1. When reaching the first bar it was most encouraging to find that the beer was 2 francs a glass, as was the *vin blanc* or *rouge*. With the result that by the end of the afternoon, many an 'ambassador' was found flaked out on the road back to the ship. Nevertheless, nobody did, or came to, any real harm, despite our having been warned that we'd better stick together in groups of six or more to avoid loners or couples being set upon by the lawless mobs said to be roaming the streets around the dock area.

The only lawless people I remember was a small crowd of us off *Redoubt* who, having left it a bit late for getting back to the ship from the Casbah before the end of our leave, rushed out to look for means of transport to cover the couple of miles involved. There was only a ramshackle gharry with a decrepit mule and an Arab driver, who protested wildly as we climbed aboard, shouting, "Dockyard, dockyard!", at the prospect of his poor old moke transporting ten happy, singing matelots through the streets of Algiers. As he wouldn't start away I seem to remember us climbing out of the car, unshackling the horse, tossing its reins to the still protesting driver on the cart, grabbing the shafts, and doubling all the way to the dockyard pulling the cart and singing like mad, with the driver – who by now had joined in the spirit of things – calling out when we had to take a turn to the *gauche* or *droit*. I believe we stopped to pick up one or two 'ambassadors' on the way. Reaching the dockyard we let go the shafts, chucked whatever spare Occupation cash we had left into the cart for the driver, and dashed through the gates back aboard *Redoubt*, leaving our hi-jacked guide to

143

get his act together again before returning to the Casbah in search of a similar stroke of lucrative luck.

Can't remember if we beat the clock, but we certainly deserved merit points for trying!

Redoubt then did some work around the Mediterranean before receiving orders to return post-haste to Gibraltar in company with *Quickmatch* and *Racehorse*, and from thence, after re-fuelling, to the Clyde. On the way back *Racehorse* signalled that torpedoes were approaching our port side. Turning hard-a-port they were spotted in time from the bridge as they sped past the ship and no harm was done – otherwise somebody else may have had to write all this!

Harry Potterton, one of my current ex-*Redoubt* pals, relates that when approaching Gibraltar he was on watch as a coder in the W.T. office – and was given an instruction to code up a signal for transmission to Fleet Officer Commanding at Gib., giving our ETA (expected time of arrival). All signals carried a 4-figure prefix denoting order of priority. He'd been working long spells of watch-and-watch – four hours on and four hours off – since leaving the Clyde and was feeling the strain, with the result that his coded signal began with the prefix figures signifying 'enemy sighting report'. Within ten minutes the duty W.T. officer came charging in all of a panic to say that signal was on top priority being repeated from F.O.C. every couple of minutes to every vessel and shore base in the Fleet and the whole of the Med. was on 'Red Alert!'

The matter, of course, was reported to the Captain who was summoned to report to the Base Communications Officer as soon as we got in. Harry heard no more of it but was later given to understand the Captain explained that the rating responsible for the coded misplonk was all of nineteen years old and until a couple of months previous was a junior clerk on the London Midland & Scottish Railway!

Speculation was rife on why they wanted us back so quickly and opinions ranged from the belief we were going to be decorated and marched to the Guildhall under ticker-tape for the way we handled the *Cortellazzo* affair, to the possibility that the three ships had been selected to spearhead an attack on the Gestapo HQ at Brest as our German prisoners had provided vital information on how the defences could be pierced from the sea. Needless to say, nobody told us anything until, after having re-fuelled, watered and provisioned at Greenock, we put to sea again late on the evening of December 20th – just twenty-four hours after our arrival from the Mediterranean.

British shipyards were overcrowded and vulnerable to enemy air attacks, so that when it came to laying up our newest, largest and most powerful aircraft carrier for a badly needed major refit – about six months work – the powers-that-be felt they had to look outside Britain.

It was just a year after Pearl Harbor and naval liaison between Britain and the USA in the combined effort to defeat the common enemy was a credit to both countries. So much so that when the Admiralty told the Pentagon about their problem in getting *Victorious* back into good fighting trim they got a laconic "No problem", in reply. "Just you get your carrier over into our yards at Norfolk, Virginia, as soon as you can," it went on, "and we'll fix her up real good. After that, let her come out into the Pacific with our Fleet and help us knock the bejasus out of them Japanese S.O.B's! That s what we call good ole American horse-trading. Now what time shall I tell my boys in Norfolk to expect you?" "Just as soon," was the prompt reply, "as I can get *Redoubt* and a couple of her destroyer pals back from Algiers to look after *Victorious* while crossing the Atlantic."

So there we were ploughing our way through one of the worst and most prolonged sessions of ocean violence ever encountered. Night and day we staggered and zig-zagged through those waves, but mostly under them, closed up in two watches in readiness for any U-boat stupid enough to come out in that weather. *Quickmatch* and *Racehorse* were seldom visible and even *Victorious* claimed she was shipping it green across her flight deck – seventy feet up in the air – but still managing to get planes on and off for anti U-boat patrols.

Galley fires were impossible to light, so Christmas Day came and went with corned beef and pusser's kye as the *table d'hôte* speciality, set off with a little pusser's rum from what some put aside from the daily tot over the past week or two. Father Christmas would have needed a wet-suit to get down our funnel as I believe half the Atlantic Ocean was slopping over the top of it.

The organiser of the HMS *Victorious*-veteran magazine kindly sent me the following from his write-up of their ship s commission:

"On the day before Christmas Day the gale was consistently recorded at 95 mph. The ship was being battered unmercifully. The effect of the constant movement was very debilitating. Apart from the stomach-wrenching emptiness at the rising and plunging, the problem of maintaining a proper balance as the ship also rolled and cork-screwed brought on headaches and nausea.

*The destroyers [*Redoubt, Racehorse *and* Quickmatch*] were undergoing absolute torment almost halted at times by the enormous seas. Continuous shipping of water meant that conditions on board were atrocious, their crews working and resting in sodden clothes, and eating cold, tinned food."*

The night after Christmas it was even worse. Coming off watch – I believe I was then doing spells on the depth charges to relieve the other two L.T.O.'s – with the wind shrieking and the seas crashing all around, I reached the comparative shelter of the after lobby, opened the hatch and descended into the friendly warmth of the switch-room lit by a low-wattage blue security light. Thankfully, as it turned out, I didn't fully-close or fasten the hatch-cover clips behind me. Little time was wasted getting sodden clothes off down to my socks, and then I took them off too. After a rough towelling from head to food, ignoring the creaking, pitching, rolling and banging all around and, naked as a new-born babe, I jumped into my hammock and knew no more.

But not for long. I was awakened by sparks flashing and spluttering akin to a fire-works display with the switchroom engulfed with yellow smoke, while torrents of sea water were sploshing in from somewhere. Bare 4" x ½" copper busbars brought the ship's DC 240 V electricity supply from the engine room generators to my switch-board. These bars were run at high level and supported at intervals by Tufnol insu-lating blocks. The brute force of wind and sea over the previous four days of gales had so weakened the welded deck joints where the after-superstructure – on which 'Y' gun was mounted – joined the open upper deck, that they'd finally given way and sea water was slurping into the switchroom with every lurch of the ship. The leak was immediately above the busbars where they entered the switchroom through the engine room bulkhead and sea water poured across the positive bar down the insu-lating block and on to the negative bar. With no protective fuses or circuit breakers the resultant short circuit had created a miniature Fourth of July as I scrambled from my hammock and grabbed the fire-extinguisher clipped to the bulkhead alongside my pin-up of Ann Southern.

Pumping the CO2 jet as hard as I could at the madly hissing flames, with acrid yellow smoke all around, I don't remember much more until I found myself, still starkers and freezing cold, stretched out on the iron deck with turbulent seas crash-ing over me; and the Chief Stoker, one of a small crowd holding me from being washed overboard, asking how I was feeling now.

Apparently, one of the gun's crew had made his way to the after galley to brew up the kye for those on watch and noticed smoke billowing out of the half-closed hatch. The adjoining hatch led to the Chief Petty Officers' mess and he promptly knocked the clips off the lid and called out that he thought there was a fire down in the switch-room. They tumbled out and apparently somebody thought I might be down there. Wearing breathing apparatus a couple went down the ladder and found me stretched out on the deck in all my pristine glory. The lads gallantly manhandled me up the ladder, but it wasn't until hit by wind, rain and ocean that I came to suffi-ciently to learn what it was all about.

That seemed to mark the end of our storm-tossed voyage for by the following morning the sea was relatively calm and all ships could be seen riding rhythmically on a long easy swell. The bad weather had taken a lot of our fuel supplies and it was decided that we would take it in turns to replenish from *Victorious*. *Redoubt* would be first. It involved both ships – 'mini David' and 'maxi Goliath' – steering a dead par-allel course, about ten yards apart, and maintaining an identical speed of about

146

three knots. A difficult thing to do on a flat inland lake, never mind in a heavy Atlantic swell, and the slower the speed, the more both ships rolled at the mercy of wind and sea, and the more apprehensive everybody became.

Once the two ships were in position, a gun-line operator from *Victorious* fired a cord across to us. To this was tied a thicker line, and then a rope with which the vital 'umbilical' oil-hose was pulled across.

Getting that 6" diameter armoured hose linked up between the two ships was quite a feat as – for all the world like a skyscraper and a bungalow – they tried to avoid over-straining or over-slackening it during the evolution. Our Chief Stoker, with a large axe, stood by the hose where it was coupled up to *Redoubt*'s deck valve, just in case we got wind of a lurking U-boat and had to galvanise into action.

But danger came from a far friendlier source than an enemy submarine. Hardly had *Victorious* began pumping the precious stuff through that 'umbilical' link that the huge aircraft carrier started to lean toward us in a playful wallowing roll. Her massive grey wall heeled over to starboard and seemed never to stop descending, as she blotted out the sky and crunched her AA gundecks into both our bridge and after-superstructures. Stricken with awe we waited to be flipped on our side like an old sardine can, but just when that looked almost inevitable she stopped shoving, paused, and started to rise, before going into her reverse roll. A string of orders from *Redoubt*'s bridge had the engines scream into full-speed-ahead, the deck take a 30-degree list as the wheel went hard-a-starboard, and horrible black sludge gushed everywhere when the Chief Stoker sliced right through that hose in one crashing swing of his axe! As a result we were well out of the way by the time *Victorious* decided to roll back for another playful nuzzle up against her little friend.

It's an ill wind, etc. Seeing that both destroyers were now too low on fuel to risk continuing to Chesapeake Bay without a top-up, it was decided that *Victorious* would go it alone through the comparatively safe waters of the western Atlantic until she could rendezvous with a couple of US escort ships – now on their way out of Norfolk in answer to her signal. Meanwhile *Redoubt*, *Quickmatch* and *Racehorse* headed for the nearest 'filling station' – Bermuda.

It was 9.00am New Year's Day 1943, when they moored-up in the harbour at Ireland Island, the Allied naval base in the most westerly of the chain of islands that make up that idyllic archipelago. The sun shone, we swam and fished from the ship s side and from the pink sandy beaches ashore for the next three days, during which time the ship underwent first aid repairs from the dockyard staff.

It was 700 miles from Bermuda to the Chesapeake, where the two 'R'-boats and one 'Q'-boat made a spectacular high-speed 'Admiralty-sweep' into its sheltered waters at 7.00am on the morning of 5th January 1943. Harbour ferries plying between Norfolk and Newport News were crowded with early-morning travellers on their way to work. They were seen to heel over dangerously – the ferries, that is – as

147

the said early-morning-travellers threw down newspapers and rushed to the sides, cheering and waving, at the unexpected spectacle of three British warships racing through the dawn's early light – each with a huge white 'bone in its teeth' and a brand new white ensign streaming aft above its boiling wake. A most impressive piece of showing the flag, that.

The general belief over there at the time was that Britain was clapped out and almost on the point of defeat – which didn't quite fit in with our swashbuckling grandstand entry into their 'holy' waters, as was said more than once during the ensuing five days that *Redoubt* spent in dock at Newport News, where technicians, shipwrights and mechanics made good the damage caused by both the Atlantic and HMS *Victorious*. Those of us who went ashore wallowed in good old Southern hospitality, while gawping in disbelief at the displays of food and confectionery in the first brilliantly-lit shopping streets seen for almost three-and-a-half years.

When entering dry dock in Newport News to have storm damage put right by United States dockyard staff, the senior engineer in charge of repairs to the switchboard became a good friend and couldn't get over the primitive nature of our equipment. He reckoned they'd never get an American sailor to go to sea and face electrical hazards such as we took for granted. As a token of his respect he suggested we meet in his favourite bar when I went ashore later that first day, and this we did. He was standing up at the bar with a couple of friends when I entered and introduced me while calling for a beer. Ordering a cigar he invited me to have one. "No thanks," I replied politely, "I don t smoke." "Don t smoke?" he echoed quizzically. "Sailor, it ain't a matter of smoking, it's a matter of a guy being properly balanced with a glass in one fist and a good five-cent ceegar in the other!"

Testing it out and finding there was a lot in what he said I tried staying 'properly balanced' for the ensuing forty years or so, during which time my daily 'balancing pole' grew longer, fatter and cost a little more than 5 cents. But I gave it up when a little coronary bother started up back in the early 80's culminating in a triple-bypass in '91. Don't miss it either, except when, after cutting the lawn on a summer's evening, I'd pour myself a malt, sit on the back porch, light up a cigar, and contentedly survey my handiwork and surrounding rural scene from my hilltop vantage point. I still do, of course, but since '82 there's been no accompanying lazy curl of blue smoke from a choice Havana leaf!

From the Chesapeake, *Redoubt*, *Racehorse* and *Quickmatch* took a convoy of tankers down to Curacoa in the Dutch West Indies and about 100 miles off the coast of Venezuela. The island was virtually a huge oil refinery and German U-boats were operating off the US coast preying on ships using those waters without a proper escort. The previous convoy had a weak escort force and half the tankers plus the

148

one destroyer were sunk. So we had to wait around a few days while another group of tankers were prepared for taking the much needed fuel about six thousand miles back to Europe.

While waiting – about three days – it was found that the temperature of the air and the sea water were the same – about 86 degrees. Diving into the harbour from the ship's side was about as refreshing as diving into the warm sump of an old banger! It certainly smelt and tasted like one. What I always remember about Curacoa was that a packet of English cigarettes was better than any currency and the shopkeepers did a brisk business undertaking to supply, wrap and send the presents we selected to our loved ones for a tin of 50 cork-tipped Craven 'A' – although my wife wasn't too enamoured with the sheer silk slip and knicker set, kimono and dainty slippers I'd got for her, as she said the heel came off one of the slippers the first time she wore them – almost pitching her down the stairs – and the undies virtually disintegrated the first time she went to wash them. Still, as I said in reply, you can't win 'em all and even if I wasn't about 6,000 miles from Curacoa by the time her letter reached me I couldn't have got my money back as the shopkeeper had probably smoked them all by this time!

From the Curacoa refineries the three destroyers successfully escorted the six heavily-laden tankers across the Atlantic without undue incident, to the best of my memory. Travelling in the tropics on a flat calm sea with brilliant hot sunshine all day and soft warm starlit nights, the trip across was almost the exact opposite to our previous transatlantic crossing. Just like they describe ocean cruises in the luxury brochures, only the second class cabins were just a little more crowded (there were eighteen in ours – 39 if you count the blokes in 15 mess from whom we were separated by just a row of low lockers) and the food could have been a little more exotic! But we had a canvas pool rigged on the fo'c'sle filled with sea water where those off watch could cool off in the heat of the day.

Re-fuelling every couple of days, too, was also the very opposite to our first experience when trying to do so from *Victorious* in that diabolical east/west crossing. A tanker would slow down, we'd move up as she dropped a grass rope astern to which the line holding the oil hose was attached. Once we'd taken it aboard via the capstan it was child's play connecting up to the fuel inlet on deck and filling up our tanks. This had to be done three or four times during the 14-day crossing.

Approaching the western bulge of North Africa our Asdics picked up an echo which had the ship at Action Stations in a trice. Despite patterns of depth charges being dropped, the amplified 'pings' echoed ever nearer round the ship, until – putting the helm over to align with the last reported bearing – 'full speed ahead both engines' was ordered and everybody braced for collision as *Redoubt* tore in at 30 knots right on target! There came a sickening thud and everybody cheered as they rushed to the ship's side to gloat over our success. Slowly an ominous black shape

149

drifted to the surface and the cheering gradually subsided as we gazed upon the two halves of a rather large and much-bloodied whale!

Unfortunately the captain refused our artistic Chief Engine Room Artificer permission to go over the side in a bosun's chair to paint a sperm whale above our much-buckled bows!

During the ramming quite a lot of no-good had been done to vital underwater equipment. The Asdic dome and Pitometer log come immediately to mind (the former is the means of detecting, locating and monitoring submarine activity, while the log records the speed a ship is travelling through the water), which meant *Redoubt* could not be of much use, escort-wise, until she got herself into a dry dock.

Fortunately, Casablanca in French Morocco had been captured by United States sea-borne forces only a couple of months earlier from the Vichy French, and were operating a well-established shipyard complex there, whereby we could receive first aid repairs before proceeding to Gibraltar for our own people and stores to get us properly set up again. The Americans had moved in from the Atlantic on Western Morocco at dawn on November 8th 1942, and the unfinished French battleship *Jean Bart* in Casablanca basin had engaged the US battleship *Massachusetts* in a game of long-distance 'bowls' with her four 15" guns. She was finally overcome by the American accuracy and her gutted hulk towed and tied up against the wall not far from where the liberty men came ashore from *Redoubt* a couple of months later. The Vichy French ships, having refused to surrender, had put to sea and fought bravely but suffered over 1,000 casualties before they threw in the towel.

It was into this volatile atmosphere that the starboard watch of *Redoubt* set out on a run ashore where once again we were told that the majority of people, whether French, Arab or American, had not had previous contact with the British and probably didn't like us on principle. We again got Occupation Money at 300 francs to the £1 and, as at Algiers, beer and wine was two francs a glass. And again as at Algiers, we were exhorted to conduct ourselves as true ambassadors.

I think the fight started in the Casbah when one of our party asked an American sailor how come he had all these medal ribbons on his chest, when they hadn't been in the war five minutes. To which the reply came that they were battle honours won in action. "Battle honours won in action?" echoed our man scornfully. "Why I've seen more battles and action on a Saturday night in the 'White Horse' at Harwich than you're ever likely to know about. Why don't you tell the truth, and say they give 'em away for 'nutty'* wrappers in your canteen!" Well, it's amazing how soon their white-suited and gaitered shore-patrol came roaring into the bar. Half of them clobbering

---

* 'Navalese' for chocolate and sweets.

ABOVE: *1923. Mum proudly surveys my big sister and two younger brothers with me, all of 6, on the right. That's our one-up, one-down cottage, in which six of us lived within sound of Bow Bells.*

BELOW: *The council flat where mum and dad were killed by the last V2 to hit London in March 1945. I was with the Far Eastern Fleet at the time.*

THE FAMILY FLAT

LEFT: *A civilian when wed at Christmas 1939.*

BELOW LEFT: *Home on leave, six months later.*

BELOW: *'Early naval encounters.' The reverse of the medal says:*
HMS Raleigh 1940
Ordinary Seaman SJ Morley
Middleweight
Finalist
(See page 93).

The Unknown Warrior's homecoming, November 1920.
ABOVE: *The* Verdun *docking at Dover.* BELOW: *The body borne in procession from the quay.*

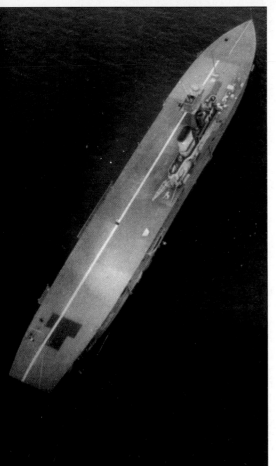

ABOVE: *HMS* Verdun, *October 1940 to May 1942.*

LEFT: *A birds eye-view of Fleet Tender 'C', the dummy aircraft carrier HMS* Hermes-Two *before it was left by HMS* Verdun *off the mouth of the Humber in June 1941, perched pic-a-back on a sunken trawler for the ensuing ten years or more.*

ABOVE: *HMS* Redoubt *September 1942 to May 1944.*

RIGHT: *Bullseye!* Redoubt *torpedo hits* Cortellazo – *Italian blockade runner (p142).*

BELOW: Redoubt *and* Racehorse *members remember the fallen while on leave at Kimberley, South Africa (p158). (Author back row, extreme right).*

ABOVE: *Roedean School for Girls and* alma mater *of Roedean Old Boys Association (ROBA)!*

BELOW: *The waxwork tableau in Sentosa, Singapore, portrays the Japanese surrender to the Allied forces of SE Asia in September 1945.*

TOP: *The Royal Yacht, HMS* Britannia *enters Durban Harbour on Friday 24th March 1995.* Photograph with compliments of Natal Newspapers.

BOTTOM: *Sam Morley is presented to Her Majesty the Queen and HRH the Duke of Edinburgh alongside* Britannia, *and the one-and-a-half ton bronze 'lady' behind Sam proclaims her approval of the meeting.* Photograph with compliments of Richard Siedle – nephew of the Lady in White and brother of the artist.

ABOVE: *The finished Monument on its temporary base by the stern of the Royal Yacht.*

ABOVE RIGHT: *Barbara Siedle, the artist, is presented to the Queen.*

BELOW: *A final word to Barbara from our radiant Queen before leaving the scene to board* Britannia.

The engraved plates read:

DURBAN'S LADY IN WHITE

THE STORY BEHIND THE LEGEND. "BETWEEN 1940 AND 1945, THREE MILLION WW2 PERSONNEL SAILED THROUGH PERILOUS WATERS TO DURBAN EN ROUTE TO BURMA AND MEDITERRANEAN WAR ZONES. WITH MORALE AT LOW EBB, THEY WERE GREETED BY PERL SIEDLE GIBSON, INTERNATIONAL CONCERT SOPRANO, SINGING A WELCOME TO THE CROWDED DECKS GLIDING BY. SHE NEVER MISSED A CONVOY. NOT EVEN THE ONE THAT SAILED THE DAY SHE LEARNED HER ELDEST SON HAD BEEN KILLED WHILE SERVING WITH THE BLACK WATCH IN NORTH AFRICA.

PRIOR TO ITS UNVEILING ON AUGUST 15th 1995, THIS MONUMENT WAS STOOD ALONGSIDE HMS 'BRITANNIA' IN DURBAN HARBOUR TO BE VIEWED BY HER MAJESTY QUEEN ELIZABETH THE SECOND AND HRH THE DUKE OF EDINBURGH DURING THEIR STATE VISIT TO DURBAN 24TH MARCH 1995.

their own men with night sticks and dragging them off into the waiting jeeps, while the others waved loaded Colt 45's under British noses while shouting, "Back-off, limey, else I'll blow your head off!"

Being ambassadors, everybody duly backed off and I seem to remember a few questions being asked back on board that evening, but don't believe anything much ever came of that little *entente*-not-too-*cordiale*!

By this time the highly efficient American 'See Bees' had pumped out the floating dock and then our partially flooded engine room. It was then clearly revealed that destroyers should think twice before charging in on full-grown whales. The plates of the ship's side under water were bent and buckled for about fifty feet back from the once graceful stem-piece and all for'ard watertight bulkheads needed shoring-up before we could go to sea again for dry-docking and more permanent repairs else-where.

It meant maintaining a steady speed of eight to ten knots for the 300 mile run to Gibraltar for every yard of which we were a sitting duck to those countless invisible U-boats we felt were hovering around. With no Asdic dome there was no way to detect an underwater marauder and even if we had done so it would have been self-destruction to drop depth charges. At that speed we d have done our already battered hull a lot more damage than might have been inflicted by the enemy.

Entering harbour at Gibraltar it was soon painfully obvious that some time would elapse before we could leave it again as a self-respecting ship. At that stage of the war at sea Gibraltar was the nearest dockyard that could service damaged ships in the South Atlantic, Mediterranean and Indian Oceans. Badly damaged warships of many shapes and sizes lay around waiting their turn for one of the two dry docks or for vital parts to be flown out from England. The buzz went round that as we could still get along, albeit sedately, we'd be sent back to England to be mended.

But that was too much to hope for and the days passed while we waited and allowed even our long overdue backlog of mail to catch up. With twenty or thirty letters to deal with from loved ones the important thing was to get them in date order before starting to read, otherwise you'd learn that the baby had completely recovered from that nasty cold before knowing she'd gone down with it!

After a couple of weeks the arrival of a new Asdic dome from England had us into dry-dock, where the opportunity was taken to clean and repaint our well-fouled bottom while a new stem-piece was fitted and all underwater replacements and repairs executed. Then followed a concerted effort to get the ship topped up again with stores, ammunition, fuel and water before leaving Gibraltar on 21st March 1943, ready in all respects to play our part once again as a fully wound-up warship.

151

The first part was to join up with and help protect a large convoy on its way to South Africa and beyond, breaking away to escort a couple of ships into Bathurst, Gambia, about 2,000 miles from Gibraltar. It's funny how we all have different memories of the same place. I remember miles and miles of wide beaches with fine white sands and tall palm trees, just like in the holiday brochures. The sea was a beautiful blue, warm and delightful to swim in. For a West African penny the native boys would climb the trees and throw down a coconut, into which a hole could be punched just to drink the milk.

As it was Sunday, a party from those off watch marched to church service. With work to do on one of the engine room fans, I was right pleased to get out of that one, as those who went were obliged to wear pusser's tropical rig – the likes of which I had never seen before – or since, other than on a Morecombe and Wise show! Like white twill shirts with spinal pads, knee length voluminous shorts, and white solar helmets!

While lying alongside in Bathurst the ship was engulfed by a swarm of locusts that turned brilliant daylight into swirling twilight. Like extra large crickets or grasshoppers they settled everywhere and all hands turned to sweeping them up by the chirruping bucketful and chucking them over the side. Then, just as suddenly, they whirred up and away leaving just a few thousand dead and dying to be collected and disposed of. We were certainly learning good and fast that Africa didn't have much in common with Scapa even though both are washed by the same ocean.

Leaving Bathurst we took some ships to Freetown, about 600 miles further south. The only good thing I remember about Freetown was that we moored offshore, had a beer at King Tom's – a shack canteen on the beach – and that the naval base there was an old depot ship called *Edinburgh Castle* that was overrun with rats acting as though they owned the ship! After the war I understand she was towed out into deep water about twenty miles offshore and the sea-cocks opened up, but true to tradition, the horrible creatures left the sinking ship and struck out for the distant shoreline – probably ending up as the *plat du jour* for the giant sharks that abound in those waters.

There followed two and a half thousand miles of steaming under the Southern Cross and over the Equator until reaching Pointe Noire in French Equatorial Africa. George Mack, a fellow shipmate off *Redoubt* described Pointe Noire in his memoirs as

> *"a terrible, dank, steamy river mouth where it was easy to believe all those stories of 'Trader Horn" and the 'White Man s Grave'; A hellhole that stank of dead vegetation, of slimy things in the water, peculiar eerie noises from the jungle, which came down almost to the waterline and the rusty tanker from which we re-fuelled."*

152

It was a blessed relief to form up with the convoy again and breathe the good fresh ozone of the open sea over the next 4,000 miles.

Cape Town was a most beautiful experience. Lord knows how many impressions of Table Bay and Table Mountain have been written by those approaching it from the sea for the first time. None can ever do it justice. It is uncanny how tidily the 'white cloth' was laid on the 'table' – as though to welcome us to 'high tea'. The 'white cloth' is a dense white cloud, formed suddenly by barometric changes, that sits on the plateau top of the mountain – and just as suddenly swirls away leaving all the rocky gorges and fissures standing out in bas relief against the sunlit mountainside.

Leaving the troop and merchant ships to await their turn to enter the harbour, *Redoubt* and the other escort destroyers in company steamed round the peninsular to the naval base at Simons Town in False Bay (so named because until 300 years ago it was mainly British and Dutch ships that used those waters, and then only to get between England or Holland and their trading interests in the Far East. With the result that the South African coastal waters were poorly charted and many a homeward-bound ship was inclined to make a right hand turn when facing the open and apparently welcoming waters of the Bay instead of carrying on and not putting the wheel over to starboard until well past the Good Hope peninsular. Whereby both the trip and the ship were brought up short as the latter ran out of ocean and ploughed into the rock-strewn coast round about where Muizenberg High Street stands today!)

Simons Town was a long-established Royal Navy dockyard with all the shore-side equipment and facilities befitting the needs of warships belonging to an Empire upon which the sun was said never to set. But other than a couple of bars and a sea-man s hostel there wasn't much high-life around to contribute to the shore-side needs of healthy young sailors coming off those warships. For that, one would walk half a mile from the dockyard gates to Simons Town station, and take the fifty minute train ride to the Cape Town terminal in Adderley Street. Simons Town was the other end of the line on that particular route so with two or three trains an hour it was no difficulty for Jolly Jack, after wrecking his health with an excess of the good life midst the wild and woolly opportunities offered by the big city, to climb aboard his train and know no more until aroused by hoarse shouts of "Simons Town (or Snooky) – all change!" 'Snooky' being the colloquial Afrikaans for Simons Town.

Thousands of sailors who did that train ride between 1940 and 1944 remember it far more clearly than most other places visited on account of a dog – a Great Dane named Nuisance, or to give him his official title Able Seaman Just Nuisance. It is also the title of the dog's life story by Terence Sisson. Here's my descriptive introductory blurb from another book in which I write of him:

JUST NUISANCE AB

Introduction

This is the remarkable life-story of one of the most famous Great Danes of all time. Able Seaman Just Nuisance was formally inducted into the Royal Navy at Simons Town in August 1939, shortly before the outbreak of World War II, and his exploits during the war made him a legend in his lifetime. More than fifty years after his death and burial with naval honours at Simons Town, the legend lives on.

In Chapter Ten of **If it Wasn't for Golf ...!** *I describe a nostalgic return to Cape Town in 1987:*

"Another war-time memory was to be seen at Simons Town, where the Royal Navy had erected a monument to a Great Dane called 'Nuisance'. When sailors would take the train from Simons Town to the 'big time' in Cape Town during those war years, many would be a little the worse for wear by the time they caught the last train back aboard (well, with Château brandy five shillings a bottle one can understand why!) The approach to Cape Town station and the trains themselves would be haunted at night by vagrants known as 'skolly boys' – youths waiting to pounce on drunken matelots – like one of our stokers who was found in the gutter of Adderley Street with a bloodied head and robbed of his boots, money-belt and false teeth!

But Nuisance was the sailor's friend. He'd wander around the concourse of the station from early evening and attach himself to anybody in blue who looked vulnerable; walking by his side and snarling at non-naval types within twenty feet. He'd see him on to the train and then wander up and down throughout the 50-minute run to Simons Town, passing from carriage to carriage at the many stops en route; and woe betide any civilian trying to disturb a sleeping matelot. At Simons Town he'd accompany the lads on their walk in the dark to the dockyardand then back to the station for the next train to Cape Town to repeat the process. Sounds a bit like *Rin Tin Tin* or *Lassie Come Home*, but this is all unvarnished truth. I know – I was there!"

HMS *Redoubt* is even featured in Terence Sisson's story of Nuisance as he names the ship as one of the only two vessels of the hundreds visited by the Great Dane where the ship's pet was killed by the visitor. I remember the occasion well and described it in the same chapter as the foregoing excerpt from "If It Wasn t For Golf ...!"

"During the day Nuisance would feel free to come down to the dockyard and board any ship alongside in order to wander around its decks at will. Unfortunately he incurred the wrath of some of us on *Redoubt* when our little mongrel, Fritz, took exception to Nuisance tucking in at his own food dish and foolishly went for him. Picking Fritz up as a terrier would a rat, the Great Dane administered a couple of quick shakes and our poor little pet was no more.

The surprising thing was that the two dogs had often romped together previously when we were in Simons Town but I suppose poor old Fritz caught the big fellow on one of his bad days."

'The Cape' epitomised a unique holiday from the war for those that could afford drinking at the Delmonico, dancing at Muizenberg, and swimming at Fish Hoek, *ad infinitum*, but fortunately we seldom spent more than two or three days there before it was off to work again, thereby allowing funds to accrue a little before the next run ashore. On that first occasion we picked up a convoy from Cape Town and escorted it for a further 1,200 miles round southern Africa and into the Indian Ocean until we reached Durban on the East Coast.

CHAPTER FIFTEEN

Durban

Six hundred years ago Mary Tudor was reputed to have said, "When I am dead and opened you shall find Calais lying in my heart." In my case I think it'll be Durban. Not that I had an inkling of it when *Redoubt* glided into its spacious harbour to the welcoming strains of 'Land of Hope and Glory' from a white-clad lady with a superb soprano voice singing and waving from the pier as we passed. Over the ensuing years we entered and left that harbour many times, to be greeted, both entering and leaving, in a similar fashion by the same lady with an endless repertoire of songs, ancient and modern. Her story and the part it has played in my affairs since 1990 is told later.

Of course, few on *Redoubt* knew anything of this 'redoubtable lady' and her reputation as we sailed past her for the first time on the 21st May 1943.

It wasn't long after we had tied up against the mile-long stretch of Mayden Wharf that leave was piped and I went ashore at 1.00pm. Strolling towards the town centre on a warm sunny Sunday I reached Durban's main thoroughfare – West Street. Hardly a building was more than a couple of storeys high. I preferred going ashore alone the first time in a strange place as it gave opportunity to stop and stare, whereas doing it group-wise with shipboard cronies, first stop is invariably the first bar – and quite often the same bar goes on to be the last one, too. Which doesn't give much to remember. I'd brought a pair of trunks and a towel with me and sauntering in the general direction of the ocean, a civilian came over and asked if I'd had my lunch yet. On learning I hadn't he said, "That's very good news as me and my family are about to sit down and have ours and there's nothing we'd like more than to share it with one or two of you young men so far from Sunday lunch with your own families. Just you wait here a moment and I'll be right back." He'd seen a British soldier passing on the far side of the pavement and gone over to rope him in as well.

He was brought over and after we'd all exchanged names our new-found host led the way to his home two or three blocks from where we d been 'picked-up'. There's nothing I can remember now about the house, the people in it, or what we had for lunch, except that they were a family of five with two grown-up boys and a girl, plus

156

another couple who lived close by. We were offered fruit juice or lager when we entered, and were then seated at a large table in the garden while the sons cooked steaks and sausages on the white hot embers of an open fire. Asked about the kind of life led in the old country I told of my trade, at which our host and his neighbour earnestly maintained that I should think seriously about coming to live in South Africa after the war, as the opportunities would be endless. In fact they gave full names and relevant details with the request that I let them know just as soon as I was ready to come as they were sure there'd be no difficulty with finding a home or employment. Well, I never ever did put the offers to the test and believe it's probably a little too late to do so now.

One memory of that first Sunday lunch in Durban was the luscious help-yourself salads piled in large bowls around the table. It was the first time I'd ever seen or tasted avocado pear. Nobody around the table believed me when I said as much until my fellow guest – the 'squaddie' from, I believe, Derby – confirmed that he'd never ever heard of avocado pears, but was frightened to say anything until he'd heard me do so. Of course, being an imported luxury not many had ever found their way on to British plebian tables – especially during the shortages of war time shipping space.

Lunch over and having taken leave of my kind hosts with promises to keep in touch, I carried on to the beaches and gazed with awe at the huge Indian Ocean rollers pounding endlessly over the surf and sand. It was hot, and the waters looked tempting. Diving through the first roller I was swept head over heels into a maelstrom of swirling water that sucked and threw me in every direction until, more dead than alive, I was thrown up on the beach with almost every square inch of my body lacerated by the gritty sand. It was several days before the soreness went and although in the ensuing wartime years I visited Durban a dozen times or more, those Hawaii-Five-O type rollers were always treated with healthy respect.

About three days later we left Durban with a convoy of troopships, parting company when another escort force took over en route for Aden while we went into Mombasa. Having lost HMS *Prince of Wales, Repulse, Dorsetshire, Cornwall* and *Exeter,* the nearest what was left of the British fleet could get to setting up a base for the South East Asia Command was at Mombasa, 4,000 miles west of the original one at Singapore. It was from Mombasa we were intended to operate, but at about this time those in charge decided that in view of the growth of vulnerable shipping approaching and leaving the Cape, an escort and patrol service should operate from Durban and Simons Town. *Redoubt, Racehorse* and *Quickmatch* were three of the destroyers fortunate enough to be attached to the South African bases for the ensuing nine months. From Durban and Simons Town we would sail the seas as far north as Pointe Noire and Freetown and as far east and north as Aden, Bombay and Colombo, with an occasional three or four-day sortie down south to the 'Roaring Forties' to rendezvous with one or two of the really big troopers – like *Reina del Pacifico, Ile de France,*

Nieuw Holland, Mauretania, etc, that sailed alone at high speeds on erratic courses through the high winds and restless waters of those latitudes. Once contact was made we'd lead them back up north to Durban or Cape Town, and what a comfortable feeling it brought to all when Table Mountain was once again in sight.

With something like 100,000 miles 'on the clock' since we first came out of the Clyde the time was nigh for *Redoubt*'s first refit for which, with *Racehorse*, we were sent into Simons Town dockyard in November 1943.

As explained in the *Verdun* story, a refit usually took about six weeks, with each half of the ship's company on 14 days leave at a time. In this case, those due to go were given three options: (a) billeted in the Union Jack Club, Cape Town, from which volunteer groups of civilians would organise sightseeing tours, dances, dinners, etc; (b) invited guests of a South African farming family somewhere within a hundred and fifty miles of Cape Town; or (c) invited guests of a civilian family in an inland town. Wanting to get as far from the Navy as possible for a while I chose (c), and with three messmates was made welcome at Kimberley, about six hundred miles up-country from Cape Town, at the home of Jim Palmer – the town's Postmaster General (at least, I think it was Jim). The South African Women s Auxiliary Services – of which Mrs Palmer was a member – organised everything, including the 18-hour journey on what is now the super-luxury Blue Train.

I remember leaving the ship and boarding the train at 12 noon with only seconds to spare, having dwelt too long in the Del Monico bar across the road to the station. I'd bought a bottle of Limosin brandy for the journey and had it nicely tucked into the pocket of my Burberry raincoat. We hurtled across the road into the station, found the platform and, waving our tickets madly raced past the inspector at the platform gate just as he was closing it. In doing so I felt an ominous thud as the raincoat, slung over my arm, hit the half-open wrought iron gate. Once into a compartment and enveloped in the all powerful fumes of 'vintage' brandy, I warily checked the damage (well, I knew it was vintage because it cost seven shillings and sixpence a bottle, whereas its cheaper rival, of which it was unkindly said 'Not a drop is sold until it's two days old', was only five shillings!). Carefully extracting the larger bits of broken glass from what was left of the pocket and watching my lovely raincoat disintegrating before my eyes I gave the lot to the guard and told him to put it through a wringer and inhale what dripped through. Nevertheless, we didn t go short of a drink on that train as it pounded along for hundreds of miles through the arid Karroo desert, where the temperature could reach 130°F in the middle of the day. There was a sing-song in the dining room of the train after supper before turning in on the bunks found prepared for us by the porters when we got back from the dining car.

A reception committee awaited our arrival at Kimberley Station and we split up to accompany the people who called our names from a prepared list.

Hospitality knew no bounds and every day was a gala event – from the time we finished breakfast and took a mile-long stroll to a friendly pub for our first Castle beer of the day, to the time we fell into our welcome beds from wherever the action happened to have been that evening. Which brings me to the one anxious moment with which each day started during that fortnight in Kimberley.

At the beginning of the 'sea-saga', there's a mention of the risks accompanying the urge to 'crash down' on lockers or mess tables rather than go through the hassle of slinging one's hammock. Well, one or two of those risks might be fairly obvious – like when the one above gets a bit careless and drops his books, fags or a grotty seaboot on your unsuspecting head; or sinks his large and smelly foot in your face when anxious to scramble out for some urgent reason or the other. Urgent calls of 'Action Stations!' 'Abandon Ship!', or just one of nature, come immediately to mind. But the most hazardous – in our mess anyway – was caused by one of its most inoffensive and longest-serving members, who also happened to be somewhat incontinent. And nothing can be more disconcerting when crashed-out on the lockers shortly after completing a four-hour middle-watch, than awakening to a steady drip-drip-drip on one's weary 'crust' through the fabric of the hammock above!

The poor devil couldn't help it, and tried all sorts of ways to overcome his problem; but he'd be a good boy for weeks and then, usually after a run ashore, there'd be a relapse. And now – here he was with us in Kimberley, drinking solidly throughout the day and sleeping each night on snowy-white linen in the home of generous and kindly people.

They'd given us three rooms – two of them each had a single bed, and one a king-size double. It was decided unanimously that Robin, to give him a fictitious name somewhere near his real one, qualified for one of the singles (nobody in his right mind was going to share a double bed with Robin!) My old Cockney mate, Alfie Gould, whose home back in London was not too far from my own, shared the big one with me, thereby leaving 'Doc', the ship's SBA (Sick Berth Attendant), with the sole occupancy of the other single, as befitted an ex-St John s Ambulance man and current 'first mate' to the ship's doctor.

Those 14 days in Kimberley were absolute heaven. All we had to do was go to bed at night, get up in the morning, get dressed, eat the breakfast served us in the dining room below, and let the good times roll. There were a number of servants around to prepare and serve food, clear tables, clean rooms, make beds, tend gardens, and generally see to the household needs of both the family and its guests.

Every night, however late it happened to be, we'd check on Robin to ensure he'd done his bathroom drill before turning in, and anybody feeling the call of nature through the night would give Robin a friendly shake on the way back from the bathroom, on the basis that if a disciplined cistern needed emptying, an undisciplined one might well be near leaking point. It meant his sleep was broken more often than ours – something he didn't enjoy, judging by the harsh and unfriendly things said when so awakened – but if it got him through the night without mishap all was forgiven. Each morning we'd show an anxious face at his door, to be greeted by a cheery smile and a thumbs-up sign. At least for the first seven days or so.

Then came one big party night, when everybody got back well loaded and just fell into bed. The next morning, one look at Robin's face was to know the worst!

As it is no use crying over spilt ... well, anything, we went into a council of war to spare old Robin further embarrassment when the girl came up later to do the rooms. It was decided to breakfast quickly, get back to his room before she got there, lock the door, make up his bed, and tuck the dry bedspread tightly all round over the damp sheets, whereby she'd see there was no need for her to tackle it. Then, once back at the house after the morning session at the pub, the bed could be stripped and sheets hung around the room to dry during the hot afternoon. Later, and before getting ready to sally forth on the evening's festivities, it could all be put together again before she came up to draw the curtains and turn back the beds – as was her wont. That way, nobody would ever know of our mate's little accident.

So, all light-hearted and carefree, we strolled through the quiet lanes back to base for lunch and turned the final corner with what we thought was a situation well under control, only to be greeted with – like a string of bunting fluttering from a flagship's signal deck – the sight of all Robin's bed-linen, freshly laundered, blowing gaily on the line at the back of the Palmer house! But never a word was said or implied. Nor would the laughing girl responsible accept the bit of cash Robin tried to give her in appreciation of the trouble he'd caused her.

Those Kimberley folk spared no effort in keeping us entertained. Dinners, formal lunches, dances, conducted tours of the diamond mines and one or two outlying farms, were crowded into each day. More than one citizen explained that we might well have been his or her guests, as far more of them had wanted to host the Navy than there were officers and men visiting Kimberley from our two ships. We were balloted for apparently, and one woman complained that it wasn't fair for the Palmers to have four while others didn't get any. The reason given by the organising committee was that – like brothers and sisters in an orphanage – messmates from the same ship might prefer not to be separated (it would have been doubly embarrassing for old Robin if he hadn't had us around in his hour of need!).

There were 22 of us off *Redoubt* and *Racehorse* billeted within a 20-mile radius of the town centre but we'd meet up from time to time at civic functions where we d foregather as hon. guests. One was the Armistice ceremony on November 11th at the town Cenotaph, for which George Mack, newly promoted to Petty Officer and with good foresight, took it upon himself to put us through a bit of 'square-bashing' practice up a side-street about half an hour before the 11.00am 'still'. Well, it was years

160

since most of us had done any, but thanks to George and our own anxiety to put on a good show for the old country we came swinging in step round the corner to line up three deep in front of the Cenotaph to the applause of the large crowd of Kimberley residents that had assembled. A press photographer took an excellent picture, reproduced in the illustrated section of this book. The civilian in the middle row was a Kimberley citizen who served in the Royal Navy in World War One. The *Racehorse* officer lost his cap at a party in our honour on the previous night. I'm standing on the extreme right, George Mack is standing third from left, and Alfie Gould is front row centre.

By the time our 14 days in Kimberley were over many had been offered a trouble-free future if only we'd come back and settle there when the war was over. In one or two cases there were appeals not to wait until then but to 'jump ship' and make a new life in the hinterland of the country with a new-found young lady, where 'Daddy', moved by his daughter's tears at the imminent parting, promised to set them up where the authorities could never find the naughty, missing sailor. It was always a temptation with a lotus-eating life on the one side against Lord knows how many more years of hardship and danger, but our particular *Redoubt/Racehorse* contingent was 100% present and correct when it came to reporting back aboard at Simons Town dockyard. There were, however, stories of Naval personnel who succumbed to the 'good-life' and went 'walkabout'. Inevitably the resultant escape from discipline and ship-board life was of short duration. With temptation all around, the seek-and-find members of the RN Regulating Branch were highly skilled in tracing deserters and before long a weak-willed young man was back aboard his ship, under escort, and facing a term of harsh imprisonment in which to contemplate the folly of self-indulgence.

In our absence the ship had acquired a new mast bristling with the latest Radar equipment and any amount of new gadgetry both above and between decks. The work continued while the other watch went on leave. Those of us that had returned went into a routine of turn-and-turn-about of 24 hours local leave and 24 hours of self catering midst limited resources while the dockyard workers swarmed over, under and around the ship. But there were few with means for the good life still available after 14 days living it up in Kimberley, etc, so frugality was the name of the game in those daily runs to and from Cape Town. Like free concerts at City Hall; high tea at the Victoria League Services Club and a shilling for a bed at the Seaman s Mission. At Kimberley we had been befriended by the Area Manager for Castle Brewery who would call about noon once or twice during our stay and drive us around his patch on a very wet pub crawl, and on other days, the Area Manager of Lion Brewery would do something similar. Everybody was most generous but one was obliged to make reciprocal efforts. By the time we were on overnight leave in Cape Town every other day, it was a question of feeling for the milled edge of a coin in your pocket before entering a bar. Once the ship was back to full complement with the opposite long-leave crowd back on board, we still did another couple of weeks against the harbour wall while refitting went on. By this time going ashore was a tiresome plod that I cheerfully forewent in order to put in useful time on the backlog of electrical studies for the correspondence course started a couple of years earlier. It's an ill wind, etc.

Eventually, it was back to taking on stores, oil, water, fuel, ammunition, swinging compasses and undergoing the usual tests and drills before setting out around the Cape with a convoy up the Mozambique Channel to Mombasa. From there it was to escort a troop convoy via Aden to Bombay. Then more convoys and patrols until there came a run to pick up a large convoy from Pointe Noire.

On a lovely summer's afternoon with the sea like a mill pond, tragedy struck when a man slid overboard while, with those off watch, he was playing tombola (lotto) by the after torpedo tubes. It was customary for some to squat seated on the lowest of the three wire ropes between stanchions that formed the guard rails running fore and aft. Each wire rope was passed through clearance holes in two stanchions and secured to the third one with spun yarn (tarry hemp) lashing. In this case the weight of a row of four men squatting on the taut wire caused the well-weathered hemp to part suddenly and they all slowly toppled backwards. Those on the ends of the row managed to grab at the nearest stanchions and another was held by a couple of men close by, but Able-seaman Shute slowly did a backward somersault just a few feet away and the last seen of him was his astonished face looking up from the water as the ship sped rapidly by. A lifebelt was thrown and 'Man Overboard' alarms sounded, but we must have travelled half a mile by the time the ship had turned, retraced its course, and called away the lifeboat. The search went on for more than three hours until dusk, and although the lifebelt was recovered, never a trace was seen of poor Shute. Some of his messmates said he couldn't swim. His personal possessions were auctioned a few days later and a goodly sum sent to his next of kin, with a letter of sympathy from our Captain.

By this time, the tide of war had turned and the Eastern Fleet had moved its base to Trincomalee on the north east coast of Ceylon. Every day more ships and stores were arriving from the UK, US and Australia, with hit-and-run raiding parties setting out to harass the Japanese in their occupied bases on the islands of the East Indies. We took part in convoying troops and supplies from Madras to Chittagong in support of the 14th Army in Burma, and providing covering fire for landings on the Arakan coast there.

Then came a convoy to Bombay where we stayed to boiler-clean, while some were sent to a rest camp on the coast about twenty miles north of Bombay.

Three days were spent swimming, playing football, and loafing around, during which time I found an Indian peasant leading a fine young horse, fully saddled and bridled, along the sands. I'd never ridden before but this seemed too good a chance

162

to miss. "How much for a ride on your horse?" I asked. "Is very good horse," he said, "You have for two hours – give me fifty rupees." So we settled for five and, after being helped into the saddle, I rode him carefully (the horse that is) to an agreed point about two miles along the beach, and with a bit more confidence back to his master at a gentle trot. By which time I felt ready for the Horse of the Year Show once all the strained and sore parts had healed. Well, I'd come straight out of the ocean and nobody considers a pair of wet flimsy cotton shorts as ideal equestrian garb. I was rather pleased at not falling off and even my Indian friend was impressed. Well, he said that I would be a good rider one day and suggested he come to see me on the morrow with a bigger and more docile steed on which he would teach me good for ten rupees. But no deal was struck because everything was already stiffening up and I didn't believe I'd ever be able to climb into a saddle again. Even if I wanted to. And I never did until twenty-seven years later, on a cowboy's quarter-horse, on a ranch in Arizona – how's that for a throwaway line! (All described in my first book *Start Off Smashed!* published in 1972).

On the third day at the camp a thick cloud of black smoke was to be seen coming from the general direction of Bombay, 20 miles away. Soon after came a prolonged and heavy explosion. It turned out that two ships had caught fire in the commercial harbour in Bombay. One was an ammunition ship. It blew up and, just like the Great Fire of crowded London in 1666 spread as building after building was ignited by the raging inferno, so did ship after ship and the laden warehouses feed the Great Fire of Bombay in April 1944 – considered by many to be the most damaging one of the War not caused directly by enemy action. The official figure was about 350 dead and a thousand wounded, but with the unknown teeming hordes of floating boat-people and dockside coolies living in shanty towns around the harbour buildings, the casualties were more likely to have been three or four times that quantity.

Redoubt had finished its boiler clean by the time we returned and little time was wasted in getting away from the depressing surroundings, especially as India was in the grip of a deadly famine, with death and disease ashore necessitating RN personnel being jabbed and re-jabbed against all known tropical disease until the visible tell-tale sores on the arms showed the necessary results. It proved successful as I don't believe anybody succumbed to anything much by way of disease other than those associated with 'playin' where they shouldn't have been a-playin'!

With convoys and patrols taking us in all directions I particularly remember pulling into the island of Seychelles on the morning of 5th August 1943. Not that anything of an earth-shattering nature took place, but it happened to be my 26th birthday and I'd toured the messes both for'ard and aft taking a sip of rum with each of my pals, until a sudden weariness overcame me and I slept lying on my back in the sun on top of the racked depth charges. The sun had set when I woke in the dark under a gentle fall of tropical, but chilling rain, my roasted skin as taut as a drum, my

163

back – following the contours of the charges – like a ripple curvature of the spine, and with a parched throat, and a mouth tasting like I'd lunched on the raw hind leg of a skunk!

Some six months earlier, *Redoubt* went into dock at Durban for a 'mini-refit', resulting in nine days leave as guest of the owner of a small hotel in Vryheid – a country town in Natal about three hours by train from Durban. What I remember most about that was meeting a little schoolteacher who taught me a lot about South Africa, including the words, in Afrikaans, of the country's most popular song – if not actually its national anthem. And in the ensuing years, right until my most recent visit in February 1988, many's the Springbok who's been taken aback by my rendering of *Sarie Marais* in neat Afrikaans!

I used to write and tell my wife that when the war was over we'd go and live in South Africa, where I'd made so many fine friends (I don't believe specific reference was made to the little schoolteacher) and had the offer of more than one job if I came back to settle. But when I did return to England in May 1945, two years and seven months after leaving it, war-torn England was still far too beautiful a place to consider living anywhere else.

The refit over it was back to join up with the Fleet at Trincomalee, where exercises and anti-submarine patrols were the norm. Returning to harbour, activities were limited to perhaps a game of football or water polo against another ship, or a 'Sod's Opera' at the canteen, where beer could only be had by surrendering an official ticket issued on the basis of one ticket per bottle per month. We had a good football team on *Redoubt* and being the match organiser usually put myself in the team at outside left. But I was too slow for the water polo team which didn't displease me at all. Not in 'Trinco' it didn't, where the two goals were dropped on booms from the ship's side, with a scrambling rope ladder at the centre line for getting back aboard at the end of the match. By which time I could just about find the wind and strength to pull myself up it, after frenziedly treading water waiting to be next to start the long ascent. And all the time aware of the size and ferocity of the sharks so often visible from the ship's decks. But I think it was the uninhibited shouts and bad language of the players that kept the evil denizens of the deep down where they belonged.

Vic Gardiner, a fellow veteran-pal, wrote of one of those water polo matches – Seamen versus Stokers – where a man was posted amidships with a loaded .303 rifle with instructions to open up directly he spotted anything with a dorsal fin trying to interfere with the game! Fortunately he didn't because there would have been chaos with everybody trying to be first up that ladder after the initial ranging shot. But it was important that the match be played to a finish as each of the winners was to collect a precious beer ticket from the losers!

164

In those days huge Flying Fortresses were making high altitude daylight raids on enemy held positions and when such raids were planned destroyers and similar vessels were spaced out at about five hundred mile intervals across the Indian Ocean along the route they were to take. The Fortresses would leave a Pacific base and after their raid fly on to an Indian Ocean one. On receipt of a signal that one had crashed, the nearest destroyer would make for that position and search around for survivors. On one occasion we found the plane sinking but picked up eleven of its crew from an inflated raft that had to be destroyed once we'd done so, it being too big for stowing on the upper deck of *Redoubt*. A number of souvenirs were taken by the lads before piercing the skin and chucking it over the side, and George Mack still has a small American flag on which was printed the following message in sixteen languages:

"I am an American fighter. I did not come here to do any harm to you, who are my friends. I only want to do harm to the Japanese and chase them away from this country as quickly as possible.

If you assist me my Government will reward you when the Japanese are driven away."

CHAPTER SIXTEEN

Aden

In June 1944 we were about a day out of Aden when I was told to prepare to leave the ship there; a three-badge LTO had been in charge of mine-sweeping there for nearly three years and I was to replace him. Aden was universally regarded as the most God-forsaken hell-hole, especially when a refuelling base in the days of coal-fired boilers – as described by Woody in Book One. But although oil bunkering was done well away from the Navy base at Steamer Point, the heat and tropical 'pong' was every bit as debilitating as ever.

The man I relieved gave me a rough outline of what the job entailed. There were three very old coal-burning trawlers, *Jamuna*, *Rio Narvian* and a third and smallest whose name I don't remember, with a total of about fifty local Arabs to crew them. The senior hand was Ali, the serang, or coxswain, as it were. He always wore khaki drill with a red fez and the more I knew him the more I respected him.

An ex-Merchant Navy serang of many years standing, Ali would hire and fire members of the crew as Navy casual labour at 40 rupees (£3) per month for an able seaman. And when I say 'able', I mean very able; many could run rings around the average 'Jack-me-Hearty' when it came to working ship. He would come and see me in my 'caboosh' – a corner of the Naval stores run by an Anglo-Indian Manager – and tell me that 'perhaps' we needed another seaman because somebody had not returned from visiting a sick aunt a few hundred miles up country in Yemen, and introduce a barefoot bright-eyed lad who was his cousin's son who he swore would do the job very well. (I don't doubt that once hired, a small percentage of the new lad's pay would go towards Ali's lifestyle!)

My 'boss' was an RNR three-ring Commander in the Navy House at Steamer Point. I messed and slept in the depot base, a series of single storey timber sheds behind perimeter fencing on the bottom left hand corner of Arabia, facing the Indian Ocean and designated HMS *Sheba*. Well, I didn't sleep in those hot and humid huts after the first few nights because Ali delegated one of his nephews, Ahmed, to be my batman at the camp, and I never again had to do anything for myself. He did my dhobeying and ironing, and as I preferred to sleep under the stars rather than in the humid huts, my folding canvas bed would be put up on a sandy bank every evening, and a cup of tea brought to me at 6.00am each morning. Catering in the camp was run by an Indian firm of contractors and we ate very well. There were usually about 150 naval personnel in *Sheba* but ever-changing as they left one ship or waited on the arrival of another for a multiplicity of reasons. They mostly seemed puzzled over how I qualified for 'QE2-treatment' and wondered how to get it for themselves, but accepted it as my perks without quibbling too much.

Whenever a convoy was due in or about to leave I would receive a signal message from the Commander's office to take my 'fleet' out at first light next morning and sweep the specified channel for mines. Ali would then be told that we'd take two of the trawlers, usually *Jamuna* and *Rio Narvian*, and double sweep the set course for about five miles. Ali would ensure that the crews were aboard in good time with steam up by the time I got aboard my 'flagship', with all running gear shackled up and paravanes ready to stream. I'd look at my watch, sing out to cast off and away we'd go. The latter was just swank because Ali knew much better than me when to cast off and what course and speed to travel. Same as he did on when and how to stream PV's and, I fervently hoped, what to do if ever we swept up a mine (we never ever did and I had it from my predecessor that he hadn't either!) All I did was flash a signal to the Navy Office with Aldis Lamp on what course we were sweeping, and have two black balls hoisted at the start of the sweep as a signal to other craft that we were not under control. On one or two occasions due to too good a 'thrash' with friends the night before, I was still flaked out in the camp when I should have been out in command of my 'fleet', only to learn that Ali had done the whole thing as scheduled without me, having learned from Ahmed that I hadn't touched my tea and was still asleep. I don't believe he ever bothered to send the Morse signal, but nobody seemed to care!

We carried a box of $3\frac{1}{4}$lb gelignite charges and I believe that, in some way, one was to be the means of destroying a drifting mine, if ever we'd swept one up. If that was so it would need a very long fuse – like a couple of miles! – before I d be prepared to light it. With a full head of steam and a following wind I doubt if *Jamuna* could knock up more than 5 knots. What I remember of blowing up a drifting mine when aboard *Verdun* or *Redoubt*, we'd do it with rifle or Oerlikon fire from the signal deck from about 200 yards and the resultant bang would shake us up more than somewhat. Enough to have me wanting to be a long way away if ever needed to do the same thing from the good ship *Jamuna* – or *Rio Narvian*.

But as already said, it was never necessary to put to the test. Instead, when finishing the outward leg of the sweep I'd take one of the gelignite charges, light and prepare the five-second fuse, and lob it over the side. A couple of the lads would then take away the dinghy and gather in the harvest of dead and stunned fish floating in a large circle above the resultant explosion. They were all shapes and sizes – the fish that is, not the lads – but if a shark happened to be among them it would be left severely alone to recover and swim away when fit enough to do so. Nobody wants to be too close to a shark with a sick headache in a leaky old dinghy. The largest and best of the catch would be delivered to the Commander via the chef in the wardroom galley down at Steamer Point. After, of course, the 'pick of the litter' had found its way to the Indian caterer at *Sheba* for his kitchen staff to prepare for me and my special cronies. Ali would arrange for the trawler crews to have the remainder after he and other senior personnel had taken their share. The senior personnel were the Anglo Indian Stores Manager, from whom we drew the gelignite charges, and the driver of our 3-ton Dodge truck who would run me down to pick up the trawlers in the morning and do the 'fish deliveries' on our return. Yes, besides the three trawlers, my 'fleet' included a 3-ton Dodge truck for collecting and delivering ship's stores and a 25 ft motor boat for 'swanning' around the harbour and checking unidentified objects.

Talking of sharks, a stretch of the beach alongside *Sheba* was fenced off under water with heavy galvanised chain-link fencing to form three large shark-proof swimming enclosures for all Service personnel. One for officers and Wrens; one for non-commissioned officers; and the third and largest for other ranks. It was only when it was found that sharks were also using all three enclosures without permission that divers discovered that much of the netting and angle-iron vertical supports below the water-line had corroded away to virtually nothing, leaving huge gaps through which curious sharks could enter at will and study the undersides of adventurous water-borne members of the human race. I say adventurous because although it became generally known that a bather was not as safe as he or she would like to be, the cooling waters provided heavenly instant relief from sticky humidity and the bodily discomfort of prickly heat, so that the braver or more stupid among us were inclined to swim come what may.

Another of my duties was to run the open air cinema in *Sheba* camp, with a change of film every week. To do this it meant sending the truck to the American Air Force base out at Sheikh Othman, about fifteen miles inland from Steamer Point. Every week they would get the latest Hollywood films on 16" reels and allow us to borrow them over Sunday night, providing they were returned next morning in time to catch the Flying Fortress shuttle to their next destination.

As we only had one projector it would mean up lights, a cynical cheer from the audience, and a musical interlude on record while I changed a reel or spliced a break; but it was all worth while just to see and hear more of the Andrews Sisters, Bing, Durante, or other greats from the golden days of Hollywood. Once able to drive I would take the truck over to Sheikh Othman myself and enjoy the Aladdin's cave of an American PX, while sharing an ice-cold juice or coffee with the man who dished out the films.

Yes, one day when being transported somewhere and feeling like a latter-day 'Alexander Selkirk' (William Cowper's poem of that name which starts with "I am monarch of all I survey.") I said to my driver, "Busty, you must teach me to drive." 'Busty' is colloquial Arabic equivalent to 'Tubby'. His name I believe was Ahwad, but thanks to a comfortable girth all his friends called him 'Busty', as did I, being both his friend and employer. "Yes, sahib," he said, stopped the truck, got out, got in through my door, and had me slide across the bench seat until I was behind the wheel. "I didn't mean right now." I protested sitting up there gazing fearfully down on the bonnet of that huge 3-ton Dodge and now looking even more fearful under the control of a terror-stricken beginner. He gently put me at my ease and told me to do everything 'deladela' – slowly! For about five minutes I went through the motions of gear-changing and double de-clutching before switching the engine on. He had guts in more ways that one, that Busty, sticking it out for the next six weeks or so of one ghastly near-disaster after another, with a trail of cursing camel-cart drivers, chicken crate carriers, taxi operators, herds of goats, etc, giving me as wide a berth as possible in those teeming market streets. Amazingly I had not yet killed anybody, damaged anything, or scraped paintwork – not even off my own vehicle – by the time I 'went solo'. True, Aden being somewhat mountainous with narrow streets and passing places with sheer drops to the rocky foreshore far below, there were times when inexperience on hill-starts led to a stalled engine, and the said sheer drop had me appealing to skilled drivers whose progress I'd blocked to get me going again. But this they'd do cheerfully and Busty would tell when we next met just where, when and with whom I'd had my last adventure. Apparently every road user in Greater Aden knew just who the blue Dodge and its white naval driver belonged to and as Busty was a pretty popular man with the locals they felt it their duty to look after his boss, no doubt setting him back 'a-half-of-sherbet' in the village tavern when they did so.

Football is an international game and played by the British in any weather. We had a good team at *Sheba* and there were big representative matches played between Army, Navy, RAF and native teams, in which I'd play on the RN left wing. On big match days the local inhabitants would be out in force and each time I'd make a bid there'd be a thunderous roar of "Sam, Sam!" from the Arab ranks echoing across the sands. No doubt all good friends of Busty!

Then came March 27th 1945, the fateful day when Lt. Creasey (I think), my divisional officer, came down from Steamer Point and sent word that I was to see him in the duty office there as quickly as possible. A most unusual request that filled me with apprehension, not knowing which of my breaches of K.R. and A.I.'s (Kings Regulations and Admiralty Instructions) had just been discovered.

Things looked even more grim when he told me to sit down and said, "I was going to have a whisky and thought you'd like one too", pushing a glass half-full of the amber fluid across the table to me. Taking a sip I thought it was like serving the prisoner in the death cell with a steak, eggs and chips breakfast before starting out on the eight o'clock walk. He then fished from his pocket a sheet from an Admiralty signal pad and said, "You'd better read this. It arrived from London by WT two hours ago."

It was dated 27th March 1945 and simply said,

> *"Your Mum and Dad killed outright by enemy action this morning. Please come home. All my love, Pat."*

"I'm very very sorry," said Lieutenant Creasey. I remember sitting there dazed, wondering why there was no dramatic sense of tragic loss. When things started rolling into place I explained to the good lieutenant that it was now over two and a half years since I left England which meant that to all intents and purposes my parents had already been out of my life for that length of time. I'd often thought that if one of them died the other would be left with a sad and lonely old age and hoped that when the end came for them they'd be together and feel no pain. For six years they hardly ever left London, enduring the nightly bombing, the V1 buzz bombs, and now the V2 rockets – the very last of which to fall on London claimed them and 122 of their friends and neighbours who lived in those three blocks of flats. They knew nothing, they felt no pain, and when the rubble was cleared they were found still in bed with not a mark on either of them. They were each sixty-four years old.

I was told that Commander Harding was already pursuing the various authorities to get me on a quick passage back to England but it was still another three weeks before I shook the sands of Aden from my shoes and embarked alone, aboard the MS *Sarmiento*, a fast new motor ship of 10,000 tons, leaving that night with Glasgow as its first stop. During those three weeks I carried on as usual, hastily turning over the mysteries of my various duties and perks to an appointed replacement, the only snag being that as a South Afrikaner, his apartheid tendencies didn't help him achieve too natural a rapport with my Arab crews. In any case I learned later that within three months of my leaving, the minesweeping duty was abandoned together with the free issue gelignite charges; *Jamuna* and *Rio Narvian* were sold to enterprising Arabs who no doubt put them to work on smuggling and slave trafficking; and the Dodge truck went to the RAF base at Khormaksar. I maintained contact for about a year with Ali, who wanted to get back to sea and would write with all the news. I remember describing him to the purser on *Sarmiento* during the long journey home and saying what an asset he'd be to any shipping company that employed him. In the end, I believe, he did get a berth with them as a serang in charge of the Lascar crew on one of their ships.

When the time came to leave Aden half the Arab population were down at Steamer Point waving me off. A very touching departure and one I will never forget. I was given a cabin down aft and told to take it easy and enjoy the voyage as though it were a holiday cruise. The Royal Navy had agreed to pay the shipping line all my expenses but I understand that when all the circumstances were made known, including the years spent on destroyers escorting merchant ships such as theirs, the shipping company waived all charges.

Halfway up the Red Sea came the news that Germany had surrendered unconditionally, as a result of which once out of the Suez Canal and sailing due west on the Mediterranean, after nearly five years of life on an ocean wave I was actually seeing the lights of ships that pass in the night for the very first time. What a beautiful and exhilarating experience it was to sit spinning a yarn on the quarter deck with a glass in one hand, a cigar for a 'balancing pole' in the other, passing vessels with portholes ablaze with light from stem to stern. The 'balancing poles' were a farewell gift from my American friends at Sheikh Othman.

We stopped at Gibraltar for fuel, water and provisions but I stayed on board as (a) Gibraltar was never my idea of a good run ashore, and (b) no way was I going to step ashore off the ship that was taking me home – not even for a minute! But what I did do was to buy a big stalk of green bananas from a bum boat that came alongside about 30 ft below our quarter-deck rail. We haggled a bit, but with agreement reached I dropped a line to which the bunch was tied, and passed the money down the same way. The fruit was green and hard but I took the bunch below to hang from the deckhead in the bilges and had about twenty 'hands' of bright yellow ripened fruit when bringing them out into the daylight at Glasgow.

But although I didn't go ashore in Gibraltar there was still a puzzle to clear up, arising from memories of previous visits. One of the favourite ports of call for the naval fraternity when ashore in Gib. was the Universal Club, or the UV as it was universally known by men who go down to the sea in ships. It was a noisy bar with a live band and a sexy blonde drummer. Some said she was a male pervert but I think she was the real thing. The UV was always full of matelots, most of whom would seek to get seated as close to the said drummer as possible, staring intently at her 'upper-works' bouncing about as she thrashed those 'skins'.

Stretching across the bar from wall to wall above Blondie was a canvas banner reading, "Free beer for all in the UV on VE Day!"

What I wanted to know was (a) was Blondie still performing at the UV, and (b) did they honour their sign on VE Day? Taking it up with one of the RN personnel that came aboard the *Sarmiento* for some official reason or other I learned that (a) yes, Blondie was still thumping the drums, and (b) the day before VE Day they switched off the lights at the UV, locked all doors and shutters, and didn't re-open until seven days later!

It was a warm Tuesday afternoon in May when I took my leave of MV *Sarmiento* alongside the wall in Glasgow Docks and stepped on British soil again for the first time in two years and eight months. And I was alone in this strange land with only a letter from the Commander RNHQ Aden saying, to the best of my memory,

> *"Leading Seaman Samuel John Morley is on emergency draft to HMS Pembroke, Chatham Barracks, after serving over two and a half years with the Far Eastern Fleet. Both his parents were killed when their home was destroyed by enemy action on 27th May 1945. Please give him all the assistance he might need to reach his family as quickly as possible."*
> *Signed Commander Harding RNR*
> *HMS* Sheba, *Aden*

That letter was a passport that broke down every barrier that might otherwise have still had me locked up in Glasgow till the end of the War. Apparently nobody was used to British sailors turning up on their own in a merchant ship from foreign parts without prior advice of his coming and official rubber stamps over masses of documents. Other than that letter I had nothing.

I'd asked the 'sparks' on the *Sarmiento* if he'd ring out on the ship-to-shore telephone to get me a taxi, and a couple of the lads off the ship gave me a hand getting my gear, including that bright yellow stalk of bananas, safely stowed when it arrived. Back in Aden before leaving, I'd been given £25 English money to help with expenses in getting down to Chatham once reaching the UK.

Much suspicion and interrogation at the dockyard gate by security officials ended in handshakes and shouts of, "Good luck, Jack," when I produced THE letter. Next stop was St Enoch's Station, Glasgow, where the taxi-driver, having heard my story en route, refused payment but accepted a bunch of bananas. Turning away after waving a fond and grateful farewell I looked around for some means of moving my baggage into the station building, and started out to find a porter's truck. But I didn't get far. Two belligerent looking sailors, led by an even more belligerent-looking two-badge petty officer – all wearing R.T.O insignias on their red armbands – approached and started asking awkward questions; questions answered with a minimum of information, that only increased their suspicions until I pulled out my magic piece of paper. The petty officer instructed his minions to pick up my bits and pieces and bring them through while, strolling by my side, he led me to his boss, the Master at Arms in the RTO office. En route he told of his days at sea in the tropics and on the South African and Far Eastern Stations.

The RTO office bustled with activity and there must have been a dozen or more of the Naval 'Gestapo' in various stages of terrorising sailors on the move. Before leading me into an inner office he roared, "SILENCE, EVERYBODY!" When he had it, he pointed at me and said, "Take a good look at a lost species – a REAL sailor!" It was embarrassing. Well, they were mostly in their late teens and early 20's with me rising 28, I had an ingrained tropical tan under my white cap compared to their wintry pallor under navy blue ones, and gold badges on my No. 1's depicting I was a one-badge leading-seaman torpedoman compared to the red insignias on those that qualified for them – gold badges had long since gone 'under the counter' in Britain's wartime shops.

Funny how human and friendly a Master at Arms can appear when facing him with nothing to feel guilty about. He studied my letter, looked through my paybook – without which nobody can claim an existence in the Royal Navy – and had some tea brought in while he and the PO discussed what do to with me. I could find no fault with their decisions, which provided me with an official draft chit to show I was actually en route to Chatham from Aden, via Glasgow. This qualified me for a railway warrant via the London termini of Euston and Waterloo. "You live in London, so if I put you down to report at Chatham in ten days from now, that should give you enough time to get home for a cup of tea with the missus before proceeding on your way?" said the Master at Arms, beaming like a good fairy. "And if you report to Chatham early enough you should be able to get out again the same day on your Foreign Service and In-from-sea-Leave, not to mention a bit of compassionate leave tacked on! Just make sure they give you a decent whack of Subsistence Money before you leave Chatham, otherwise you're going to eat your missus out of house and home before it's time to report back!"

The petty officer stayed to take care of all the paperwork while he sent me off to the station restaurant with a chit for an evening meal. He came along to join me there with the documents and we sat spinning a yarn till it was time for my train, in which he d even arranged for me to have a first-class compartment. "Well," he said, "this being your first journey on a British train in nearly three years we can't poke you in among a load of drunken squaddies sitting on their kitbags in the overcrowded third class corridors, can we?"

His loyal companions had brought along my gear and my last memories are of them all three each waving a bunch of bananas they were delighted to receive for their kindnesses, as the train pulled out for the overnight journey to London. It would be pleasing to know that one or more of those four characters – the Master at Arms, the petty officer and the two 'crushers' are still around and happen to read this book, thereby knowing how far and how long a good deed CAN shine in a naughty world!

The train rolled south and by noon the following day I was reunited with my wife and three year old daughter, Sue. Although it took almost a week before the latter accepted the fact that Daddy was no longer the framed picture on the sideboard but this big sailor who had given her two bunches of bananas on arrival and slept in bed with Mummy ever since. Yes, time I'd passed a bunch or two on to people who were nice to me – like the taxi driver from Euston who charged me a couple of quid to take me to my home in Forest Gate instead of at least double that amount – two handsome canary-yellow bunches were all that were left from that crowded green stalk I'd bought in Gibraltar.

After a week I made my official return to Chatham Barracks and, like the man said back in Glasgow, before the day was out I was home again on lots of leave. Once again the time had passed all too quickly when I returned to find what awaited me there. Asking if they had a driving job, my luck held out because they wanted a responsible driver to do the early and late runs with the mail van. A badge and hook was considered sufficiently responsible but being unable to provide a driving licence they sent me to be examined at the MT office in the dockyard. Explaining to the civilian officer in charge that I'd learned on a 3-ton Dodge in Aden he looked a bit sceptical but decided to try me on a 5-ton Bedford. I think they heard me crashing those gears in Bedford town itself, but nevertheless I was cleared to drive RN vehicles. And until to today whenever obliged to complete a form asking the name of the authority holding proof of my ability to drive I've written HMS *Sheba*, Aden, and MT office, Chatham Dockyard. There's never been a query.

Back at Chatham Barracks I was attached to the MT office by the Gymnasium and put on the mail run (collecting the outgoing mail at 5.30am at the mail room, and taking it to Strood Station, where I'd collect the incoming bags for delivery back to Chatham). There were usually three runs a day besides collecting and delivering people on draft. I worked noon to noon with 24 hours at home on the alternate days. It was a dream of a cushy number but like all cushy numbers it couldn't last. Early in September I returned from 24-off and found a notice to report to the drafting office. My stomach dropped. The War was now over and I knew my demob number would be coming up soon. Where on earth were they thinking of sending me? My fears were soon confirmed at the Drafting Office. Report for medical preparation to leave for HMS *Lanka*. "Do you know where HMS *Lanka* is, Chief?" I asked the bloke in charge. He said he didn't so I told him. "It's the RN depot at Trincomalee on the west coast of Ceylon and I'm not long back from serving on a fleet destroyer working out of there for the past two and half years!" (Well, you've got to pitch it strong if you're out to win). "What's more, they'll be calling my age and service group any time now so what's the sense of sending me seven thousand miles away if you're going to have to get me back for demob. before I'm halfway there?"

It was to no avail. He'd heard it all before. So I put in a request to see the Drafting Commander on compassionate grounds. He said I'd be wasting my time – and his – and that the DC didn't take kindly to having his time wasted. But I insisted and the following morning, cap in hand, I stood before him. After the usual pre-

174

liminaries he said, "Come on Morley, you know the Navy. This is certainly a 'green rub' after the time you've already spent out there but a leading torpedoman of your experience is needed in those waters for a short time and I give you my word that if your demob comes up we'll have you on your way back here within a couple of weeks." "Oh yes," I thought, "something jolly, like mine or bomb disposal, and if I happened to survive that there would be eight weeks on a crowded trooper when allowed to come home."

So I pulled the 'magic letter' out of my pocket and passed it across to him. He read it carefully and passed it back, thinking hard. Eventually he said," I'm very sorry to learn about your parents but this happened in March. There's no real reason why you should be kept in this country now." I then played my trump card. "There were 122 people killed when that rocket exploded, many of whom had families, like me, thousands of miles away on war service who could not get back to pay their last respects. A multi-denominational Memorial Service is planned for 27th September, exactly six months after it happened. Having missed the funeral I think I should be allowed to attend the Memorial Service."

He folded and returned my letter and without a pause said to the Master at Arms, "Request granted. See this man's name is taken off the Awaiting Draft register!"

Then came the 29th day of October 1945 when, with those of my age-and-service group, I mustered for the last time in that traumatic tunnel under the perimeter hills of the barracks, only this time there was no claustrophobic depressing pong-laden atmosphere – just animated laughter and excitement as we filed by desks and job stations collecting paperwork, money and medals while shedding kitbags, hammocks, and what we each had left of original kit issues and uniforms. Which reminds me of what befell my old shipmate, Jim Webster, when he returned to England after three years on *Redoubt*.

On his first day in Chatham from his foreign service leave, he walked across the 'holy' parade ground and heard the stentorian shout of, "That man!!" He looked around to see a two-ring lieutenant approaching and pointing at his white cap while saying, "You're improperly dressed!" Explaining that he'd just arrived back from leave after 3 years in the Far East was a waste of time. "Kit muster at 4.00pm," roared the officer and marched off.

Laying out what gear he had, Jim received a list of all the things he was short and their cost of replacement. "But I've just come back from my foreign service leave and have no money!" protested Jim. "Here's a chit," said the other, "and take it to the clothing store." "That's very nice of him," thought Jim when he found himself with a full kit again. But he didn't go on thinking that when he mustered next pay day to find there was no money for him when his name was called. Just a 'North-Easter' (Not Entitled). He remained in debt to the pusser for the next four pay days, by which

175

time he, too, was about ready to start *his* release routine and hand back his recent purchases in exchange for a trilby hat and a demob suit.

I must admit that every help was given by those in attendance when selecting hats, shoes, suits, ties and coats on display – but only one or one pair of each. Finally, clutching a railway warrant and an attaché case containing my personal property I walked out of Chatham Barracks for the last time and without a backward glance, into a bus waiting to take a number of ex-sailors to Chatham station. I was on my way to start a new life as a home-loving civilian.

EPILOGUE

Fifty Years Later

T he 'one-man-band' of an electrical engineering business started with my war gratuity in October '45 employed some sixty personnel when I sold out to a public company in October '82. In 1984 my second book *In Search of Eastern Promise* was published by Quiller Press. It dwelt on the highlife experienced between 1978 and 1980 while marketing my products to large construction projects in the Far East. On pages 54/55 I explain an evocative link with WW2 when visiting Sentosa Island, Singapore, with my wife:-

Sentosa (the word means 'Tranquility') could not be better named. It is a lush and unspoiled island, maintained by the Government for leisure and relaxation. Our first sightseeing visit was to the Surrender Building, a two storey, white-painted, timber-built, Colonial-style structure, with wide verandas on both levels, situated a hundred yards or so from the cable-car terminal. It was now a museum, commemorating the occupation of Singapore by the Japanese in 1942, who then surrendered to the Allies in 1945.

Displayed were a variety of relics, photographs, newspapers, official notices and memorabilia. They were of more than passing interest as I had served on H.M. destroyers in those waters from the beginning of 1943 to May 1945, and well remember the daily toll of men and ships.

The crowning scene in the Surrender Building is a large glass-walled room with a viewing gallery round all four sides. It is a replica of the Chamber in Singapore City Hall, when the 'Act of Surrender' was signed in 1945.

Two large polished tables form the central feature. Full-size waxwork replicas of the senior offices of the Allied High Command, in full dress uniform, are seated down one side of one table, with Admiral Lord Louis Mountbatten in their centre. Facing them on the other table are the senior officers of the Japanese forces. Name, rank, command, documents and pens are set before each of the seated figures. A Japanese ceremonial sword lies across the Allied table with its hilt close to Lord Louis' hand. Uniformed waxwork sentries from the various allied forces are spaced around the room.

Public address loud speakers quietly described events leading up to the tableau set before us.

I stood spellbound, eyes misty with sentiment and memories. The background music was Elgar's 'Pomp and Circumstance No 1'. As the taped commentary drew to its end, the music gradually swelled in volume until the crashing strains of 'Land of Hope and Glory' set us gulping with emotion. Brushing a sleeve across my eyes I thought of those who suffered and survived the days when Japan dominated the East in World War Two. They would find a pilgrimage to Sentosa rewarding.

By 1987 I'd written three hardbacks and was half way through a fourth with hedonistic involvement in racing, travel and golf as its theme. In one chapter, set in South Africa where our party went racing at Clairwood, Durban, I described my wartime memories of Durban and expanded somewhat on the mysterious Lady in White who used to sing to the ships in those bleak and awful times. I was telephoned by Helen Wightwick, the young lady in our village who prepares my finished typescripts. Born, bred and educated in Cape Town she had settled in England twenty years earlier. "What do you mean," she demanded, "by describing Perla Siedle Gibson, the aunt of my very best friend and the lady I remember so well from my youth, as 'mysterious'?"

But going back to the Introduction to this book, it was 1969 when I first started thinking Navy again after a gap of twenty four years since demob. Preparing Lt. Comm. Wood's story for my Club Magazine involved considerable research in our Naval and War Museums during which time I took out a subscription to 'Navy News', and joined the HQ Branch of the Royal Naval Association. Both Captain Jim Rayner, general secretary of RNA, and Jim Allaway, Editor of 'Navy News' have become good friends and hardly a month goes by without seeking help from either on latter-day ex-Navy commitments, like *Redoubt* Veterans Association, Roedean Old Boys Association, **"Durban's Lady in White"**, **"99 Years of Navy"**, and the Lady in White Monument Appeal – to name but a few.

In January 1990 I heard John Dunn interview Joy Liddiard, daughter of the one-time 'mysterious' Lady in White on his chat show, in which mention was made of an autobiography published in South Africa thirty years earlier – now long since out of print, and never distributed abroad. I made contact with Joy, explained there were many like me who would have bought that book and could she send me one of her precious souvenir copies to consider publishing it in Great Britain. I had by this time started my own publishing company – Aedificamus Press.

When it arrived I went from cover-to-cover in two wet-cheeked sleepless nights and still can't glance at a random page without having to contend with yet another lump in the throat. The three million British and overseas veterans who sailed through Durban would, I felt, react like me if they, too, could read this book. It just had to be revised and re-published even if it did relate to fifty year old events.

'Durban's Lady in White' hit the bookshops on St George's day, April 23rd 1991. Unfortunately I couldn't attend the launch due to a triple coronary by-pass on the previous day, but that didn't stop the orders flooding in thanks to excellent reviews in newspapers and veteran's magazines all over the world. And with those orders came hundreds of letters from ex-soldiers, sailors and airmen expressing heartfelt fifty-year-old memories.

From the beginning, **'Durban's Lady in White'** provoked 'itchy feet' for the WW2 veterans among its readers. Soon after publication enquiries started arriving on the possibilities of a return visit to 'Memory Lane'.

On 27th June 1991 I wrote to Durban City Council explaining that a 'Lady in White' Memorial Visit was under consideration and would it be possible for the party to have its memories of her and the City renewed in a number of specific ways as set out in my letter.

At the same time, Durban residents who had helped in my research for the book were also approached on the logistics of arriving in the company of two or three dozen fellow 70-year-olds (give or take a couple of years) in search of history. They'd be from all parts of the country and complete strangers to each other, but with one experience in common. All the men would have served in the Royal Navy, Army, Air Force or Merchant Navy in the War, and would have seen or heard the 'Lady in White' on their way through Durban.

One of those Durban residents, Reverend Millen Adams, full-time Secretary to the International Sailors Society at Durban, received a "Yes, please!" when enquiring if he could be responsible for organising things when we got there, and from then on he was my sole point of contact.

My first requests was for a memory-link to those over-crowded troopships, warships, hospital ships and cargo ships on their way to Mediterranean and Far Eastern war fronts, and entering Durban's harbour after forty or more stressful days at sea.

Whether Navy, Army or Air Force, everybody first heard and saw the 'Lady in White' from the deck of a ship. Could the visiting veterans be taken a short distance out to sea on the deck of some vessel or the other and on return find a look-and-dress alike 'Lady in White' singing to them from the North Pier? *Good idea!* came the prompt reply, *We'll make that the highlight of your visit.*

In addition, he wrote, *and to mark the 70th anniversary of the South African Navy, its largest fleet of warships yet to enter Durban would be scheduled to arrive there on Friday 20th March at 12 noon. Shortly before that time the British veterans would be embarked aboard a naval tug and taken out into the Bay. Its return would be synchronised to lead the arriving fleet past a top concert soprano who, dressed to resemble Perla, would go through her routine as the ships glided by. North Pier would be decorated for the occasion with coloured awnings and bunting, a Navy band would play, public address equipment would be installed, and hundreds*

179

of chairs hired and laid out in rows for invited civic dignitaries, the Services and the various ex-Services associations. Coverage by TV, radio and the Press was anticipated.

Enthusiastic editorials regarding the forthcoming visit were run in the ex-Services magazines, the national and provincial Press, on the BBC Charlie Chester show, and I was interviewed on a number of local radio chat-shows. Over 200 postal requests came in for more information and all were told that the register would close and a waiting list start for cancellations on receipt of the 40th deposit.

In all there were 38 registrations, and I told the story of that Memorial Visit in **"Back to Durban – 50 Years On!"**

Four months later I wrote to Durban s *Daily News.*

"Perla Siedle Gibson – Durban's Lady in White – well merits a more suitable memorial. The only one in existence to my knowledge is a sombre heap of stones at the extreme end of a bleak pier that nobody visits. I need hardly tell you how many would travel from afar to attend an annual or biennial Remembrance Service at a more fitting monument in a more accessible place. Perhaps the Daily News might care to initiate a campaign to this effect." (They obviously didn't for they never replied, so I set up my own campaign.)

Visiting Durban again in March 1993 involved *ad hoc* meetings with the Director of Culture at Durban City Council and other responsible citizens. The project and its timing was received enthusiastically, as North Pier was to be part of the first phase of developing Durban's waterfront into a major commercial and leisure centre – aimed at attracting business and tourism to its scenic setting.

Costings, design, type of material, siting and other factors were discussed whereby it was established that a life-size monument could be cast in bronze for an overall cost of £20,000. The South African economy was not particularly buoyant so they were told that a fund-raising scheme would be launched in Britain to help raise the sum.

The **Lady In White Monument Fund** was set up on my return to England in April 1992 and the ensuing two years were more than hectic. Especially as there was, in addition, the challenge of having this book ready for publication by Spring 1995.

The RN Philatelic Society at Portsmouth Naval Base made plans to issue a Commemorative First Day Cover, featuring Durban's Lady in White, on 15th August 1995, the 50th Anniversary of the Japanese unconditional surrender and unveiling day for the Monument.

Soon after starting the Appeal to raise funds for a Lady in White Monument I asked Buckingham Palace if the Queen would consider unveiling it on V.J. Day 1995, especially as Perla had written of greeting King George the Sixth and his family on their State Visit to Durban aboard HMS 'Vanguard' in March 1947. In reply Her Majesty's private secretary said how well the Queen remembered the occasion, but explained that Royal visits were organised by her Ministers. There

180

followed considerable correspondence with 10 Downing Street and the Foreign Office without effect. Well, it was a very long shot and I never expected much of it.

Then came a change of Government in South Africa and its re-entry into the British Commonwealth, followed by news of a State Visit planned for March 1995. As Durban was to be included in the programme I asked if Her Majesty might consider unveiling the Monument were its construction accelerated accordingly. This time it was implied by the High Commissioner that with only twenty four hours in Durban there would hardly be enough time for the Queen to show interest in projects related to the new image of South Africa without flaunting 'undesirable links with the colonial and Imperial past'.

Graham Linscott, assistant Editor of Durban's *Daily News*, wrote a stirring leader on 9th December 1994 accusing the British High Commission of the 'quaintest bit of politically correct thinking we've had for a long time.' 'Colonial?' he went on, 'the Lady in White was a citizen of a British dominion (as was every South African, white or black, in those days) and I am sure she thoroughly approved of that status. But High Commissioner Sir Anthony Reeve judged her to be too colonial! Were it not for World War Two nobody would have heard of Perla Siedle Gibson. Her memory is inseparable from that of the war. Was World War 2 then colonial?'

But despite obvious desire on all sides in South Africa for the Queen to renew her memories of the Lady in White the politicians continued to oppose. So I called in the Royal Navy.

King George the Sixth had been shown in the uniform of Admiral of the Fleet at a Durban 'walkabout' in 1947 and now the Royal Yacht, 'Britannia', was to be moored alongside T jetty in Durban Harbour as the Queen's H.Q. during her stay. Captain Mike Cooper, Port Captain, offered us a temporary dockside position alongside 'Britannia' to display the Monument where the Queen could preview it on first boarding her yacht. When approached, senior naval officers approved the idea and wires were set humming in all directions between Buckingham Palace, Whitehall, South Africa House, Capetown, Durban, and Sam Morley.

On March 8th 1995 came a telephone call from Buckingham Palace to ask if we were ready for Her Majesty the Queen to be given a preview of the Lady in White Monument alongside 'Britannia' at 4.0 p.m. on Friday, 24th March 1995 and hoped that Sam Morley and Barbara Siedle would be there to be presented to her. They certainly were – as indicated by the following excerpt from the Durban *Sunday Tribune* of 26th March and the black and white photographs portrayed in the illustrated section of this book.

'The Queen was also given a private viewing on Friday of the bronze statue of the Lady in White, the late Perla Siedle Gibson, who sang for troops during World War Two.

181

The sculpture was made by Durban artist Barbara Siedle, a niece of the Lady in White. The statue was commissioned by the Lady in White Memorial Fund in the United Kingdom whose Chairman, Sam Morley, came out for the occasion.

They were both presented to the Queen at 'T' jetty alongside the royal yacht 'Britannia' where the monument was temporarily placed. It will be officially unveiled on 15 August, the 50th anniversary of V.J. Day, which signalled the end of the war.'

This latter-day sequel, added to my war years of Book Three, plus the time served by the authors of Books One and Two, explains the title chosen for this trilogy:–

As **NINETY NINE YEARS OF NAVY** was scheduled for British bookshops for May the story and photographs relating to this historic event came on the scene just a little too late to be done full justice in these closing pages, but a coloured supplement is being prepared and those interested are advised to contact: Aedificamus Press, 113 The Ridgeway, Northaw, Potters Bar, EN6 4BG. Phone 01707 872720, Fax 01707 873444.

182

We Were Expendable! Dieppe, August 1942

By W P McGrath DSM

"Not though the soldiers knew
Someone had blundered.
Theirs not to make reply,
Theirs not to reason why
Theirs but to do and die."
Alfred Lord Tennyson

'Jubilee' was the code name for this Combined Operations action launched in the early hours of Wednesday, 19th August 1942. I was one of 350 members of the Royal Marines 'A' Commando, formed in January of that year. Every one was a volunteer and this was to be our first combat mission. We had been conditioned by rigorous training in Scotland and in the Isle of Wight and were now ready for action. Our platoon briefing for the operation did not reveal the target area – Dieppe. We only knew that it was to be some place on the coast of France.

Before we sailed, Admiral Mountbatten, Chief of Combined Operations, came aboard. Perched on a vantage point, he gave us a pep talk before dashing off for repeat performances on other ships.

On that awesome summer's day, we were baptised in the blood and thunder of war, and those who survived the carnage will never forget it as long as they live.

* * *

There was no moon and few stars visible on Tuesday night, 18th August 1942, as an armada of over 200 ships made up of destroyers, troop carriers, infantry landing ships, Free French Chasseurs, a river gunboat, HMS *Locust*, and a host of smaller assault landing craft, left the southern shores of England and made course for

Dieppe some 70 miles distant. In front of them, minesweepers were engaged in clearing safe channels through the German minefields. At about 0300 hours, some 8 miles off Dieppe, the armada began to position itself for the coming battle and the various assault groups took up their stations for the run in to their allotted beaches. The headquarters ship was the destroyer HMS *Calpe*.

On the left of the line, some 6 miles east of Dieppe, No. 3 Commando had the task of landing on the beaches at Berneval and Belleville-sur-mer, which had been given the names 'Yellow 1' and 'Yellow 2'. The Commando had to climb the formidable cliffs overlooking the beaches and destroy a German heavy gun battery, dominating the eastern approaches to Dieppe and code-named Goebbels.

About four miles to the right of No. 3 Commando, the Royal Regiment of Canada was to land on the 200 yards long beach at Puy, ('Blue' beach), overcome the 12 feet high sea wall, cut their way through a barrier of barbed wire, scale the heights, destroy another German gun battery code named 'Rommel', and attack and secure the high ground immediately east of Dieppe.

The frontal attack was to take place on Dieppe's mile long beach. Two Canadian Regiments were to remove the enemy from their defensive positions on the front whereby the Calgary Tank Regiment would then land with their Churchill tanks to support them in the capture of the town.

Royal Marines 'A' Commando aboard HMS *Locust* and several Free French Chasseurs, were given the job of driving into the harbour, attacking and capturing the German naval headquarters based in a dockside hotel, and extracting specified contents therefrom, removing a number of German invasion barges for towing back to England and generally aiding in the capture of Dieppe.

Some 2 miles to the right of Dieppe lay the seaside village of Pourville, and its beach, 'Green', was the landing area for the South Saskatchewan Regiment and the Queens own Cameron Highlanders of Canada. Their task was to capture a fortified position known as 'Les Quatres Ventes' farm and overrun the high ground immediately east of Dieppe which dominated the town and sea front. They were also to capture the airfield at St Aubin about 3 miles inland and attack what was mistakenly believed to be the headquarters of an enemy division located at Arques-la-Bataille, a further 2 miles inland.

The right of the line, two miles to the west of 'Green' beach, was allocated to No. 4 Commando. The Commando was split into two attacking groups. One group of about 90 men were to land on a small beach designated 'Orange 1' a few hundred yards west of the village of Varengeville-sur-Mer, and the other group would go ashore 2 miles further west on 'Orange 2' beach situated some hundreds of yards east of the village of Quiberville. The Commando assignment was to attack and destroy a coastal battery of heavy guns which dominated the western approaches to Dieppe, code-named Hess.

The overall objective of operation 'Jubilee' was for the attacking forces to capture Dieppe and the high ground on both flanks, consolidate and hold their positions before withdrawing at about the time of the next high tide.

Apart from the magnificent performance of No. 4 Commando in achieving their objective, the bulk of the attacking ground forces were overwhelmed by the German firepower. In broad daylight, without the element of surprise, with considerable physical obstacles to overcome, and with inadequate firepower, the result was a horrifying disaster.

HMS *Locust*

In the gloom of the night of 18th/19th August 1942, HMS *Locust*, a river gunboat of some 500 tons, had carried us safely across the English Channel. Now she was making straight for the narrow entrance to the harbour of Dieppe over which hung a menacing cloud of black smoke.

It was about 0700hrs. The morning was dull and cool with a high layer of thin cloud. The sky swarmed with fighting planes. Ours were bombing and strafing the German defences in and around Dieppe, laying smoke screens a hundred yards or so off the beaches and yet others were engaging the German war planes in what was to be the greatest single action fought by the RAF's Fighter Command throughout the war. The noise of exploding bombs, screaming engines and chattering machine guns violated the ear drums.

I was lying on the top deck of HMS *Locust*, belly pressed hard against the steel, rifle clutched in my right hand, my pulse at the double and waiting with others of 10 Platoon X Company Royal Marines 'A' Commando for the moment to leap on to the quay side and go about our business.

The platoon was commanded by twenty three year old Lieutenant H O 'Peter' Huntington-Whiteley. He was a regular officer, softly spoken with a languid air, his spare frame reaching a little over six feet high. He was popular with the men, who had nicknamed him 'Red'.

Alongside me lay the platoon sergeant John Kruthoffer. Twenty one years old, a six footer, tough minded, as fit as a fiddle, with a penchant for Anglo Saxon expletives. He had a fresh complexion, straw coloured hair and usually carried a slight scowl on his brow, more as a badge of authority than of ill temper, as he was essentially a sociable bloke. We were to serve together throughout the war, interrupted only when he forsook the ranks and took a commission.

Sitting against a bulkhead some fifteen feet away, not deigning to lie down, was marine Sam 'Ginger' Northern. He was a stocky lad, sturdy and aggressive with hair to match his nickname. Other members of the platoon lay prone on the deck, adrenalin pumping and primed for action.

We had been assigned the job of attacking the German Naval Intelligence HQ lodged in one of the dockside hotels, and seize secret documents before they could be destroyed. It called for speed, firepower and surprise, but as we raced towards the harbour mouth it was clear that the last and most vital ingredient was stillborn.

The previous morning we had left our civilian billets in the seaside towns of Sandown, Shanklin and Ventnor on the Isle of Wight. I had shared a comfortable billet with three other commandos in the Fort Tavern pub in Avenue Road, Sandown. The hostelry hosts, a husband and wife of middle age, had given us a hearty breakfast believing that we were going on another of our day long field exercises.

It was a nice summer's morning and fully equipped, we had made our way to the railway station to take the train to the town of Ryde situated on the north coast of the island opposite Portsmouth. I was 19 years old, an inch under 6 foot and weighed about eleven and a half stone. I was carrying some 60 pounds of equipment which included a Lee Enfield .303 rifle with two cotton bandoleers containing 100 rounds, a fighting knife strapped to my right thigh, several fully loaded bren gun magazines, a number of shrapnel grenades, a 'sticky bomb', a fighting pack on my back full of other items and, of course, a tin hat.

The 'sticky bomb' was a curious weapon. It had the shape and size of an Ogen melon with a straight handle about 4" long. Its protective metal outer casing which was detachable, covered the bomb s glass interior. It was to be used by me in the event of a tank attack. When confronted with a tank I was to remove the outer casing, run up to the beast and smash the bomb against its side. The glass would break and release a gluey substance causing the bomb to stick to the tank. I then had some few seconds to make myself scarce. Today's terminology would label it 'user unfriendly'.

From Ryde our platoon boarded HMS *Locust*, and joined an armada of small ships – destroyers, landing craft, motor gun boats and Free French warships of some 150 tons called Chasseurs on which most of our RM commandos embarked. Towards late evening, all bows were pointed eastward and we set off to meet the Germans somewhere on the coast of France.

We had practised our impending action several times in Portsmouth's dockland. Charging in on a gunboat, leaping onto the quay, scurrying to various buildings assigned as objectives and bewildering and alarming the dockies in the process. We knew our drill and now here we were, within several hundred yards of putting it to the test against the enemy, but with most of us not knowing that the pall of black smoke in front of us covered the town of Dieppe.

On the right were high cliffs overlooking the shingle beaches and promenade waterfront. To the left were lower escarpments dominating the harbour and the crooked channel leading to the inner harbour about a quarter mile from the entrance.

Both heights were stiff with German guns whose crews, relatively safe in their concrete bunkers, kept up a savage bombardment.

As HMS *Locust* charged on towards the harbour entrance, a shell struck the ship on the starboard side some twenty feet from where we lay. The noise of the explosion was gigantic. I lay on the deck with a sort of premature rigor mortis, immobilised by the awful thought of an immediate and terrible death. The game of war which I had been enjoying up to that point, had suddenly turned deadly serious. Of course, I had been aware that the game had its perils but getting killed was something that happened to other chaps. Now, for the first time, it burst like a thunderbolt upon my consciousness that my life too, was in danger of being abruptly snuffed out. The sods were actually trying to kill ME! (The quality of terror induced by that explosion was to be a unique experience for me as, despite several more frightening encounters with exploding missiles that day and in subsequent actions throughout the war, I was never again overwhelmed by such an awful, paralysing fear).

The air was thick with the smell of burnt explosive and alongside me Sgt. Kruthoffer lay motionless. He was covered with small debris thrown up by the explosion and at first glance I thought he had been hit, but he grunted, stirred and expleted. He was shocked but unhurt and, like me, trying to collect his wits. Other members of the platoon lay nearby, some wounded and all in a state of shock.

Meanwhile, HMS *Locust's* captain had made a quick appreciation of the situation. To press on through that murderous fire would have been suicidal, so he aborted the attack and turned sharply away from the harbour mouth approach.

Still lying on the deck I raised my head and saw 'Ginger' Northern slumped against the bulkhead. One of the ship's crew – a sick berth petty officer – had appeared and was kneeling beside him taking out the contents of his pockets. I thought that was rather odd and was a trifle suspicious, so I prised myself off the deck and went over to him. "What are you doing?" I enquired. "He s dead," he said, "And I am taking his personal stuff to be sent back home." When the petty officer had collected all the items he muttered, "Orders to throw the dead overboard." Then, in a louder voice, "Here, give me a hand." We picked up the corpse and threw it into the sea. Northern was probably the first RM commando to be killed on that day.

Before HMS *Locust* withdrew to the pool of ships lying a mile or so offshore, the ship's 3" gun crews went into action and bombarded the German gunners in and on the cliffs. We crouched on the deck, hands over ears in an attempt to muffle the enormous cracking sound made by the exploding guns. It was a relief when they ceased firing.

It was now about 0730hrs. From the pool of ships the sound of machine gun fire and detonating bombs and shells on the pebble beaches in front of Dieppe was barely audible above the greater noise of the war planes overhead as, like demented flocks of birds, they flung themselves about the sky.

As our briefing had dealt solely with our own special assignment, we were not aware of the big game plan for the Raid. We didn't know that Lt. Col. Lord Lovat's No. 4 Commando were already homeward bound, having taken out the German coastal battery of 6" guns situated some three miles west of Dieppe. The action had cost them 12 killed, 20 wounded and 13 missing/prisoners.

A similar coastal battery to the east of Dieppe had been the target for Lt. Col. Durnford-Slater's No. 3 Commando. They had had the bad luck to run into an armed German convoy shortly before they were due to land. The resulting action had destroyed the Commando's capacity to carry out their assignment. Even so, a small party of survivors led by Major Peter Young had got ashore and had peppered the gun battery with small arms fire before withdrawing. This brave assault had helped to nullify the battery's activity during a critical period. No. 3's casualties were 37 killed, 21 wounded and 82 prisoners.

Meanwhile, in the early daylight hours and in full view of an alerted enemy, Canadian soldiers from some of the proudest regiments in Canada had attacked, were still attacking, and were being slaughtered in their hundreds on the beaches east, west and in front of Dieppe.

On the HQ Destroyer HMS *Calpe*, the Military Force Commander Major General John Roberts, a Canadian soldier, had received a message the result of which was to send us into hellfire on another desperate venture. The wireless message seemed to indicate that the long beach situated directly in front of Dieppe was under the control of his Canadian soldiers and that an extra shove would enable them to take the town.

It was decided that Royal Marines 'A' Commando was not only to give that extra shove but also to fight its way through Dieppe, and attack and destroy the gun battery which had been No. 3 Commando s objective. But the message had been misinterpreted. The Canadians were not in control but were pinned down by intense machine gun and mortar fire. Their dead and wounded were strewn all over the beach.

"We are going in!" As the order was passed on, a marine turned to our platoon commander Lt. Huntington-Whiteley and plaintively enquired, "For Christ s sake sir, where the f****** hell are we?" "I suppose I can tell you now," was the cool reply. "That," he said, pointing to the cloud of black smoke, "Is Dieppe, and I want to see you in my office tomorrow morning for using improper language."

We were now ready for action. Let's get the bastards.

Heavy laden with arms and equipment, we climbed down the rope netting which hung from the portside of HMS *Locust* and dropped into an LCM assault landing craft. The boat was about forty feet long and some twelve feet wide, its bottom was flat and its sides about four feet high with a flange at the top, several inches wide, coming inboard. At the bow end was a ramp designed to fall forward on to the beach to enable rapid disembarkation. At the stern was the propulsion machinery. It was crewed by three young men, a Sub Lieutenant and two naval ratings.

When 10 Platoon had transferred from HMS *Locust*, one of the Free French Chasseurs approached. Down its sides came 11 Platoon commanded by Lt. Derrick Over. We gave them a cheery welcome as they joined us in the LCM. One of the platoon was Leslie 'Lofty' Whyman. He was in his middle twenties, a plus six footer, lean and sinewy with a complexion that seemed to turn nut brown between the rising and setting of the sun. His teeth were large and white and flashed out of his face when he smiled. He was a regular marine with a King's Badge to his credit. We served together throughout the war.

Then came the Commanding Officer of RM 'A' Commando, Lt. Colonel J Picton Phillips. In his late thirties, of medium size, wiry, he was physically and mentally as tough a 'bootneck' as any, with the nickname 'Tiger'. With him came the Adjutant, Sgt. Major and several other HQ staff.

The boat filled up with about 70 commandos, crowded together in the narrow confines of the LCM. The gravity of the occasion hung in the air. We were going into our first combat action against the German enemy and every man was 'stiffening his sinews and summoning up his blood' for the coming baptism.

"Cast off!" cried the boat's skipper and the LCM slowly drew away from HMS *Locust*. The rest of the Commando had transferred from the Chasseurs into give other assault craft and they formed up behind us for the mad charge to 'White' beach. Several hundred yards ahead a long, thick bank of smoke, laid down by several small craft belching the stuff out of their backsides, obscured the shore. The sea was choppy and as the boat gathered speed the waves kept up an irregular thump thump thump on its flat bottom as it careered onwards towards the carnage. Above our heads flights of fighter bombers roared in to attack the German defences on the cliffs which dominated our approach.

I was in a crouched position on the starboard side near the stern. Immediately to my left was the Adjutant and to his left the Sgt. Major. Behind us was Lt. Col. Phillips and the boat's crew. Up near the bow I saw the platoon's bren gunners 'Brad' Bradshaw and 'Alex' Alexander. Near them were Sgt. Kruthoffer, 'Lofty' Whyman and Ken 'Jock' Finlayson, a twenty-one year old Scotsman. He was a disciplined six-footer, always impeccably turned out and with a mind conditioned to see only the black and white of any argument. He too was also clutching a bren gun.

I knew he was a rifleman like me so, what was he doing with a bren gun? It turned out that when the shell had struck HMS *Locust*, it had not only blown his rifle overboard but had wounded 'Pusser' Hill, another of our platoon's bren gunners. Ken, not wanting to face the Germans with only his fighting knife, had borrowed the bren for the occasion. We were to serve together until he went off to fight the Japanese in 1944.

189

Our small cluster of assault boats – engines at full rev – galloped on. The senior naval officer of the Chasseurs who had been watching us through powerful binoculars, was moved to report that he thought it was, "A sea version of the Charge of the Light Brigade". Certainly, "Cannon to the right of us, cannon to the left of us, cannon in front of us, volleyed and thundered".

Suddenly, we were enshrouded in the smoke screen. It muffled the sound of the boat s engine and for a while we were in an eerie, fog bound capsule of time. For some reason the words of an Irish song came to my mind. It was 'Danny Boy'. "Oh Danny Boy the pipes the pipes are calling" – my brain kept repeating the refrain as if seeking some release from the increasing tension.

When we burst through the smoke screen into the clear air we were some two hundred yards from the beach and the German gunners, from their cliff-top strongpoints, had a perfect view. Almost before the boat had shrugged off the smoke we were assailed by a storm of machine gun bullets, mortar bombs and cannon shells. The bombs and shells cascaded down around the boat and exploded in the sea but some of the bullets struck home. There were gasps and groans and slumped bodies.

I instinctively crouched lower. My head was touching an upright pipe which rose from the deck at the side of the boat. The pipe was about four inches across and at the other side was the head of another marine. As we looked at each other a bullet struck the pipe dead centre between our noses. I tipped my tin hat lower over my nose and crouched even more.

As our assault boat, now some 100 yards from the beach, charged on 'Into the jaws of death, into the mouth of hell', there was a movement behind me and I saw our C.O. Lt. Col. Phillips climb onto the stern of the craft. He began waving his arms in such a way as to signal to the crews of the other boats astern that they should abort the attack. He had rightly judged that our mission was impossible. However, to stand in full view of the German gunners at such short range was suicidal. The courage of his action was awesome. Within seconds he was dead.

The Sub Lt. who skippered our boat seemed unaware that the action had been called off. His job was to deliver us onto the beach at the designated point and he continued to drive forward at full throttle. The chaps at the bow were bracing themselves in anticipation of the ramp falling in front of them, to be followed by a frantic scramble up the beach over potato sized pebbles when, about thirty yards from the shore-line, the boat stopped abruptly. It was impaled on one of the many underwater obstacles that were submerged beneath the high tide.

The LCM swung portside onto the shore. Those of us on the starboard side were now bereft of cover from the bullets pouring down from the cliff-top. It is certain that if the Germans had maintained the rate of fire with which they had greeted our charge, even fewer of us would have lived to fight another day. No doubt seeing us dead in the water and no longer menacing, some of the German gunners turned their attention to more urgent targets. Even so, other gunners kept up a brisk delivery of missiles which thrashed the sea, the side of the boat and some of its human cargo.

I then saw the young Sub Lt. in command of our craft, dressed in white plimsolls, blue trousers and a dirty white roll-necked pullover, (I see him now as I write) climb on to the top flange on the port side and take quick strides to the point where the boat had collided with the obstacle. His intention was quite clear to me. He wanted to free the boat and complete his own particular mission, that of depositing us on the beach. His sense of duty was sublime. His act of immense bravery matched that of our C.O. but before he could achieve his objective he, too, was shot down and he fell into the sea. Indeed, if he had succeeded and the craft had beached and the ramp had fallen, it is doubtful whether any one of us would have survived.

"Get the bren guns working!" I think the order came from the Sgt. Major who was to my left side.

Up near the bow our platoon bren gunners Alexander and Bradshaw, both good looking lads with dark wavy hair and cheerful smiles, lifted their weapons on to the top ports side of the boat and went to work. We couldn't see the enemy, at least, I couldn't see them even though I had taken a quick peek towards the beach. All I could see were the bodies of some of those gutsy Canadians who had gone before us. Nevertheless, the very sound of the bren guns spitting back defiance was encouraging. Within moments Alexander was killed.

Bradshaw continued working and was to earn the Military Medal for his contribution that day. Meanwhile, 'Jock' Finlayson realised that he, too, as a temporary bren gunner, had a job to do. He was at the bow on the starboard side and not having a place to rest the muzzle of his bren gun, he had to fire it more or less from the hip. The boat, rocking to the movement of the waves, was an unstable platform and those in front of him crouched lower as he sent several bursts over their heads. It was a brave effort.

About seventy yards away, in a small cave at the foot of the cliff, a German gun crew were working a cannon. I didn't see it from the boat but when I returned to the spot with then Capt. Huntington-Whiteley in early September 1944 (a few days after this visit he was killed in a street fight in Le Havre) we both agreed that it must have been the gun which administered the coup de grace to our boat.

A shell struck us in the stern. It killed the two crewmen and started a fire. The Adjutant who was at my left shoulder, rose up from his crouching position presumably to take command. Before he was fully erect he fell forward and I saw that the back of his skull had been sliced like a melon. Either a bullet or a piece of shrapnel had destroyed him. I observed this with my mind curiously detached from the scene, as if I were a spectator and not a participant. I discovered later that this mental phenomenon is frequently experienced by people exposed to life threatening conditions.

As the fire spread a shout went up. "Everybody overboard. Every man for himself!" As I dropped my unused rifle (no order had been given to the riflemen to open fire), one chap, his mind blown, stood up behind me crying, "It's no use, we'll all be killed, we'll all be killed!" He was helped overboard and I hurriedly unslung the two bandoleers of bullets, unhooked my belt and flung my webbing containing the bren gun magazines, grenades and my 'sticky bomb' onto the deck and took off my boots.

I tightened the straps of my Mae West, a rubber tube with a canvas cover, which had been worn under my webbing, tied around my chest. I raised myself in order to roll over the starboard side so as to keep the lowest possible profile. It should have been a moment's work but the scabbard of my fighting knife, still strapped to my right thigh, became wedged in the flange opening and several long seconds were to pass before I dropped into the cold sea.

The Sea

We crowded close to the boat's hull for protection against the bullets. I quickly inflated the Mae West and, not being a good long distance swimmer, its buoyancy encouraged me. Some voices were heard, "Let s go for the beach". Other voices, among them Sgt. Kruthoffer's urged, "Come on, let's make for the ships." The ships were visible on the horizon and the beach was but several strokes from the other side of the burning LCM. Decisions were then made which determined each man's fate. On the one hand he had the option of staying and being shot or taken prisoner of war, and on the other, that of being shot, drowned or rescued.

Among the first to strike out to sea was 'Lofty' Whyman. He was a superb swimmer employing an overarm stroke coupled with a scissor leg kick. If the ships had not been there he reckoned he would still have tried to make it back to the Isle of Wight. No doubt he might have too! 'Jock' Finlayson, 'Brad' Bradshaw, 'Lofty' Dwan, Harry Gosling, 'Jock' Farmer, 'Spike' Watson, 'Killer' Kilbride (who was to die in Sicily), Lt. Huntington-Whiteley, Lt. Over (who was killed before he had taken many strokes and whose body was one of the few the RM Commandos recovered and identified by the Germans and is now buried in the Canadian War Cemetery near Dieppe) and other bold lads struck out for the ships. I joined them. We left behind those who had taken the other option.

In my battledress suit and with my Mae West full of the air from my lungs, I set off breast stroking through the water. The Germans, gazing down from the cliff-top, seeing our party swimming out to sea, kept up a desultory rate of fire. But, as we no longer threatened them they soon turned their attention to other targets. Slowly we pulled away from the shore. The strong swimmers moved ahead and within a hundred yards or so our group had changed formation. We were now, more or less, in line astern and I was at the rear of the line accompanied by a diminutive Scotsman from 11 platoon.

We plodded on in silence and several hundred yards out I began to weaken. My companion pressed on, and after a trying period when I was stationary in the water, removing my trousers in a clumsy and exhausting manner, I found myself alone. I turned on to my back and floated for a while, thankful for the buoyancy of the Mae West. Above me a pilot had flung himself out of a burning Spitfire, and I watched as his parachute opened and he floated downwards into the water.

I continued my slow progress out to sea, breast stroking for about fifty yards, then floating on my back to recuperate from the effort. Whilst in this position I kept moving my legs so as to maintain some forward momentum albeit painfully sluggish. I kept up this routine until I had covered about three quarters of a mile, and as the ships loomed larger on the horizon so my confidence increased. Once whilst floating, I looked back to the shore and saw our burning assault boat in which the bodies of the men who had died were being incinerated. To my left was the harbour mouth which we had tried to enter a bare two and a half hours before. And now, I saw a motor speedboat catapulting out of the harbour at a frantic rate of knots, in a desperate and doomed attempt to escape. I saw three shells explode in perhaps three seconds. One behind, one in front, and one on target which disintegrated the boat. The German gunners were on form that day.

When I turned over on to my stomach again and took the first stroke, I looked towards the horizon and was astonished to see it was empty of ships. All our craft had disappeared! I trod water and must have panicked a little as I swallowed sea and vomited (I was later informed that the ships had withdrawn to escape enemy gunfire but had returned after a while). The question demanding an immediate answer was, should I retreat to the beach and be taken by the Germans, or continue out to sea in the hope, now somewhat tenuous, of being picked up? I decided to press on.

The Mae West which had so far given me good service, now seemed to be losing its buoyancy, as I appeared to be lower in the water. My legs, instead of being fairly horizontal behind me, now inclined deeper as they tried to thrust me forward. I rested more frequently, and instead of trying to float on my back I found that it required less effort just to stop swimming and gently tread water. I don't know how long this continued. I was cold, had swallowed too much sea, my vomiting was painful and my eyes felt raw. Gradually, I lost the strength even to tread water, and after floating legs down for a while, I became aware that I was drowning. My brain seemed to accept the thought without fuss as if my will to survive was about to 'throw in the towel'.

To add to my confusion I was suddenly enveloped in a smoke screen. The acrid stuff caused more vomiting and coughing and more swallowing of salt water. Now, still partially buoyed up by the Mae West, only my nose was above the surface of the sea. It is said that drowning people are visited by a kaleidoscope of snapshots of their previous experience. This mental phenomenon came to me and the pictures it brought were so clear it was as if they were the reality and my drowning was only a dream. Then, the dream abruptly dissolved into a new reality.

Around me a gap appeared in the smoke and there, not twenty yards away was a small craft with smoke spouting out of the canisters at its stern. The sight of it galvanised me and I let out a croak and raised an arm. The crew, two matelots, among the unsung heroes of the day, saw me. They dragged me inboard over the stern and over the smoke canisters whose little flames burned my stomach. I welcomed the heat and flopped prone and squelching on the deck, my sodden mind almost hysterical with relief. God, the sense of security which filled my being was sublime.

As I lay there vomiting and coughing and counting my lucky stars, I was unaware that the small boat was carrying me back to the beach. After a short while I felt the craft stop and over the sides tumbled Canadian soldiers all of whom seemed to be walking wounded. The picture of one of them remains with me. He was bare to the waist, and from the base of his neck, a diagonal red slash of a flesh wound crossed his back and ended at the top of his buttocks. They gathered around me and when the boat was full, the crew hurriedly backed it off the beach, and with the engine doing its utmost we raced out to sea. Not a word was spoken as we bounced over the waves to the ships and away from the machine gun bullets, mortar bombs and cannon shells.

HMS *Calpe*

We were taken aboard HMS *Calpe* the HQ destroyer. It was crowded with survivors rescued from the bloody beaches by the courageous naval lads who had maintained a ceaseless ferry service throughout that terrible morning. Many of them had been killed by the accurate cannon fire of the German gunners.

I was taken to a small cabin on the top deck which was full of other survivors. Some were wounded, and a young doctor and sick berth petty officer were busily engaged giving morphine and dressing injured flesh. I slumped into a corner, coughing and shivering. However, I was alive, in one piece, and going home.

Before withdrawing from the scene, HMS *Calpe* turned towards the shore and bombarded the German defences in an effort to help the beleaguered Canadians. It was in vain. The day was lost. It was time to go home. The ship turned away from the bloody beaches and headed out to sea.

With my head between my knees, I must have dozed off for a while as I came to with a jerk that nearly dislocated my neck. A bomb had exploded alongside the ship. We were being attacked by German fighter bombers who were strafing the ship with machine gun fire as well as delivering bombs. The outside deck was covered with survivors from the beaches of whom many now had the cruel luck to be struck down.

One of the wounded was carried into the cabin by the sick berth petty officer and

194

placed on the small table in the centre. He was conscious and moaning with pain. The doctor came and stripped the top clothing off the wounded man to examine the bullet injuries after which he spoke to the petty officer and left the cabin. I was looking at the wounded man when he opened his eyes. With a voice full of despair he said, "Oh God, don't let me die." He paused and looked around the cabin. "Oh God, he said again, I'm only nineteen, please don't let me die. Please God, don't let me die." His voice trailed away into silence, and a short time afterwards he was taken from the cabin.

We were again attacked by the German war planes and this time their strafing struck down the sick berth petty officer who had been out on deck attending to the wounded. He was brought into the cabin and placed on the table. He lay there with several bullets in his torso and one in his right heel. It was this wound which caused him to groan with pain and ask for morphine. After a while he too was taken from the cabin.

HMS *Calpe*'s boilers, although damaged by bombs, were working overtime. She steamed on through the darkness and in the early hours of Thursday 20th August we entered Portsmouth harbour to the sound of the 'All Clear' which followed another destructive German air raid on the historic naval port. It seemed an appropriate welcome home. With a blanket over my shoulders, I was taken to a dockside building and spent the rest of the night drinking hot cocoa, munching sandwiches, and recounting some of the scenes at Dieppe to the dock marines who were entertaining me.

At about 0800hrs, dressed in some clothes given to me by my hosts, I caught the paddle ferryboat which carried me over the sun dappled, calm waters of the Solent, to Ryde. From there I took the train to Sandown, and walked back along the same road, up which I had walked two long days before.

I entered the Fort Tavern and passing through the saloon bar to the private dining room I was greeted by 'Lofty' Whyman, 'Lofty' Dwan and, if I'm not mistaken, Harry Gosling. They were seated at the table eating a meal. "Christ Mac," said Dwan, "We were told that you'd had your bloody head blown off." I smiled, sat down, and tucked into a hearty breakfast. God it was good to be alive.

The following day our company held a roll call in the street we used for parades. Many names called remained unanswered. The Commando had lost 66 men killed or captured and 31 wounded.

For statistics, see page 133.

Index